An East Kent Quintet

Voices from
Sturry, Fordwich, Hersden, Broad Oak and Westbere

"Last year's words belong to last year's language
And next year's words await another voice"

LITTLE GIDDING by T.S.Eliot (1944)

Edited by
Heather Stennett and K.H.McIntosh

Down On The Farm

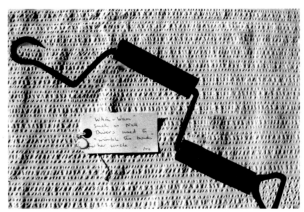 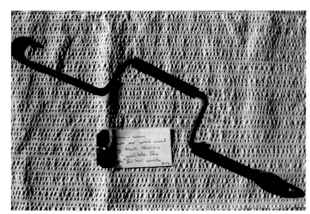

A wimble and a wim-wam, hay-making tools, as referred to by Nell Divers on page 5

A Weeks-Dungey tractor built in 1915 by William Weeks and Sons, engineers of Maidstone, for fruit and hop farmer, Mr Dungey of Cranbrook, (thought to be Clement Dungey, grandfather of David Dungey of Popes Lane, Sturry) It had a four cylinder engine at the front and a large cylindrical water tank next to the driver's seat. This very obviously posed photograph came from the album of the late Mrs Maud Bourner, of the Island Road, Sturry.

Five Villages – One Parish

This collection of interviews and articles, accumulated over many years, provides an intimate glimpse into the past and is intended to complement the several other books already published about the villages of Sturry, Broad Oak, Fordwich, Hersden and Westbere. These publications are listed elsewhere in this volume.

Any reader unfamiliar with the area should know that each of the villages, all of which lie to the north of Canterbury and are now in the same ecclesiastical parish, has its own unique characteristics and is very different and distinct from its contiguous neighbours - and that we have taken the view that, in the words of the poet, "history is a pattern of timeless moments".

The interviews and other contributions provide a conspectus of events as they have been remembered in these villages over the last hundred years. We hope that the historian C.R.Cheney's famous dictum "documents don't speak to strangers" won't deter those who do not live here from reading them. They provide a real insight into happenings considered important by those who experienced them as well as casting an accidental sidelight on the personalities of their various authors. A happy temperament in circumstances that others might consider dire indeed shines through in several interviews, whilst stoical accounts of the Second World War as it affected Sturry – thought to have been one of the most heavily bombed villages in the South-East – inspire great respect.

Heather Stennett and K.H.McIntosh

Beating the Bounds about 1891.
Front row second from left Thomas H.Pope, Headmaster, Sturry Primary School October 1888 to September 1923

A Contented Woman

Nell Divers

Interview with Ellen Ivy Divers, (always known as Nell), of 6, Chapel Cottages, Chapel Lane, Sturry, by Monica Headley at an unknown date.

Now, Nell, tell me about yourself

I was born at the Four Wents Ways, Westbere, in 1895 and lived there until those new houses in Bredlands Lane were built. I stayed at home until my sister, Daisy, got married and had to come home so I went into service. I was fourteen then and I stayed there until November 1918 when my Mother died of that terrible 'flu they had, you know, in the First War. [1]

What they called the Spanish Flu?

That's right. My brother [William James, aged 29] died on the Thursday and my Mother [Matilda, aged 57] died on the Monday. So I had to come home and look after Dad.

That was very sad

My brother, Perce, had died in the war, too. They never found him. [Percy John Gore Divers, died 1 October,

1916 in Egypt, Lance Corporal, Queen's Own Worcester Hussars] We came to this cottage [6, Chapel Lane, Sturry] in 1914 and rented it at 4/4d a week, that's all, and Dad went to work at Mr Homersham's gravel pit.

Is that the same family who were hurdle-makers?

Yes. And when Dad couldn't work he went on the 10/- a week pension and I used to have to get most of the living.

When you went into service at fourteen what was your work and how many staff were there?

I was supposed to be house parlour-maid to the Reverend Evill at St Dunstan's Vicarage, in the London Road, at Canterbury. [The Revd. William Ernest Evill, B.A. This vicarage is now The Red House Nursing Home.] There was a cook and a gardener as well. I got £1 2s 6d a month there. Then they went to Biddenden and I went with them.

Was it the same house as my parents lived in when my father [the Revd. Samuel Risdon-Brown, Vicar of Sturry, 1938-1949 and later Rector of Biddenden] was Rector there?

That's right, Miss Monica. I was the only one then. The cook left, you see. Yes, it was a big place. And then they retired to Hythe and I went with them until 1918 when I had to come home.

You were still very young, surely?

Oh, yes, I was only twenty-three when I came home and I took on the Parish Hall after Miss Marsh died about 1920. [The Sturry Parish Hall in Church Lane, opened on 1st December, 1906, by the Bishop of Dover, was totally destroyed in the bombing of November, 1941]

What were your working hours in Biddenden?

Well, I used to get up at six and keep on until bed. I fell into bed half past nine to ten those days.

What free time did you have?

They were so strict, they didn't let you out, you know. When I was in Canterbury I used to come home for half a day, but I had to be back for nine o'clock and that was all I had.

Were they kind to you apart from being strict?

Yes, but they never let you have any followers. No, you didn't used to have to have any.

What if you were ill, Nell?

I was never ill, no, I wasn't ill. No, I can't ever remember being ill.

Did you ever get home at all when you were at Biddenden?

I don't suppose I did come home much then because there was a war on.

But how would you have travelled when you did?

By train. Go to Headcorn and then on to Canterbury.

But how would you have got to Headcorn?

There was a little railway from Hastings then. [The Colonel Holman Fredk Stephens Light railway] [2]

Tell me about your family.

My father [Jesse John Divers, born at Sturry about 1861] was a waggoner at Bredlands Farm. He had two horses and he used to have to get up at three o'clock in the morning to give them their food – we used to call it "serve up" – you know, do the horses, feed them and water them, I suppose. There was waggoners at Tile Lodge Farm and Hoades Court Farm and Joiner's farm – that was all Mr Wotton's property in those days.

And then what did he do?

The ploughing and cut the corn and cut the grass. They used to have to cut the grass on the marshes down at Westbere. He had I don't know how many black bullocks down there, they never had coloured ones down there only black, Mr Wotton did. And then he used to have to take the hay to Ramsgate Brewery. [Thomas Wotton of Tile Lodge Farm, Hoath Road, Sturry, was a partner in the Ramsgate brewery, Tomson and Wotton. Until they were taken over by Whitbread in 1968 they boasted the title of Britain's Oldest Brewery (c. 1635)].

How did they cut the hay, Nell?

With machines, big machines. They'd got a long knife on them, and the horses pulled the machines. [Known as a reciprocating mower]

Did they just let it dry in fields and then pitchfork it up onto the wagon?

No, it had to be turned, you know, and then it was taken down to the farm, and made into stacks and thatched.

Did your father do the thatching?

No, no, Dad never did. My old uncle used to do the thatching. He did all the thatching for Mr Wotton and then he used to cut the hay out in trusses as they called it.

With a big knife?

Yes, and I used to go and wimble the bonds for him. [Wimble, a sort of augur] I used to have this thing on my waist with a hook on it and he used to put a bit of this hay over the hook and then I used to twist it and it made a long thing and you used to tie the trusses up with this bond made of hay itself.

Did you get paid for that, Nell?

No, I used to do that for free like! In September when we had the holiday from school we used to go hop-picking. At Tile Lodge [Farm] this was, Miss Monica, there was three hop-gardens there. There was the string hop-garden and poles, the bines used to go up the poles and in the string hop they used to go on a sort of angle and then to another wire and then down to where the hops were.

Why did they have different ones?

I don't know why. There was just the biggest hop-garden was on strings and the two smaller ones was up the poles. That was the way Mother used to get our winter clothing.

Nell Divers' cottage next to the churchyard

Plaque in her pew in the choir of St Nicholas Church, Sturry

Were you paid by the basket?

Yes, that's right. . . . five bushels for the basket. And then they used to be priced, about 1/6d [about 8p] that was the highest for five bushels, those days. Well, there isn't any hop-picking now, is there? Then, of course, when the hop-picking was finished it was time to go back to school.

Tell us about the school

My sister and I went to Westbere School. Now it's a house, I think. There were 31 of us as a rule and one teacher. I went there until I was 14 and then I went into service.

Was it all ages from five to fourteen in one room?

Yes, in one room. Boys and girls mixed together, you know, two in a desk. We used to have Scripture in the morning from the Rector of Westbere, [the Revd. George Lindsay Wallace, M.A. 1900-1921], first all together and then I suppose we went on to Dictation and Arithmetic. The girls used to do a lot of Sewing and Knitting.

Well, it stood you in good stead, Nell, because you still do!

I used to think, Miss Monica, in those days only one teacher! It must have been terrible for them, mustn't it? I got the cane more than once! Yes, I did!

Was it a man teacher?

No, a woman, but she still hit us. We got into the habit of putting our hands out sloping like and it [the cane] used to slide off the hand and hit her on the knee! She got wise to that, though, and used to knock our hands up with the cane first before she whacked us.

And what sort of things did you get hit for?

Talking.

Did you write on paper?

No, on slates.

With chalk?

No, slate pencils.

Earlier on, Nell, you were saying that your Father worked these immensely long hours seven days a week, and you, too, had a tremendous lot of work to do, very little free time and precious little money. What was your attitude in those days? Did you resent it at all? Did you ever think things should be better? What did you think about it?

I don't think we ever resented anything, Miss Monica, well, we didn't know any better. We didn't used to think of it.

Did you not get colossally tired?

Don't remember, Miss Monica, at all.

You can't have got colossally tired or you would have remembered it!

No, because we didn't get up like Dad used to, you see.

But you had very long hours and worked very hard at Biddenden Rectory. Didn't you resent that?

No, I don't remember resenting anything at all.

What about the attitude to the people who employed you? They were much better off financially than you.

Oh, if we met them anywhere, Miss Monica, we used to have to curtsey to them.

Did you not mind doing that?

No, it used to come sort of natural, I suppose.

But why did you think it was natural? I mean, why should you curtsey to them any more than they should curtsey to you?

I suppose they were better than we were.

Why?

Ah, I couldn't say.

Come on now, Nell, why did you think that at the time? Did you think they were cleverer?

I suppose I thought they were richer! That's all. But at Westbere House, you know the big house there, Colonel Hill [Colonel Peter Edward Hill, C.B., R.A., buried 15th July, 1919, aged 85, served in the Crimea, the Indian Mutiny and the Afghan War, 1878/9] used to live there and when his funeral was on Mother said it reached from Sturry Station to Westbere Church. Of course, we thought that was wonderful. I can remember him being buried at Westbere. He had six sons who carried him.

Did you, in a way, share in the glory of the people that you worked for? Did you so to speak take a pride in the fact that they had got all these things?

I suppose so.

So the fact that it wasn't yours didn't matter?

I don't think I was ever jealous of anything.

I'm sure you weren't, Nell, you aren't that sort of person! On the whole you feel you were happy people?

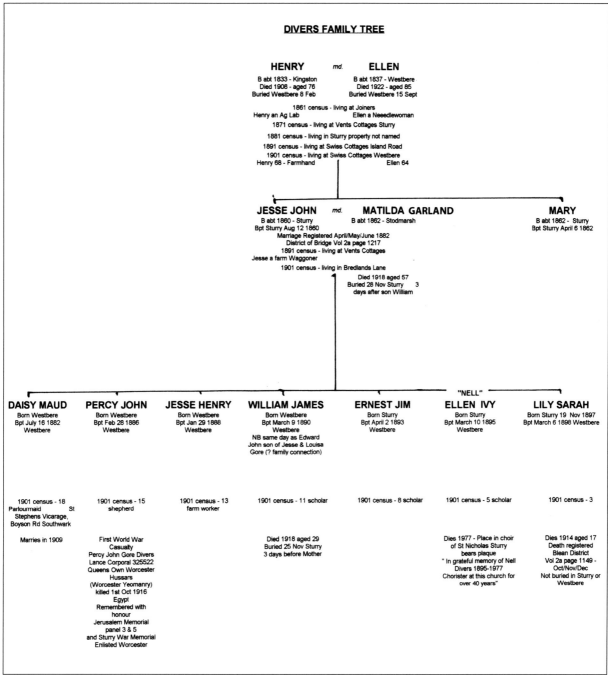

DIVERS FAMILY TREE

HENRY *md.* **ELLEN**

HENRY	ELLEN
B abt 1833 - Kingston	B abt 1837 - Westbere
Died 1908 - aged 76	Died 1922 - aged 85
Buried Westbere 8 Feb	Buried Westbere 15 Sept

1861 census - living at Joiners
Henry an Ag Lab   Ellen a Neeedlewoman
1871 census - living at Vents Cottages Sturry

1881 census - living in Sturry property not named
1891 census - living at Swiss Cottages Island Road
1901 census - living at Swiss Cottages Westbere
Henry 68 - Farmhand   Ellen 64

JESSE JOHN *md.* **MATILDA GARLAND**   **MARY**

JESSE JOHN	MATILDA GARLAND	MARY
B abt 1860 - Sturry	B abt 1862 - Stodmarsh	B abt 1862 - Sturry
Bpt Sturry Aug 12 1860		Bpt Sturry April 6 1862

Marriage Registered April/May/June 1882
District of Bridge Vol 2a page 1217
1891 census - living at Vents Cottages
Jesse a farm Waggoner
1901 census - living in Bredlands Lane

Died 1918 aged 57
Buried 28 Nov Sturry   3
days after son William

"NELL"

DAISY MAUD	PERCY JOHN	JESSE HENRY	WILLIAM JAMES	ERNEST JIM	ELLEN IVY	LILY SARAH
Born Westbere	Born Westbere	Born Westbere	Born Westbere	Born Sturry	Born Sturry	Born Sturry 19 Nov 1897
Bpt July 16 1882	Bpt Feb 28 1886	Bpt Jan 29 1888	Bpt March 9 1890	Bpt April 2 1893	Bpt March 10 1895	Bpt March 6 1898 Westbere
Westbere	Westbere	Westbere	Westbere	Westbere	Westbere	
			NB same day as Edward			
			John son of Jesse & Louisa			
			Gore (? family connection)			
1901 census - 18	1901 census - 15	1901 census - 13	1901 census - 11 scholar	1901 census - 8 scholar	1901 census - 5 scholar	1901 census - 3
Parlourmaid St	shepherd	farm worker				
Stephens Vicarage,						
Boyson Rd Southwark						
Marries in 1909	First World War		Died 1918 aged 29		Dies 1977 - Place in choir	Dies 1914 aged 17
	Casualty		Buried 25 Nov Sturry		of St Nicholas Sturry	Death registered
	Percy John Gore Divers		3 days before Mother		bears plaque	Blean District
	Lance Corporal 325522				" In grateful memory of Nell	Vol 2a page 1149 -
	Queens Own Worcester				Divers 1895-1977	Oct/Nov/Dec
	Hussars				Chorister at this church for	Not buried in Sturry or
	(Worcester Yeomanry)				over 40 years"	Westbere
	killed 1st Oct 1916					
	Egypt					
	Remembered with					
	honour					
	Jerusalem Memorial					
	panel 3 & 5					
	and Sturry War Memorial					
	Enlisted Worcester					

Divers family tree

Oh, yes, we were happy enough.

Some people just have happy natures. Do you think perhaps in a way you were sometimes happier than the people who were richer?

Oh, yes, I do. Yes, I do. I do, yes.

But all these people you knew well, did you feel they lived happy lives and were happy people?

They never looked happy, you know, they never looked happy.

What did you think made them less happy?

Well, it must have been a miserable life for them, mustn't it, Miss Monica, you know to have all that money and have nothing to do. Oh, I think we were happy enough...I can't remember being anything else.

[1] Richard Collier THE PLAGUE OF THE SPANISH LADY (Macmillan, 1974)
[2] Kidner, R.W. THE COLONEL STEPHENS RAILWAY (Oakwood Press, 1936)
    Oppitz, Leslie THE LOST RAILWAYS OF KENT AND SUSSEX 2 vols Newbury reprint (2006)

Knights to Remember
Sir Charles Warren

In 1913 after a long military career General Sir Charles Warren, G.C.M.G, K.C.B, F.R.S, moved to The Oaks in Church Lane, Westbere, following the death of his brother-in-law, the Revd G.P.Haydon. Born on 7th February, 1840, he had begun his service in the Royal Engineers, working first on a survey of Gibraltar.

He led excavations in Jerusalem for the Palestine Exploration Fund, where the Warren Gate in the Western Wall, the main entrance to the Temple Mount, is named after him. He then went to Africa to carry out surveys in Griqualand West, and the Orange Free State. He commanded the Diamond Field Horse in the Transkei War and then was sent to investigate a rebellion in Bechuanaland (now Botswana). The town of Warrenton in the Northern Cape Province of South Africa is named after him.

Following several later successful expeditions and the solving of the mysterious disappearance of an archaeological expedition in Sinai, Sir Charles was appointed Commissioner of the Metropolitan Police in 1886. Here he was blamed for his failure to catch the multiple-murderer, Jack the Ripper. (Sir Charles has been portrayed in films about the Ripper over the years by the distinguished actors Basil Henson, Anthony Quayle, Hugh Fraser and Ian Richardson.)

He resigned from the office of Police Commissioner in 1888 over the lack of support from the Home Office and in 1889 was sent to command the garrison at Singapore. When the Boer War broke out in 1899 he was appointed to command the South African Field Defence Corps and later attracted criticism at the Battle of Spion Kop. Even so he was promoted to General in 1904 and Colonel-Commandant of the Royal Engineers in 1905, retiring in August, 1905, at the age of 65.

A keen Freemason and a great admirer of the Scout Movement, he donated a camping ground in Westbere to them. He died on 27th January, 1927, Scouts and Rovers from the Canterbury District forming a guard of honour at his funeral in Canterbury Cathedral. Two hundred troops from the Canterbury garrison were present. A further two hundred troops lined the streets as the coffin was taken on a gun carriage in a procession over half a mile long out to Westbere.

Sir Charles was buried in Westbere churchyard beside his wife, the former Fanny Margaretta Haydon, who had died in 1919. They had two sons and two daughters. A grandson, Watkin W. Williams, wrote his biography - THE LIFE OF GENERAL SIR CHARLES WARREN which was published by Blackwell, Oxford, in 1941. His handling of the Trafalgar Square unemployment riots of 1887 is the subject of a work of fiction by crime writer Joan Lock called DEAD CENTRE (Hale, 2008). She writes that his role has since been re-examined and that he is now seen as one of the better, if unluckiest, of Commissioners of the Metropolitan Police.

Dead Centre reproduced by kind permission of Robert Hale Ltd., Publishers.

Sir Charles Warren

Mrs Margaret Neame (née Lawrence) of Fordwich

21ˢᵗ November 1894 - 12ᵗʰ November 1977

Interviewed by Mrs Daphne Partington at an unknown date.

We left school at 14 in my day and I was 15 when I went away from home. That would have been about 1909. I went to Cliftonville College, Warren Place, at Margate really as a storeroom maid and I worked mainly with the proprietor's wife. After I had been there a few weeks she said "Do you know matron is leaving?" There was a matron, a second matron and an assistant matron. She said "That would be a better job for you if you like". So I said I think I would like to – I knew the matrons – they were very nice people and I always wanted to be a nurse – that was my ambition. In those days parents had to pay for the training and it wasn't a small item. You had to work 3 years in training. Anyway I took this job – I was very happy and I stayed with them for 3 years. Then I left them and went to a smaller school in Herne Bay called Herneville doing the same work. I enjoyed it very much. In Margate you worked with the boys and some of them were quite young – the parents were abroad. We always had to see that they had their baths and each morning that they were washed and ready to go down to breakfast. During the day we used to make the beds and then get ready whichever dormitories were going to be cleaned – we used to prepare those. I was 3 years at Warren Place and three years at the other. Then I left to get married. I didn't do any more work after that. I had a family. The second one was born on the first one's birthday. I had a pretty busy time with the children – altogether I had eight children. Four boys and four girls.

The name of the place I worked in Margate was Cliftonville College and Herne Bay was Herneville. Oh, I've said that before, haven't I? We had all their clothing to attend to – mending – laying out their clean clothes. Mending the socks. Putting on the buttons. We used to get them up 7 to half past in the morning. We had to see that they were all cleaned up. See that they were in a decent state. We never really finished. There was always something to do. I used to get an afternoon and evening off once a week. We only had a fortnight's holiday, summer holiday. And perhaps the odd weekend. When the boys were away there was all the cleaning to do. We didn't do the actual scrubbing up. The maids did that. It was 4 large houses made into one. There was a maid for each house. And two kitchen people. We didn't have to prepare any food. Our work was looking after the boys. If they were sick you had to look after them. It wasn't hard work at all. I enjoyed it very much. When I first went I was paid half a crown a week. That was in about 1909. We used to wear a sort of grey cotton uniform in

the morning. In the afternoon we had a navy dress with big white aprons and cap. We had to buy them ourselves. The maids wore print dresses in the morning and white starched aprons. They had black ribbons going into streamers at the back. We had our meals with the boys. Splendid meals. The parents were abroad you see and left the boys behind to be educated. It was a wonderful life really. The boys were happy. No trouble. We took them from quite young – about 6 and 7. It was a life I enjoyed. When I first went down there – I was the youngest of the family – my sisters were all away from home - just my two brothers at home - if only I had the money I would have gone home, though. I hated being away from home. I got over it. When it was your day off you hadn't got time to come to Sturry. We had a work room. That was where we did the mending. We had our own bedroom. There was heating in the workroom, not in the bedroom. Quite comfortable really. Very cosy. There were 3 men employed – the coachman helped clean the boots and one had to wait at table. We had a cook and kitchen maid and three parlour maids. The proprietor and his wife had their own quarters. We weren't tied to any particular times. We just had the duties to do. I would go to bed about 10 by gaslight. I enjoyed it very much once I got over the home sickness. I was just the same at Herne Bay. We had no transport then. I didn't want to stay. But because they didn't want me to leave they bought me a bicycle. I used to cycle home often. They used to say do you want to go home. And then I would get away. I was with them for 3 years and I left there to get married. So I only had 6 years working. When I got married we went out to Charing. My husband Edward (born 1891, died 1953) was a confectioner. I didn't work in the bakery. I had enough to do with the babies.

Then came the war and he went into the army. My father said to my husband "You can't leave her right out in the country on her own". He fetched me home. Bag and Baggage. When I came home to Fordwich a little cottage came up just 2 doors away so I took the cottage. I went and stayed in the cottage. My husband didn't like it very much. It was the best thing I thought for the children and we were happy in the cottage. Then after he got out of the army we pushed up there in Sturry behind the Welsh Harp. It was the only shop that was there.

[There had been a bakery on the site since 1724. It closed in 1996] A man or woman in a business that makes cakes, icings all that sort of thing was a confectioner. He could do it all – bread – his father had a business of his own. My husband was the eldest boy and he didn't want to go into an office so he learned the bakery trade then after he had been with his father for some time he went to his uncle and worked with him for some time in the bakery – on the Romney Marsh near Dymchurch. He was there with his uncle for some time then he came to Herne Bay. That's where we met each other. Then we finished up in Canterbury. He became an invalid. I couldn't have responsibility for him and the business as well. So we had to sell the business and we moved into Canterbury. He liked Canterbury – it was his home. If I am ever left alone I won't stay in Canterbury for longer than I can help. It was never home to me. I've always been used to the country. Mind you it was a nice part of Canterbury. At the same time when I was on my own it was too big for me. Then I had the opportunity of this little cottage back in Fordwich so I bought that and settled in. I mean I've got the 4 boys and 4 girls. They are all so good to me. They visit as often as they can. My boys are all away now. He left everything in such a neat way. I mean I shouldn't have known a bit where I was otherwise. The children were awfully good to me. I go away in the summer time. They come and fetch me and I stay with them. I mustn't spend more time with one than the other. If I stay 3 weeks with one I've got stay 3 weeks with the other. My husband used to work early in the morning and on to half past five. I used to help him because we had help in the bake house so he didn't do it entirely by himself. He had somebody on the round with him. He always delivered the bread. He used to go to Upstreet on the Margate road and Broad Oak. He knew Mrs Headley. Her father married each of my girls, Doreen and Betty. Is he still living? He was such a nice man. What are you going to do with this – make a book of it?

Mrs Margaret Neame outside the bakery in Fordwich Road.

The Shooting Party

by K.H. McIntosh

On the night of Monday, 6th December, 1886, George Challen, the gamekeeper on the Elbridge estate in Trenley Park, was on the alert for poachers. He had with him his son, Benjamin, and Harry Boys, son of the estate gardener, both aged nineteen. He was on the alert because a man had been apprehended and charged with night poaching there the week before and he had reason to believe that there might be poachers in the wood that night.

There were in fact five of them: Henry Curtis, aged 32, a labourer in the employ of Mr Skinner, a carrier; Richard Terry, age 26 and William Grant, age 19, also labourers; and two brothers – James Dawkins, age 28, a seller of watercress and rabbits, and William Dawkins, aged 48, a hawker and night-watchman.

At 11.15 pm shots were heard below them by the gamekeepers, who were standing in the wood on the south side of Stodmarsh Road and to the east of its junction with the top of Mote Lane, Fordwich, beside Ten Acre Field. The footpath goes beside a disused gravel pit, through Mote Rough, down over the Lampen Stream and onto the Littlebourne Road.

The first part of this footpath was known locally as Hangman's Alley because of its medieval connection with the way to the King's Tree – a euphemism for a gibbet. (These were usually placed on parish boundaries as in this case to instil fear into as many inhabitants as possible).

As the gamekeepers advanced in the direction of the shots, two of the poachers came towards them, the two groups standing only some ten feet apart. As Challen, the gamekeeper, said "I have about got you" one of the poachers fired at him. The charge lodged in George Challen's left thigh, inflicting a severe wound. These two poachers then ran away over the field towards Fordwich, pursued by Harry Boys, one falling down in his flight. A gun went off again which I thought more important than the judge did.

Benjamin Challen sent Harry Boys for help while he himself stayed with his injured father. He soon heard the two poachers coming back through Homersham's wattle-working yard, (later to become Christchurch University Sports Ground). Benjamin Challen, who notably kept his head throughout, put his hand over his father's mouth to stop him revealing their whereabouts and eventually the poachers went off down the track to the Littlebourne Road.

They buried their gun and a hen pheasant just below the gates of the long-gone Mote Park (always known as the Apple Pudding Gates and now the entrance to the Polo Farm Sports Ground) and made off to Canterbury by the side road through Barton Farm that comes out by the Chaucer School.

Harry Boys brought some men and a cart up from Fordwich and George Challen, still bleeding, was carried to Elbridge House where he was attended by Mr Edward Jameson of Sturry (a doctor's assistant, who sadly was himself to be murdered in Fordwich ten years later [1]. Dr T.S.Johnson visited Challen the next day and found him very shocked, with an almost imperceptible pulse, the patient himself convinced that he would not recover. He didn't - he died the next day.

The police recovered the gun and the pheasant, which was still alive. All the poachers were charged with murder and night poaching. While James Dawkins was being taken in a cab to the County Gaol in Longport, Canterbury, he cried and asked the police if he "was to have his neck stretched".

The inquest was held in "The Swan Inn" in Sturry High Street and was conducted by the County Coroner, Mr R.M.Mercer, an old sparring partner of Dr Johnson. [2] William Grant turned Queen's Evidence and was discharged to become a witness at the trial the following February. At this, a gunsmith, Mr W. Bodin of Burgate, Canterbury, deposed that the gun fired by Dawkins had an exceptionally light pull of one pound and not the more usual four and a half pounds. The prosecutor observed rather tartly that nevertheless it had not fired itself!

Dr T.S.Johnson deposed that Challen's heart was found to be in poor condition for a man of his age.

The Defence submitted that the discharge from the gun had been unintentional on the part of Dawkins and due to his having been startled by the sudden appearance of the keepers.

Rather to my surprise in view of the second shot, the jury agreed with this and returned a verdict of "Not Guilty" to the murder charge. All four men pleaded guilty to night poaching. James Dawkins, who admitted to previous convictions, was sentenced to five years' penal servitude, and the others each to six months' hard labour, in the ringing words of 'The Kentish Gazette,' "thus bringing to an end the activities of a nefarious local gang".

[1]McIntosh, K.H. STURRY – THE CHANGING SCENE (1972) p 94.
[2]Bygone Kent, 1998, Vol 19, no 9 p 543.

The Shooting Party: Path in Trenley Park Wood

F. Stanley Homersham - Hurdlemaker

April 1903 - August 1987

Interviewed by Tim Fletcher and others at an unknown date.

Were you born here? [Silver Birch formerly Ephrath, Island Road, then Westbere, now Sturry]

No, at Addiscombe Villa, just down the Island Road from here.

How old were you when you started work?

Fourteen, I was fourteen on the Sunday and started work on the Monday.

And what job did you start with?

The sawing of logs.

How did you learn to make the hurdle and how long does it take?

Well, if you do it young, you can learn in a couple of years.

How did you start?

You mean actually making them? Well, you see, I went with my father and he did the more skilled parts and I actually nailed them together with what they used to call rose nails or cut nails. They were made of wrought iron and were pretty tough. That was before they invented wire nails. Then I was taught to use a draw shave – that's a long blade with a handle at both ends that you used for shaving off the wood that you don't need. Then you started splitting.

That's quite a skilled job surely because presumably you can split all the wood the wrong way.

Oh, yes. Very easily! What you wanted was what we called a good "run", when it split easily the right way.

What tools did you use for splitting? Wedges?

Oh no – that was my father's job. [Arthur Henry Homersham] I wasn't quite sure of the words, the names of all the tools, when I started but I learned them all later and what you needed for the wedges if a sledge-hammer wouldn't do the job was a beetle. That was a two-handed job. What was best, though, was a dowel axe. Three cuts with that and you were away. Then you had to learn how to work the saw-horse – a sort of stool

with pegs in it to lay the saw in it so that you could sharpen the teeth.

So how much were you paid when you started?

About a shilling a week.

And what could you get for a shilling in those days?

It was just a bit of pocket money. I think when my brother first started work he used to get about six shillings. [Arthur Douglas Homersham, The 1st Battalion, The Buffs (East Kent Regiment) killed in action 27 June 1917, aged 20]

What sort of house did you have? Small or large?

Well, we lived at Grove Villa on the Island Road. It is two flats now. We moved up there on 1st April 1914. My grandfather had died in 1911 and my grandmother stayed on at Grove Villa for a few years. I suppose that was until the beginning of 1914. I don't know why but

I think she financed her sons for a short while until they had got on their feet and then she moved to Canterbury. My father moved up into Grove Villa and he eventually bought it and then there were his two brothers, one who went away soon afterwards and the one that got caught up in the First World War about 1916 and went on his own when he came back.

[William E. Homersham, whose business was at Home Rest, Island Road, Sturry, was a noted professional cricketer for General Lambton's XI at Hoath in 1904 and was involved with Sturry Cricket Club from 1895 to 1956. [1,2,] [Stanley himself was a great supporter of both the Kent County Cricket Club and the Sturry Cricket Club.]

Did your father have his own business?

Yes, it came from my grandfather to the three sons, as I said.

What did you do? Get contracts from different farms or what?

No, you would buy the chestnut wood or the underwood standing.

Do you know how much you paid for it?

Well, it was sold in cants, that was an area of wood, half an acre, three-quarters of an acre or whatever, by auction. I don't know for sure how much it cost Dad in those days. About £5 an acre I would have said then.

You axed it down, I suppose?

Oh yes, you bought the wood, you see, not the land. In twelve years or so the stool would grow up again. It went up in value quite a bit.

That would be about 1920?

No before then, before the First World War, yes.

And then when you cut the chestnut you obviously had to take it out of the wood.

You would bring it where we had the wood yard just down here, you see. The horses and tugs would bring it down from the wood as green-timber.

What kind of horses?

Just heavy horses, no special breed. And the wood was brought on trailers you see, on what we would call a tug. Then they were sawn up into lengths and in the old days the chap who was on piece-work would cut his own lengths off and make up all of it

And what did he do, hope that someone would come and buy it or did he get his contracts? Do you know?

Well, he would work what we would call piece-work. I think when my father first did it for my grandfather he got 5 pence a hurdle, but then they were selling for £5 a hundred in those days.

Did they get a living out of it?

It was very hard work but it was clean work and it was healthy work.

How many hours did you put in?

They used to work from 7 to 7 and 4 o'clock on Saturday afternoon.

What was it like compared with a farm labourer's work?

Oh, better and of course they used to get the odds and ends of wood, chips and shavings to light a fire and that. Bavins and cordwood, they called that. My mum [Rose Matilda Homersham] used to cook nearly all by wood when we were kids.

That must have been quite a saving.

Oh yes, it was and we were never short of firing. We never went to bed with cold feet and my grandfather – I admired him for that, he planted up a little plantation of fruit trees and by Jove we reaped the benefit of those.

Where did he have them, in the back yard?

On a piece of ground down here where the road goes up.

And it worked and you all ate well?

Oh yes, damson trees, cherry trees, Morello trees, apple trees. He didn't do any spraying at all in those days, no, the fruit just came and came and it always tasted nice.

You won't have needed to buy any jam!

Well, it all depended on the seasons, same as Father was very fond of gardening, we always had plenty of vegetables. I know there was quite a to-do if the blight got into the potatoes or if an apple crop wasn't good.

What about meat?

We always had quite a lot of meat. We always had a good old joint.

You got it from the butchers?

Oh yes, and my father would bring a rabbit or two and we would have a rabbit pie.

I remember eating them myself during the war.

Oh, the rabbit pies! Lovely. And bottles of cherries we used to have, put down with sugar.

What about pigeons?

I can't remember having a pigeon until I had the business myself and a chap caught one in the wood one day and my Mother cooked it for me and it was beautiful.

When you took over the business yourself how old were you?

Thirty.

Thirty? You worked for your father until then. Do you remember Brett's Quarries coming here?

They were actually preparing for them during the war, making the roads in but they never started sort of getting cracking until after the war. Before then it was just some planks and a wheelbarrow – not at all like Brett's methods.

Did it harm this area in any way? And did you mind it or did it bring work to the people?

It brought a lot of work but I don't think it can have pleased a lot of families who were living down there beside the works.

And that was just before the war or after the war?

Brett's were going before the war. They were just picking up but I think the First World War made them. [3]

Can you remember any other interesting things about work around here, particularly farm labourers. When farming they obviously did a lot of ploughing. How did they do the ploughing?

With horses. I had seen a little bit of steam ploughing then but not very much.

Have you done any hop-picking?

Oh yes. Six weeks holiday we skipped and four weeks of that was in the hop garden.

Was that hard work?

Well, we would have to start walking from Grove Villa before six o'clock in the morning to get over to Elbridge and we used to have to do that every day.

Did you go as a group?

Well, no, mother and my sister, not my younger sister, she wasn't born then and of course my brother went when he was younger but he never went to Elbridge because he had left school by the time we got there and my younger sister had not arrived then. We started off at Denne's at Fordwich - they were very poor hop gardens - and then we did one year at Stodmarsh Court and then we finally got to Holdstock's at Elbridge Farm and that is where the hot weather did grow good hops.

Did you earn much money from it?

Now, I am going to tell you this. You may not believe this but I have to stop and think sometimes if it is correct, but it is. In 1913 we had five weeks of hop-picking. It was an exceptionally good year. I didn't do much in it because I was a devil for picking hops but my elder sister and my mother and we had 11 pence a basket, that was five bushels of hops – what they called a tally measure and my mother and sister and I we earned £10 in those five weeks.

It would be about £60 now I reckon, don't you?

Oh yes, oh yes. More, I would think.

The farmers, they transport all their stuff these days on big lorries, you know. As they get the grain in they transport it on big lorries. In those days they used what?

The wagons, they used to have wonderful teams of horses in those days. I don't know of many people round here with horses now but there used to be a man, do you know Tomson and Wotton, the Brewers?

Vaguely.

Well, they were Ramsgate people. Well, Mr Wotton had Tile Lodge Farm – this is going back before the First War and he always used to show at Smithfield and we used to see the big cattle walking down the road, you know. When they were too fat they used to have some transport to get them down there.

On carts?

Yes, those that were too fat. They really used to fatten them up in those days.

Where did they take them to?

To Sturry Station and on to the railway wagons.

That must have been quite a sight!

I used to see them going by. There always used to be a man named Gurney who walked the stallion horse round. I used to admire those horses. Lovely, they were.

What was this road like in those days?

Oh, very quiet. I used to play on it as a child!

Hardly any traffic?

Almost none.

Was the Island Road ever a small country lane?

No, it's always been more or less like this. It used to be a little wider. Now we have got a footpath on the other side which we didn't have in those days which has narrowed it.

But it was less busy then?

Oh, gosh, yes! There was a man named Ashley used to live across the road, he had a car of some sort. I don't know what they called them and Mr Hilton used to live at Oaklands, he was a banker. His car's number was FN 29, and Dr. Ince, he had a car, being the doctor.

They were the only three cars in the village? That is fantastic!

But as you got nearer to the First War you got sort of traffic on Sundays. Well, you talking about that, a most interesting thing – the Germans came to bore that pitch for the mine and we had three German kiddies come to Sturry School and of course when the war started they disappeared. [4] At Sturry School when we were small children we went up for examinations and we had a big boy or girl sitting each side of you so that you couldn't look over and copy.

What was school like in those days? Can you tell me something about school life? Was it strict?

Oh yes.

In what way?

Well, we were always scared, especially of the Headmaster. Until you got a bit older and then you wasn't quite so bad, but unfortunately for me my brother was good at school, especially at arithmetic. I wasn't and I was always having that drummed into me by the teachers.

Were you scared of getting the cane or anything like that?

No, I do not think Mr Pope ever caned me.

Did he cane the children much?

Not very much. Mr. Bournes used to do a bit of caning in the 3rd and 4th year. I got the cane from him, but I think what I feared most he would ridicule you in front of the other kiddies.

And that was a bad thing?

With me it was.

Chestnut growing for coppicing

Did the kiddies resent this?

Well, it used to hurt me.

What was the valley like before the quarries?

Oh lovely and green. Beautiful. You see a lot of people think that this estate down here [Fairview Gardens] is too low-lying and that it is damp but there were arable fields the other side of the railway. You can tell that where the football pitch is. It used to go right through there but as you get to Westbere it narrows off a bit. Personally I would like to see it all filled in and see the cattle grazing down there again. It used to be wonderful grazing ground for cattle.

Can you remember anything about farming around here? Hops and orchards, I suppose.

Yes, but it was more mixed farming when I was a boy, the orchards have come since. Like Mr. Brook's orchard at Broad Oak. That was a shocking derelict farm when he came into it. With more hops in those days when I was a kid and we had hops at Tile Lodge and hops at Fordwich when I was very small, and at Stodmarsh and Wickhambreaux .

So, you moved to this house fairly late on?

We moved from Addiscombe Villa on 1st April 1914 and we moved into this one on 1st April 1927.

You were very proud of it when you got here were you?

I have always liked this house. I never liked being at Grove Villa. I suppose it was during those years I used to suffer with my nerves so when I was a youngster. I suppose my mother was very nervous and my father didn't like meeting people, even though he wouldn't admit it. And my brother was killed when I was living at Grove Villa and I think that must have had some effect on me.

When you made these hurdles, how many could your father make - say - in an hour?

He used to make one in about ¼ hour.

Is there a record time in which people made hurdles?

Yes, let me think, as we progressed a bit, there was a chappie named Fred Clayson lived at Addiscombe Villas. He used to make about 14 a day. Well, he did when he worked for me.

Fourteen a day?

Yes, that is from 7 am – 5 pm.

After you took over the business I suppose you actually gave up making hurdles yourself and ran the business.

Oh no, I had to make hurdles myself. I've even got a receipt from Mr Winston Churchill for supplying him with hurdles that I made for him.

Did you make anything else as well as hurdles?

As the years went by we went in a small way into paling fencing and just before the war farming was in such a dire strait that my trade was going down and we had a job to survive and about that time they were going in for this paling fencing you see as they used to come to our chaps, us small chappies to make the palings for them. We used to make bundles of 25 and I always contended that was what put me on my feet financially. Because the first thing we started doing, and you may not believe this, for a bundle of three feets, [the height of the fence] that was 25 in a bundle, I used to get 8 ½d. for it and I used to give the chappies 4 ½d. to get them ready, but I took £200 that year, it was terrific for me.

They were easier to make, were they?

No, it was that the money kept coming in each month. With some of these jolly old farmers you would wait from one Michaelmas to the next Michaelmas and sometimes they would go to the next Michaelmas after that before you got your money. Our biggest customers were the Auctioneers, the Bensteds at Sittingbourne, and Ambrose and Foster at Maidstone. There were several of them I used to make for, but Bensteds and Ambrose and Foster were the two principal ones. They used to buy the hurdles for their Sheep Fairs and that sort of thing and then instead of having the hurdles pinched afterwards, as they did get pinched or broken, they used to sell them on afterwards and renew them the next year, and they used to sometimes make a profit on them, people used to buy a few.

Why do you think it was that the palings made so much? Did the auctioneers use them more?

I think the reason was you could cut shorter lengths for palings than you could for hurdles. Sheep hurdles were 8 feet long by 4 feet high and you couldn't have crooked old pieces, you see, while if you had palings you could cut between those hooks, you was combining the two.

Sturry Cricket Team, 1936.
Back row: R.Hopkins, Frank Holmes, Geoff Maile, Sid Burton, Len Dale, W. Wooldridge, unknown, umpire.
Front row: Roy Rose, J.Burton, C.Homersham, W.E.Homersham. Owen Wood. Scorer, F.Smith.

I see, so there was a lot less wastage. What wood did you use for palings, the same as for hurdles?

Oh yes, mostly chestnut.

How long does a chestnut tree take to grow for coppicing?

About twelve to fourteen years.

About how high do they grow?

About 30 feet, but it all depends where it grows. It lasts about 40 years – it's got tannin in it, you see.

Who owned the land, the farmers?

What, the woods? Most of them did and I think the reason we have got so much chestnut in Kent is because of the hop growing industry.

Did the farmers have to clear it at all?

Well, just clear the tracks, the lanes, that sort of thing.

Because I worked on the Forestry for some time and we had some blokes who used to do this, but it was 15 years ago, but you see it less and less now. Well, shall we leave this for now?

[1] Derek and Allan Butler VILLAGE VIEWS (1988)
[2] D.R.Butler 100 YEARS OF STURRY CRICKET (1963)
[3] Paul Tritton ONE FAMILY, ONE FIRM, ONE HUNDRED YEARS (2009)
[4] Ross Llewellyn HERSDEN – Chislet Colliery Village (2003)

Early Years in Hersden
George Lock

(Born 1906)

Interviewed in a residential home in 2000 at the age of 94 by John Line

I was born in 1906 in Union Street, Canterbury

You see you have nearly got a whole century to talk about

Yes, I know but one gets a little bit rusty.

What was life like for you as a child?

Well, difficult. My father came out of the Navy and went to the Electricity Works in the boilers and he was only keen on my going in the Navy so he could send me to College.

Did you enjoy your childhood and your work?

Yes, I did very well. I was doing all sorts of things. I was being on the end of looking after old people. Even with old miners. You see I used to run all the old miners after they had so many years at the pit. They used to be able to come to a dinner every year at the old Welfare Hall. I was in charge of that.

That is a wonderful Hall isn't it? Beautiful dance floor in there and everything

They had a Steward and Stewardess and dances and sports welfare there and I won the Championship Cup in tennis. Yes, I could change hands and I was ambidextrous.

You were a champion up there

Yes, I won it up there. That is when I was at work and when I got on further at work I used to do all sorts of things, looking after the old people, giving them all parties, everything that came under welfare.

There was an awful lot of good work done in the Welfare Centre

Oh, yes. I went and signed on to go to war as I thought, but the Coal Board stopped me because things were getting a bit tight. We had all these trainees coming. [The Bevin Boys, men conscripted into the mines instead of the fighting services]

So you had to stay at the pit

Yes, I had to rig them out and train them out in the fields. I then became a Special Constable. I was running dances there, right opposite my office and I was here when they built the first new offices.

I was told that it was heated from steam that came right up from the pit

Yes. Just outside the door there was the back pump.

So you started doing your welfare work in the Black Hut?

Yes, I started right opposite. Before my offices were built.

Were you part of the church organization there?

Well, I used to attend the Methodist Church. The Thomas' were the church in Hersden [1]

It was very interesting how it did not seem to matter what denomination people were, they all became Methodist because that was the only church that was there to begin with.

It was funny really, it was all new to me. I got roped in to do this and that and I ran all the Sports, started them off on golf.

Well, you had wonderful sports facilities up there eventually

The Welfare used to pay so much a week and everybody paid, whether they lived there or not.

There was all sorts of things. They had Rugby teams, football, tennis, the Bowls Club which is still going well

I used to play bowls. I had a go at everything, because I was responsible up there. Of course, we had a fine body of people to run it.

When I was at school there were a lot of wonderful sports people came from Hersden, footballers and athletes

Yes, that was the reason why some of the people lived here.

One of Mr Ernest Banks' buses

(A lady comes in at this point and thinks the interviewer is a reporter. He explains what he is doing):

We are trying to make a history of the last century as seen by the people who lived in our villages. It is difficult to try to think now what Sturry was like when I was a kid, say, 50 years back. It is vastly different to what it is like now.

(Lady makes suitable noises and goes!!)

Are any of the events that happened in your life that you obviously celebrated at the Welfare Club?

The men used to pay so much a week, 3d. or so, and then we used to organize those events together.

What happened when King George V1 was crowned?

Yes, we had the celebrations up there. The Coal Board donated money towards it and directly they started work, the miners would pay 2d. or 3d. a week which I was responsible for.

Did you have any famous people come down to the Colliery?

Oh, yes. These stars used to come down and give a show in the Welfare Hall. I used to engage them to come down and play in the Hall.

In those days you used to have live music, not tapes or anything

Oh yes, we used to have some good times. Of course, the Welshmen (not picking them out particularly) but the miners were mad on singing, and miners could sing.

You had a choir up there, didn't you?

We used to have all these big concerts up there. We had a colliery band. It is all coming back once you start talking. I had forgotten those things. They used to bring the ponies up for a little run round. We had ponies down the pit then.

Because there were no trains down there, I suppose. It was either pony power or man power then. Can you remember there was a railway line that went across from the colliery up to round about the North View and East View area. Can you remember what that was for, because somebody told me that they brought all the bricks and wood in via this railway to build the houses there, but they wouldn't build a railway just to build houses would they?

Oh yes, we had to have it to get the men to the mine because we had a lot of men from Ramsgate and round about that used to come to and fro. We had to give bus passes and train fares, so much a week.
I can remember Ernie Banks running the colliery buses to bring the miners in from the village and the coal

lorries and delivery. Of course, each miner got so much coal when they got a house.

Black gold that was, wasn't it? It must have been a very, very good thing for those sort of days when life was a bit tough

Well, my job was regular. When I first went there I used to come across the field to some houses on the main road every morning at 11 o'clock for a cup of tea. I was the tea boy when I first started. I used to come on the bus and my father bought me a bike, get the papers at old Ma Cork's as I came through.

What about the big strike in 1926?

I got caught going home with coal on the mudguard in a bag and when I was caught I was stopped. They wouldn't believe my word that it was part of my money. They stopped people stealing coal during the start-up on the work down the boilers.

I suppose you had to keep the pumps working

Oh yes, that was me. I worked down the pump house two or three days and did the wages for the people that were working, that was mostly officials and non-union members.

But the pumps had to be kept going, otherwise there was flooding

Oh, yes. We had safety men down there all the time.

How long did it last? [2]

(George didn't know)

It must have been quite an education for them, the people coming down from London

Yes, but The Welfare Association use to pay 3d. a week for the funds and the Colliery used to double it up.

You had a very good social life, it was very close knit

Oh yes. Well, we had air raid shelters built in the main street in Hersden where the shop is now. They said "Here he comes – children and Specials first!!"

One lady got hit by a stray bullet, I heard

Yes, she was a slight relation of mine – Ivy Lowther (nee Dalton)

Not much else damaged up there?

Not really, no. We spent quite a lot of time in the house where we built our own shelter.

I remember at the end of the war living on the farm, we had one outside. You got to the gate and just dived in

Coming off duty when the whistle warning went we all used to go to the shelters you know. Just used to go 'Children and Specials first!!' They were glorious times really, nice to remember.

We didn't have much of a war, did we?

No, we didn't know much about it.

It was more fun really, spotting the planes and the doodlebugs and the fun in the shelters

With the police, I went round drilling and God knows what.

Did you have to go out in the blackout?

Oh yes, I done most of that in Hersden and Westbere. Well, I came down here to Westbere when they got pushed. Being in the Fire Service we got four bob a week, special allowance. I have still got my medals for the police and fire service from the colliery.

Long service medals?

Yes, the men had to have the money and we had to have the coal. We had lots of trying cases. A lot to deal with here but the Welfare covered the lot. It was good.

[1] Muriel Thomas FIFTY YEARS OF METHODISM IN A KENTISH MINING VILLAGE - HERSDEN 1929-1979 (1979)
[2] see KNIGHTS TO REMEMBER, Sir Arthur Pugh below p 38
[3] Ross Llewellyn HERSDEN – Chislet Colliery Village (2003)

William Thompson of Broad Oak

1908 - 1985 (In conversation in 1971)

I entered Sturry Church of England Primary School in 1913 at the age of 5 and left at 14. There were no secondary schools, you went to the one school for nine years. I went in the war years and there were more women teachers than men because the men were in the army.

There were no such things as school meals. Children from a long way away brought their dinners in satchels and in winter used to bring a large potato which the headmistress would mark with their initials. She then placed the potatoes under the big open fire at about 10.30 a.m. and handed them out, cooked, at twelve o'clock.

As I lived in Sturry I went home for dinner. There was no school milk or any other drink and only one tap in the lobby that served the entire school. There were no flushing lavatories - just buckets and chemicals. Children walked up to three miles to school and back because until 1916 there were no buses.

Holidays were much the same as now except that there were no half-terms and if hop-picking lasted more than 6 or 7 weeks in the summer we could stay away until we had finished picking them, which could be a week or more. Children had to pick to earn money to get themselves clothes and boots. Most children, although not me, wore hobnail boots because they lasted longer and as the school floors were all wooden, the noise was incredible. Most of their fathers worked in the local gravel pits or on farms so, of course, if it rained, they lost time and therefore had lower wages that week.

Children often came to school really ragged and on wet days some couldn't come because their boots were no good and Wellingtons hadn't been invented. Nits and lice were about and I remember girls having to have their hair cut short and boiled vinegar rubbed into it – it stank on a hot day!

A good eight out of ten children, I should say, had never been away from Broad Oak for a holiday and a great many had never been on a train. I was lucky and went on holiday every year to places such as Guildford, London, Suffolk, etc.

There were exams and also two scholarships to the Simon Langton Schools and one to Kent College. Sandy Piper was the only boy I knew who went to Kent College but he was really clever. If a girl was 14 and quite bright she used to give lessons to the Infants class for a year or so instead of leaving school: otherwise we all left at 14.

The school had small windows and in the Autumn and Winter the lights were on all day; these were gaslights as there was no electricity in the village then. There were no prefects but one child would act as monitor, more or less a head boy or head girl. No homework, no ballpoint pens – desks had inkwells let into them. The Infants and lower classes used slates and chalk.

Games were different, too. At times it would be a craze for hoops and then it would be "button in the hole". Boys would make a hole in the playground about 3 inches deep and 4 inches across and then throw buttons into it. The boy who got the most buttons in the hole won all the buttons there. Then there would be a craze for tops and all the way to school children would be spinning tops right across the road. It was safe to do this because the only vehicle that could run you over was Obadiah Moat's horse-bus which went from Canterbury to Herne Bay twice a day for 4d.

The price for picking hops was ten pence a tally (which was 5 bushels) for a variety called "Fuggles", which were as long as your finger. "Goldings" were one shilling a tally – these were very small hops. A good woman picker could pick 24 bushels a day if she was very fast. All the money was paid out at the end of the "hopping" and it always seemed a big sum. I have picked hops for 7 weeks and at the end I had enough money to buy a nine shilling fretwork set. I really thought I had the earth!

You see in those days the public house was the cause of a lot of trouble as life was lived on a much lower scale. Men worked hard in the gravel pits – there were no machines to dig it out – and it was sheer hard work. Women used to wait outside the pub on Saturdays to get their housekeeping money before it was all drunk. I suppose the average wage for a lot of the men would have been about 25/- a week. A lot of the gravel digging was piece-work – so much a yard. In most villages of a Saturday and Sunday night you could see lots of drunken men in the streets but things have improved now. Outlook has changed and standards of life risen.

There was no dole in those days and until Lloyd George fetched out the National Insurance Scheme people used to pay into "Slate Clubs" run by the village pubs. They used to pay in a shilling a week and, if there hadn't been many sick in the year, there was a share-out at Christmas which might be as much as 12/-: a lot in those days. There was more sickness and colds in those days as it was the custom of many of the mothers to take in other people's washing. This entailed drying lots of clothes indoors and the children naturally caught a lot of colds.

I enjoyed my time at school but I realise that I did not suffer the hardship of being born poor and, I'm glad for the opportunities the youngsters get today.

Knights to Remember
Sir Michael Nethersole

Sir Michael Henry Braddon Nethersole, K.B.E., C.S.I., C.I.E., D.S.O., who was born in Dover, belonged to a long-established East Kent family and was a great nephew of M.E.Braddon, the famous author of "Lady Audley's Secret". He came to live at Stonerocks, Hawe Lane, Sturry, in 1947 after serving in the Indian Civil Service since 1919. Until the Partition of India he had been a Senior Member of the Board of Revenue in the United Provinces (Utter Pradesh) there and sat as a judge in Bareilly.

Born in 1891, and a gifted classical scholar at Wadham College, Oxford, he served with great distinction in the First World War, joining up in 1914. He was firstly a Major in the Royal Garrison Artillery and then became a notable Squadron Commander in No 103 Squadron, R.A.F. He was Mentioned in Dispatches and awarded the French Croix de Guerre in 1917 and awarded the D.S.O. in 1919.

He entered into village life with enthusiasm, being President of the Cricket Club in 1950 and 1951, and in much demand as a speaker. He was an especially eloquent member of the Sturry Good Fellowship.

He left Sturry in 1953 and was appointed the Chief Justice of the Seychelles Islands. There at one time he had in prison both Archbishop Makarios and Colonel Grivas, exiled from Cyprus after the EOKA conflict in 1956. He was also Chairman of the Board of Governors of Seychelles College and head of the Civil Service Commission of the Islands.

He left a widow and daughter by his first wife, who died in 1944, and later married again. He died on February 14th, 1965, at the age of 73 at his home in Mahe and is buried in the Seychelles Islands.

Michael H.B. Nethersole (reproduced with the kind permission of the Fleet Air Arm Museum).

Madeline Bates

A Sturry Memorial
by Hazel Basford

The memorial first came to my notice several years ago when I was undertaking a study at the University of Kent of the work done by volunteers in Kent to care for the sick and wounded of the First World War. I found Elsie Bates's name on a list of members of the Canterbury Voluntary Aid Detachment, (VAD), but with no further information supplied. After 1915 VAD members could volunteer for service abroad, and many served in the large hospitals that were set up in places along the French Channel coast from Calais to Rouen and it seems that Elsie was one such volunteer.

Some nurses' graves are listed by the Commonwealth War Graves Commission and I found that Elsie was buried at Shenfield in Essex. Further research revealed that she had been visiting her brother at the time of her death and had been killed during an air raid. She is buried in the churchyard under a private memorial, but her name is also on the local war memorial.

Millicent Sutherland-Leveson-Gower, Duchess of Sutherland, (1867-1955), travelled to Europe at the outbreak of war in August 1914 offering to provide medical relief for wounded soldiers. She initially met with resistance from the military authorities but managed to establish a unit in Namur in Belgium. Later the Duchess was able to form an Ambulance Car Convoy and a Red Cross Hospital, (No. 9 at Calais) which is where Elsie Bates served. All the women who volunteered for service overseas had to have some sort of financial backing since allowances, if any, were tiny.

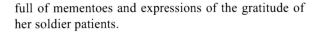

Photograph of M.E.Bates

In November 2009 a chance meeting in Folkestone led to my meeting a great-niece of Elsie Bates, who was her father's favourite aunt and proudly remembered within the family. To my eye this lady bears a striking resemblance to her great-aunt. She showed me a photograph of Elsie and also her small autograph book,

full of mementoes and expressions of the gratitude of her soldier patients.

Elsie was born in Waltham Abbey, Essex, in about 1883, the oldest daughter of William and Annie Bates. Her father was a Corn Commission Agent and she had two older brothers. Another brother and sister followed. The family lived in Essex until about 1900. The 1901 Census records show that Elsie was then working in Ramsgate for a draper and living there. However, by 1911 it seems her fortunes had changed since she was living with her sister at Southover, Island Road, Sturry, and is recorded as having "private income". Of her father there is no record in the 1911 Census, but her mother is then keeping house for her widowed brother-in law, Frederick Maxted, a farmer at Broad Oak Farm, Sweechgate.

No doubt there is more to be discovered about Elsie Bates and the tragic end to her life – what were her experiences in Calais, why was she buried in Shenfield and not brought back to Sturry where her mother and sister were living? However, it has been quite wonderful to see recently an image of the woman who prompted her comrades in France to provide this unique remembrance of her on a pillar in Sturry Church and so ensure that she is not forgotten.

Photograph of brass plate in nave of St Nicholas Church, Sturry

High on a pillar in the church of St Nicholas at Sturry is a brass memorial. Those who take time to read it will find the words

***Sacred to memory of
Elsie Madeline Bates
who was killed when on
leave, after devoted
service to her country
in France December 1917
This tablet is erected
by her comrades of the
Millicent Sutherland
Ambulance, Calais***

Life With Lady Milner

Mrs Emily Victoria May Cork (née Hillman)
Died 14 November, 1980, aged 80

Interviewed by Margaret Edmonds at an unknown date

I'd like to ask you, how did you first come to be with the Milners? You were quite young at the time, weren't you?

Yes, I was nineteen, I think. And she was on a visit to Lord Milner at Sturry Court, and I had to join her there. It was the 12th April, 1919, I remember perfectly when it was, and we stayed the weekend. But we had quite a number of weekends there afterwards.

That was 1919, was it? So in fact they weren't married then, were they?

Oh no, they were sort of friendly, you know. Helen [Lady Milner's daughter] used to come with us, Lady Hardinge, I liked her, she was a sweet girl, and she used to come there; and Lord Edward [Lord Edward Herbert Gascoyne-Cecil, K.C.M.G, D.S.O. 1867-1918] had just died, her first husband, and in those days, you know, they wore widow's weeds – you know what they are, do you? A black veil with a white band – it was French designers in France in those days, because there were so many widows during the war.

I think you gave me a black and white band. Would that be the one you gave me? I thought you said it came from one of the hats?

No, they were ordinary black and white ones. I used to have to change it quite often to keep it nice and clean. But that's what we did.

But how did you come to be in her employment anyway? Did you see an advertisement?

Oh, she'd got an aunt that lived in Fittleworh, our village, and she wrote and asked her if she knew of anybody. And I'd been for a very short time, my very first post, with a cousin of Lady Milner's, Miss McGeorge, and then she married a Colonel Somebody. Anyway, he was still in the Army and they were going to be fixed up in Ireland, and I didn't want to go, so I told this Miss Steele, this old aunt, that I didn't want to go, so she said, "Well, I'll write to my other niece to see if she wants anybody." She rang up and asked me to go up to see her in London – on the following Thursday it was, and she said 'Would I come'.

So where was Lady Milner living at this time? She was living in London, was she?

Well, she lived at Great Wigsall, the other house, and at that time her daughter, Helen, was what was called 'coming out', you know, and she used to take furnished houses for the Season, for entertaining for her. We had one in Buckingham Gate, opposite Buckingham Palace, and we had another one in Bryanston Square, which is where Lady Milner eventually married from, and I remember it perfectly, 24A Bryanson Square; and the morning that she married him I went in to call her, and she said "I've got something to tell you." She said "I'm getting married to Lord Milner at eleven o'clock." I said "Good gracious me!" She said "Yes, but please don't tell anybody until we've married and come back." Actually, it was quite sensational, because he was an elderly man at the time, he was sixty-five, wasn't he, and it was in the evening papers in London: 'Lord Milner married today.' And in the afternoon we got the train and went and stayed two nights – no, one night, it was a Saturday – one night at the Lord Warden Hotel at Dover, and crossed to France the next day. But they had the first night at Dover. [1]

Where were they married?

The church in Sussex Square, I think, yes. And the only person who was there was her solicitor, and her sister, Miss Olive Maxse. It was all that was there.

I thought there was a Lord Edward Cecil, that's where all the other people were, people like Meredith and Oscar Wilde went to –

They didn't go there.

They must have gone to her first wedding, then. I think I read somewhere –

Where did you read all that? Because I haven't – that's a different paper, this was out of the Sunday Telegraph, the bit I've got.

Yes, it says here that she married Lord Edward Cecil, this was her first marriage, and signatures to the register were Salisbury, that was –

Brother-in-law.

Brother-in-law? Or I thought it was –

No. That would be her father-in-law, wouldn't it?

It says 'Chamberlain, Balfour, Morley and Asquith; also present were Meredith and Oscar Wilde.'

Good gracious. Where did you read that?

That was to do with this auction which is coming out in some of the papers, you know, the auction which is coming on at Sotheby's this week.

Where did you read that, then?

Well, to do with that, the catalogue which is saying what the letters are. But that was her first marriage; of course, you never knew Lord Edward Cecil did you?

No, he died just as I came. He died in Switzerland, he had TB.

Did he?

Caught it during the war. And they had to send him to Switzerland, but he died there. And then I came just after.

So then – sorry, I interrupted you, we digress – they went to Dover and then went over to where?

We went to Paris, and stayed one night in Paris, and then the following day they went down to Avignon – you've heard of that?

Yes

Avignon and I believe they had a fortnight there if I remember rightly. It was a delightful place. Oh yes, it was. And she had treatment there because she'd got so stout. And in Avignon, seaside it is, underneath the cliffs, there are some hot baths, and that's where they used to give you treatment in these hot baths.

Did it help?

She didn't stick it very long. Two men used to come up with one of those chairs – what d'you call those chairs with handles?

Sedan chairs?

Yes. They used to come and fetch her, and she had to be wrapped up and covered in, she was, and they used to carry her quite a way, down to this hot pool under the cliffs for this treatment. They used to massage her there.

What did Lord Milner do while this was going on?

Well, he used to write a lot. And when they brought her back they used to dump her on the bed under the blankets and she had to lay there and sweat it out until she dried. But she didn't do it for as long as she was supposed to do it. But he wanted her to, because it was his suggestion they should do it.

The Manor House at Sturry, now the Junior King's School.

She was very slim, wasn't she, when she was younger? I mean in the portrait in the dining hall in Milner Court, she's very slim there. [2]

Yes, I mean that would be of course when she was a young woman. The MP we had here at that time [Ronald McNeill, M.P. 1918-1927] – they travelled out on the same train with us, and they were at the same hotel. . .

And did just you go? Were you the only one who went with them?

Oh, yes.

You looked after him as well, did you? Or did you just attend to her?

Oh, yes. Him, too, I liked him very much, he was a nice man. I liked him better than her.

Yes, he was a very kind man from what you said, wasn't he?

He was understanding, yes. And I think that these experiences in his early days perhaps made him rather nicer.

He was always nice with you, wasn't he?

Very, very. And when I got lost in South Africa, he was the one that was so pleased to see me back.

When was this? This must have been a year or two after they were married?

Yes, it was. He had been High Commissioner out there, hadn't he, before he married, and they went there a month. I keep thinking about them both with all this trouble going on there, because it's sad, isn't it? We started with Cape Town, of course, and we went to Johannesburg to stay just outside with some titled people, the name's gone. But then they were going up to Durban or whatever and they wanted to motor up, so we motored up, and then they were going to motor back, and coming back through what we called the Transkei, a very wild part of South Africa, and the young man, he was a solicitor's son, he asked if we might go on and get to the hotel before they did; but he got lost, and that's when I got lost. There was a thunderstorm came on, and there's no roads on the Transkei, and when it poured with rain we got stuck in mud almost as bad as that thing now, and couldn't drive out, couldn't get out of it. And there were the Kaffir huts, the round ones, you know, and I said, "I'll have to see if they can get their ox to come and pull us out." And he said, "You wanted to see inside one of these so we'll go and look." Well, we did, and it had got a fire in the middle of it and they were all sitting round. The man couldn't speak English, but he did what we wanted, and so we went back to the

car and waited, and whilst we did that three cars had come back for us, the car that had been driving Lord Milner, and he came back for us, and with these cows and oxen they pulled us out of the mud. And that's when Lord Milner was so nice, because when we got back to the hotel he said, "There you are, I've been worried about you." And he said, "Tell me exactly what happened." So I told him like I just told you about getting stuck in the mud after a storm and everything, and I always remember him saying, "Well all I say is, don't do it again. I hope you won't have to do it again," or something like that, and I said, "Well, I hope not, either." I wasn't frightened, it was very odd, but I was young and I suppose-

And you'd got all the luggage?

Yes, his, hers and mine. And I'd got her dressing bag, too, with all the treasures in it, I'd got that.

She must have had many treasures?

Well, we used to take a certain amount of jewellery and stuff around for her to wear. I had to carry it in a cardboard box so you had to keep your eye on it!

What did you have to do for her? You dressed her and did her hair, and all those kind of things?

Not so much. She used to like her clothes seen to, of course, and I used to keep them clean, all her clothes.

Did you make her clothes?

A good many of them I did, yes, but I had lessons in Paris from her hairdresser, but she preferred to do her own hair really.

You say she had pretty hair?

Very. Lovely, it was curly.

She had it done in Paris? Not in England?

No, she always had it done in Paris. And she had some of her dresses made in Paris. The dressmaker used to come to the hotel where we stayed.

You went there quite often?

Oh, we did; four times a year we used to go to Paris.

And you met Clemenceau, I think?

Yes, we stayed with him you see, because he lived in the west of France, you see. I've been trying to remember the name [of the place] where he lived. He had been a doctor, you know.

Barn interior before restoration

Yes, I knew that.

And the people there at this small fishing place it was, in the west of France, because we stayed in a hotel actually, but it was delightful, you'd see the fishing boats with their sails, every morning we could from where we were. And he came up there and we went to his place once, but he hadn't got a very big house there. He'd got a housekeeper. But he was a charming man.

You liked him?

Yes, I did, yes he was very nice. He always spoke to me when I'd seen him. And I had seen him in Paris too, he used to come there.

Did they converse in French or English?

In English mostly. I think he liked it. She liked talking in French, yes, she did.

She spoke French fluently, of course.

But that was very nice, though, the visit to the west of France. I only went there once.

So Clemenceau was nice to you, was he? You said you formed a good opinion of him?

Yes, you can soon tell, can't you? Well, as with all of them I did get to know.

There were many of them weren't there? Did you meet De Gaulle at all?

No, not because of the family I was with, but I didn't admire him because of the way he had of treating us. Because he was over here during the war, you know, De Gaulle; he was in London, I know he was.

So, who else did you meet? You met him, and you met

Kipling, of course. I used to see a lot of him.

Where did you see him?

At Batemans. And that wasn't far from Lady Milner's house at Hawkhurst. And she had me taught to drive her car. I used to have to go over to Bateman's quite often for things. I don't know what for, notes and....

Letters?

Yes, and her brother, Mr. Leo Maxse, used to edit the National Review, a monthly political magazine, and when he was ill and couldn't do it she took it on. And I used to go over to the Kiplings sometimes with a note, and wait for an answer. They were very fond of Lady Milner's children and I used to drive them over there and stay with them.

That's the present Lord Hardinge? [George Edward Charles Hardinge, 3rd Baron Hardinge of Penshurst. 31 October 1921-14th July 1997]

Yes, those children.

And Lady Elizabeth Johnstone? Because they were very fond of you, weren't they, the Hardinge children?

Well, Lady Milner used to say, "They don't come to see me, you know, they come to see you!" I liked them very much. And the present Lord Hardinge, Georgie, he was always in my room. He loved the sewing machine. I used to give him some bits of material, and in his funny little way – he wasn't very big, you know – he'd make things with it

He'd be about, what, five?

A bit more, when he was able to use the machine. But no, they were a nice little family. And Lord Hardinge was quite nice, their father. He was a nice man.

What impression did you have of Kipling when you met him?

Oh, he was a dear old thing. He had those bushy eyebrows, hadn't he? like –

Denis Healey?

That's right

And his son, I think was killed in the war?

That's right. So was Lady Milner's boy. [George Edward Cecil, 2nd Lieutenant, Grenadier Guards, died 1st Sept 1914]. I didn't know him, he was killed in France. But his picture was always by her bed.

What was your car, the one that you drove?

A baby Austin! She got a Morris 8 afterwards, but she knew if I passed my test or not, she'd got this open one. And then she got a Morris 8 that was a bit bigger.

And you drove her about quite a lot, did you?

Yes, I did.

And you had to sit and wait outside, I think, sometimes?

Yes, I did.

Wouldn't she invite you in with her?

Well, I was the chauffeur, you see. I had to wait outside.

What happened when it rained? You had a hood presumably?

Oh yes, yes, we did.

Did she converse while you were travelling? Or was she quiet in the car?

Sometimes. If she was busy with the National Review or anything she didn't.

But you did travel by train didn't you?

The only time she did was when we went down to Oxford with the valuables – you see, Lord Milner had been given through his years in office some solid gold pieces. It was solid gold! And quite a lot of things he'd got solid gold, big things. And I used to have to go to the bank in London if she'd got a dinner party on – she used to have some very smart dinner parties – and if she had somebody very smart (coming) I used to go and get some of these gold things out, and they were all put on the dining room table (as) centre pieces. But after he died and she stopped using them, she wanted them put in the New College, and so it was after I left her, and

was nursing my people, she asked me if I could possibly come back and help her do up the boxes with all these things. So I did.

These dinner parties – you say she gave a lot of dinner parties – this was at Manchester Square, was it?

Yes, they had a lovely dining room there, a big one. And they could open the table right through, you know.

So what help did she have, then? You were with her all the time, weren't you?

Yes.

Then she had the parlourmaid?

She had two parlourmaids, and two in the house, and two people in the kitchen, and me.

Who do you remember at the dinner parties? Any of these people that we hear of?

Well, Amery, you know.

Julian Amery?

His father, Leo. She was very friendly with him. And one night he was going to say something in Parliament, and she didn't want him to say it. So she wrote a note, and I had to take it down to the Houses of Parliament, and she said, "It must go, you must take it." So I went down. I had been in that big room before when one of the royals died and was in there. You could go there and see them.

The lying-in state?

Yes. There were one or two, but I can't remember who they were. At the end of it there are some steps, and when you go up these steps you often hear them now saying they all collect outside like on the landing. And when I went up there, there wasn't another woman in sight. Of course, it was years ago, and I don't suppose there were any (women) MPs. I didn't see anybody. I was worried sick, I didn't know how to get this note to him, because he'd got a room in the House of Commons, you see. And eventually a young-looking member came in at the door and I thought 'Here goes', so I walked over to him and I said "Would you be good enough to show me where Mr. Amery's private room is, because I've got a note for him." And he said "Would you mind if I took it? I would like to take it." So he probably was keen to talk to him or something. He said "You wait here and then I'll tell you if he's got it." So I waited at the said door and he went away, and he came in and said "It's all right, he's got it." But she was protesting (about) what he was going to say!

I wonder what it was.

I've no idea what it was.

Or even whether he said it or not?

But that's the sort of thing that used to go on, you know.

You mentioned Bryanston Square earlier. Did they keep that?

No, they only took that one temporary for the season. They got married from there but it was given up after that. But it was a nice house, it was a corner house 24A. I can remember being there.

So they'd known each other a long, long time, hadn't they, before they married?

Oh yes, yes. And she used to go off to South Africa – of course Lord Edward was in Egypt, and she did sometimes go there, but she didn't go there very often.

You went to Cape Town, didn't you, and you went to France. Where else did you go abroad?

Egypt and Palestine and Syria. We had nearly a week there waiting for a French boat called "The Patriot" which was lost during the war, I think, to bring us home, to Marseilles, and then we went through France up to Paris. We stayed in Paris for about a week. But Lord Milner was chairman of a large copper mine in Spain, and a deputation of people used to go out there once a year, including him and Lady Milner, she used to go with him, and of course I used to go too. And I liked that, because he'd got English people in his house over there with him, looking after him, so I knew some of the people quite well afterwards, because we met several times.

You mentioned how kind Lord Milner was to you. There was another example, wasn't there, when he was showing you, in the –

Well, that was interesting. We got the boat from Marseilles to Port Said, I think it was called "The Naldera" and I rather think that was another boat I'd been on that was lost in the war. And they stayed for dinner at Port Said, we went to the Commanding Officer's and there was all these English boys there. And of course you know I was young and not too bad-looking in those days. Well, that was all right. After I'd had my dinner – of course they were all posh with the head officer – however, at midnight we got a train and slept in the train. From Port Said we were going up to Jerusalem, and it was then that, in the morning, I was awake early, you see, and looking at everything because it was

Mrs Emily Cork

Lady Milner

Lord Alfred Milner

interesting, and Lord Milner come along and he said, *"You come and sit with me."* And he had his Bible and he said, *"I'll tell you exactly what happened all along here in a minute."* And that's what he did, which was jolly nice of him, wasn't it?

Was he a religious man?

Yes, he was a bit. He used to like going to this church.

He went to this church at Sturry?

Yes, he did.

Did he go every Sunday? Or most Sundays?

Yes, he did when he was here. So did she, but she wasn't churchy. She was not a bit religious. No, she wasn't. But he was.

Was he a very reserved man? Was he a quiet man?

Yes, yes.

And with everybody, was he like this?

Yes, yes. He took it all in everywhere, but he never had a lot to say about it. But – he was a dear man, I liked

him ever so much. I did a lot for him.

Did you? What did you do for him?

You see, before he married her he had a valet. A man valet. He gave it up when he came to us, so I had to take him on, it wasn't my job either, but –

What, get his clothes ready?

Yes, but I didn't mind. And he'd got such a lot of orders, and when they went out to these big dinners, you know, he used to put all these orders on.

What sort of orders?

Well, things that he'd been honoured with.

Yes, I see what you mean.

Then Lady Milner had two.

Did she?

Yes, she'd got a French one, Legion of Honour, they didn't wear them on all occasions unless there was French people there, in that instance. But his, he had no end of them. I used to have to put them on – I knew where to put them, because once a year there's a thing at Windsor for Garter people, isn't there, and he'd got one of those garters, and he had a blue band to wear, a sash. And then he had lots of little – they did a lot of them in miniatures. They're so big, you see, you had a little one, and he had them all across here for things he'd been honoured with.

What did she get hers, for, Lady Milner? You said she had two. What was her second one?

She had – it was a white cross and a black ribbon, and it was St. John's something. I suppose something she'd done. She used to wear them.

She was a very active lady, wasn't she? And clever. [2]

Oh, she was a very clever woman, no doubt about it. Oh yes, she was.

I think we'll leave it for today.

[1] Hugh and Mirabel Cecil IMPERIAL MARRIAGE: An Edwardian War and Peace (John Murray, 2000]
[2] R.Q.Edmonds A History of the Junior King's School 1879 – 1956
[3] A. Susan Williams LADIES OF INFLUENCE – Women of the Elite in Interwar Britain (John Lane, The Penguin Press, 2000)

The Shoebox Diaries - A Hersden Family 1920 - 1958

By Gillian Ratcliff

These small pocket diaries were found in a shoebox and bought from a Canterbury dealer in 2003 by Kinn McIntosh. When she found that my family, (Fred and Dorothy Price), who had lived at Gatesgarth in Hersden and next door to the Dawson family, were mentioned she asked me to read them and comment. There are 33 diaries covering the years between 1920 and 1957 but four are missing – those for the years 1924, 1931, 1937 and 1939. They are written by Ada Dawson except for the final three years when her husband Charles takes over after her death. A question is why these years are missing and on closer scrutiny it seems that they were exceptionally tragic ones for Ada and the family.

They are simple diaries and, on a first superficial read, seem to consist of everyday happenings - regular journeys to Canterbury on the very frequent buses for haircuts, purchase of vests and winter coats, and the much loved visits to the "Pictures"; visits from family in Nottingham,

life in a colliery village, the vicar dropping in. She makes the occasional observation on national life such as the burial of the Unknown Warrior in Westminster Abbey on 11th November 1920, the General Strike and the Abdication in 1936. We hear of the bombing of Sturry, the competitive output from the colliery and local labour disputes.

Charles as an electrical engineer is in the forefront of bringing new means of communication into the family. On 12th October 1927 Ada writes "Deo magnus-Magnissimo! New wireless set complete". Friends come to "listen in" for concerts and special events. Later come a gramophone and telephone and finally on 22nd May 1954 "Very excited, TV set arrived. We had a wonderful evening and enjoyed every minute of it."

Charles and Ada Dawson moved from Notttingham to Kent in 1913 and when the diaries begin in 1920 they had

Photograph of Shoebox

three children - Elaine born in 1914, Graham in 1916 and Rex in 1918. They lived then in Westbere, moving to a bigger house in Hersden a few years later. Already there were health problems with Rex and at times the doctor calls daily. But the first tragedy happens in September 1924 when Graham was in a playground and a heavy swing fractured his skull causing paralysis down his left side. The diary for that year is missing and no doubt events were too painful for Ada to record. His recovery was slow and much attention was given, with consultant surgeon Mr. A.B.Beresford Jones visiting at home and bringing a present while others took him out for a ride in the car - a rare treat! Graham always walked with a limp and was employed as a clerical worker all his life at the colliery, always living with his parents and moving with them to Broadstairs where a favourite pastime was greyhound racing in Dumpton Park.

Elaine's early life seems happy and she enjoys visits to the Heron family at "Wildwood" in Sturry (where my family lived in the 1950's and 1960's); she attends the small school in Westbere run by the Misses Powell and then has some training as a typist. But her ability to hold down a job is limited and in October 1937 she is admitted to a psychiatric hospital at Dartford, probably with schizophrenia. The diary for that year is missing and in the following year Ada comments "Poor Elaine went from home 4 months ago today" ; "dear Elaine at home but we had a distressing time with her and we were all very sad"; " Charles took Elaine back- nearly broke my heart". On 11th January 1941 Ada writes, "Elaine not well enough to go to the office today" so clearly she was much improved and there are no further references to her being hospitalised. Elaine is a shadowy figure in the diaries and also lives permanently at home. She died on 24th March 1966 at the age of 52 and is buried in Westbere churchyard.

As if this was not tragedy enough for this little family Rex is seriously disabled. He suffers from epilepsy and severe behavioural problems. His needs in his short life dominate much of Ada's diaries and 1922 "Rex very trying" ; 1928 "Dear Rex had a bad seizure"; 1928 "Rex fainted in Canterbury- awful shock for me" are only three of many references to his condition. In 1935 Rex goes into care in Larkfield near Maidstone and throughout the year there are visits and consultations with staff and doctors. By 1938 he is at home, "Dr [Catherine] Evans to see Rex, saw him in his tantrums"; 1941 "Rex very

ill...Rex chuntering a lot – an entirely new phase". By late 1942 he goes into St. Augustine's Mental Hospital at Chartham for bowel surgery and dies there on 23rd December.

Ada was severely bereaved and did not begin to recover for years. She scarcely left the house, no longer enjoying the bus journey to Canterbury and visits to family in Nottingham and Essex. Her great difficulties in managing Rex were forgotten and his anniversary each year brought a new grief. Her health had always been fragile with regular mention of severe headaches which kept her in bed for days at a time. She was a well-educated woman who had taught Latin and at the end of some diaries she records books which she has read during the year. She keeps the books for a local society, attends Conservative Party meetings and records speaking at one of them. She is a great letter writer and it is a sad day when no letters arrive for her.

Charles clearly is able to provide well for the family and in the early years there is a live-in help. He is called to engineering emergencies at times but also travels to meetings in London, Manchester and Nottingham. The impression given is of a strained marriage and Charles goes off on holiday on his own, often to France. He and Graham go off fishing together and at the end of the 1946 diary, Ada writes "No comments on 1946, much like 1945, a year of monotony and strain. I had one day's outing and change to Folkestone!!"
However in later years one senses much more companionship and she talks about walking by the sea in Broadstairs and going out for occasional treats.

Ada had been in poor health and pain before her death in September 1954 a few days after Charles' 70th birthday. His diary for 1955 is simply an engagement diary but for the next two years he copies closely Ada's pattern of writing and clearly feels her loss deeply.

In this small article it is not possible to interpret more. I have felt very caught up in Ada's world - her deep despair at her children's tragedies, the largely hidden problems of her married life, her joy at the letters and visits of her family and the frustration of an intelligent woman with few stimulating outlets. The quotations with which she sometimes ended a diary indicate a reflective and searching mind.

Mrs Muriel Thomas

(1912 - 2004)

Author of "Fifty Years of Methodism in a Kent Mining Village"

Interviewed in Hersden by John Line in August 1999

Where did you live as a child?

Stoke-on-Trent, Staffordshire

How big a family did you have?

I'm an only child

You're the lucky one!

Mother lost her first baby. Had she lived I do not think I would be here. My father was not going to have a large family when he was one of ten.

What did Dad do for a living?

Miner

Do you remember your grandparents?

Oh, yes, yes.

Were they in the mine as well?

No, farming in Shropshire – where you did not say "you are going in the gate" but "going in the wicket".

What was the housing like then? Things like did you have an inside toilet and was there a tin bath in front of the fire?

Oh, yes, it was that, toilet outside though.

When you came down to Kent was your Dad looking for a job?

Yes and it was a long time before he got one.

When you first got your house here was this the first house you moved into?

No. When I was married we went to Upstreet. My parents got this house because Mother was ill and living in rooms at Ramsgate.

That was when your father had to travel to Chislet Halt station?

No, there wasn't a Chislet Halt station when he came. Grove Ferry was the one he had to walk from to here and then back again after his shift - and dirty as there were no pithead baths then - and he would be wet through, too.

Having walked from Grove Ferry then two or three miles to the coal face and back then walk back to Upstreet? Filthy dirty? Is that right?

Yes and no baths there. It would be a tub in front of the fire. Don't forget before we came here to Hersden it was only a field of mud and the houses were built round as they are now.

Where did your husband come from?

Muriel Thomas

Yorkshire

Was he a miner?

Well, he wasn't old enough for that when he first came.

Your husband's father moved down to the colliery as well?

Yes, to Ramsgate first. There were no houses here in Hersden at all, except perhaps The Villas, but then it wasn't so much the workmen as the managers over there.

You both came down from up North. Did you meet your husband in Ramsgate or down here?

When we got here. Although they had a house at the top of the road and we were in rooms and we didn't know each other. When we came here there was no church only the Black Hut and no shops.

What was life like here then? Was it grim?

No, I didn't think it was. Whether my parents did or not, I don't know. We were all children playing together in the wood, you see, and coming from town and then coming into the country was good. We used to walk everywhere - there was a chapel at Upstreet and that's where we went walking on Sundays to go to Sunday School there.

Was the religion mainly Methodist in those days?

No, it was ecumenical.[1] That's how I put it in the book,[2] because everybody wanted somewhere to go and so were pleased to go to the Black Hut but I suppose there were no Anglicans, Methodists or anything like that - just people pleased to get together and work and then the Canterbury Wesleyan Methodists took an interest in it and got us into the Circuit there. We wondered how it would work out because all the churches in the Circuit were in the country and we were miners, weren't we, but they were very good to us. [3]

What about school? Where did you go to school?

If you walk down here and go down the woods and you can see the square where the original school was. Of the older ones George went to Westbere because he lived on the other side of the road and I went to Sturry to finish up on the hill.

The Primary School, that was in, I presume, Mr Thomas Pope's era?

Yes, then Mr Albert Prior.

Did you like school?

Yes, I loved it.

Where did you go after that for your schooling?

I still stayed there because, how old was I? Eleven when I came down here. I passed the eleven-plus in Staffordshire but didn't do anything about it. Well, my mother couldn't be bothered. Really she had enough on her mind to get a job. I went to Ramsgate – to Ellington Girls' School

Then when you moved down to Hersden you were sent to Sturry?

Well, I wouldn't have had long to do really before I was old enough to leave.

What age did you leave school?

Fourteen, I suppose I was then.

What work did you do?

I went down helping someone at Sturry, a Captain Grant. His mother was very ill. I was down there for a time then I went to Fordwich to Brice's farm where I developed Diphtheria and so I was sent to an isolation hospital. It was an awful place when I went there. It was on the road to Bekesbourne and I was there for five weeks. [The old Bridge-Blean Rural District Council Isolation Hospital.] My mother wanted to visit me, of course, so she took the bus to Sturry then had to walk the rest of the way. Then all that she was allowed to do was talk to me while she was in the road and they would take me to sit on a chair on the lawn and that's all. People don't realize how hard isolation is for a child of that age.

She actually had to stay on the road and talk to you over the fence?

Yes.

Because you were in isolation?

Yes. And what a distance to go and then walk back again!

Did you go back to work for Daniel Brice then?

No, I finished up at David Greig's [the grocer's shop in Canterbury].

Your husband was down the pit all the time, was he?

Yes, more or less.

What happened in the General Strike? Was it rough then?

It was really. One of the end houses over there, George, my husband, George Thomas, his parents at the farmhouse, their place was opened up as a soup kitchen where the people went. My father and another man went to all the farmers appealing for funds so they could have food to give away and then the house at the end had clothes where the children could go and get things.

What year was that?

I don't know - was it nineteen twenty-six? – no, it wouldn't be – yes, could be. . . Before my time, that's for sure. I'll check. Yes, it was 1926. The produce given by the local farmers was distributed to those very much in need and this was in the days before social services and welfare organisations were in operation. Another item of interest was when members of the Mission at the Black Hut, Mr and Mrs Ellis Roberts and Mr and Mrs Philpott, my parents, served breakfast to children in the hut so that they wouldn't go to school hungry.

So you're Mrs Thomas nee Philpott?

Yes. School for those children meant a journey to Sturry Church of England School in a horse-drawn vehicle driven by Mr. Jesse Morris from Sturry and in those days there were no school meals provided.

So the children got something to eat at the end of your road for breakfast and that was it until they got home at night?

Yes, whether they went down to the soup kitchen or their parents there I don't know.

It must have been horrendous. Did you go on holiday in those days?

Well, if we did it was back to Shropshire or Staffordshire.

To see the family?

Yes.

Did you get day trips in London or anything like that?.

No. Girls and boys went to the Royal Albert Hall when the Methodists took it over. We stayed the night in the Clapham deep shelters.

This was after the war and the shelter was being used as overnight accommodation?

That's right, yes. Just remember we had no electricity when we came here first - just lamps and candles.

Gas lamps or oil?

Oil as there was no gas laid on and just open range stoves to do all your cooking on.

The old black stove? So that was in here in the living room? When you moved up here you did all your cooking on the same stove? [4]

When I moved up here the electricity had been laid on. Of course the garden was not anything like this. It was an open field - a clay field really.

There were no separate gardens – just a field at the back of the house?

They allotted it out and it wasn't fairly done. Some had a big patch. You see those houses didn't come here for a long, long time, that was all wood there.

The church has obviously played a very big part in your life.

I think it has, and I sure that there are others who have a lot to thank the church for because there would not have been anything otherwise.

Times must have been hard in those days.

Sometimes they were.

Shall we stop and have a cup of tea?

A memorial plaque to Muriel Thomas was erected in the Wesleyan Church in Hersden, now the Neighbourhood Centre.

[1] K.H.McIntosh IN GOOD FAITH – A Commemoration of Twenty-Five Years of an L.E.P. 1970-1995 (1995)
[2] Muriel Thomas FIFTY YEARS OF METHODISM IN A KENTISH MINING VILLAGE (Compiled in 1979)
[3] Revd. P.J.Gausden "The Church in Hersden" in CHISLET AND WESTBERE ed K.H.McIntosh (1979)
[4] Ross Llewellyn HERSDEN – Chislet Colliery Village (2003)

Knights to Remember
Sir Arthur Pugh

Sir Arthur Pugh, J.P., who lived at "Gosfield", Sturry Hill, was born in 1870 and became involved with iron and steel works as a young man. By the age of 24 he was local – and later – General Secretary of the British Steel Smelters' Association. A calm and tactful man, he was partly responsible for the amalgamation that led to the formation of the Iron and Steel Trades Confederation in 1917. He became the Confederation's first General Secretary in 1917, holding the office until his retirement in 1935, when he was knighted.

A member of the General Council of the Trades Union Congress for 16 years and its Chairman in 1925-26, and essentially a moderate man, it was largely through his statesmanlike influence that the General Strike of 1926 was called off. He was a member of the World Economic Conference in 1927, and served on the League of Nations Economic Advisory Committee, the Committee of National Expenditure and on Committees inquiring into disputes in the docks, building trades, tramways and buses. In the Second World War he was a member of a tribunal hearing the appeals of Conscientious Objectors against the decisions of their local tribunals.

Whilst living in Sturry he played an active part in many local organisations including the Social Centre, the Good Fellowship, the Horticultural Society and Civil Defence. He was the author of MEN OF STEEL BY ONE OF THEM - A Chronicle of Eighty Eight Years of Trade Unionism, published by the Iron and Steel Confederation in 1951.

Sir Arthur Pugh

Sir Arthur died in August, 1955, and is buried beside his wife, Elizabeth, in Sturry Cemetery. They had two daughters and two sons.

The Milner Memorial Ground
by R.Q. Edmonds

The same afternoon that Lady Milner laid the Foundation Stone of the new building for the Junior King' School at Milner Court on July 18th, 1928, there was also a ceremony on the South side of the Parish Church in which she gave the piece of land between the main road and the Church to the Church Council for the people of Sturry as a memorial to Lord Milner . In her day it would have been possible to park the car in the road and stroll through the gates to sit and enjoy the peacefulness of the 'garden', as Lady Milner preferred to call it, before going through to the Church that in those days would have been open to all visitors.

Despite Lord Milner's having died in 1925 there was still a good deal of appreciation of him as a major local landowner and contributor to the village and so her kind offer was generally well received.

The impressive ceremony in which the land was donated to the Parochial Church Council was attended by several of the dignitaries who had earlier been present for the Stone-laying ceremony at Milner Court. The prestige of the occasion was greatly enhanced when it was learnt that the MP for Sparkbrook, Birmingham, the Rt. Hon. Leo Amery, at that time Secretary of State for the Colonies, was also going to attend and say a few words about Lord Milner and his service to the nation. Leo Amery had been a correspondent for the 'The Times' during the Boer War in which Lord Milner was much involved and was a good friend to Lord and Lady Milner.

It was essentially a village affair and the Parochial Church Council decided that as well as the dignitaries and members of the Church Council, all members of the parish should be invited to attend such an important occasion, including all the children from the Sturry Primary School. Eventually, after a certain amount of heated discussion, it was decided that only the older school children would attend. In the event one of the worries of the staff about the length of time that the children would have to stand proves groundless as photographs of the occasion indicate that eventually they sat on the ground during the ceremony except during their contribution of singing "Jerusalem" at some point in the event.

Chairs had been hired from the council at a cost of five shillings per hundred and with the exception of the special guests and members of the Parochial Church Council, who had reserved seats in the front row, the chairs were allocated on the first come first served basis.

So it was that the Milner Memorial Ground, as the village soon came to call it, was accepted by the Parochial Church Council. As this included a sum to cover the cost of looking after the land in those days, it was regarded at the time as a well-intentioned gift made after careful thought by Lady Milner.

At the opening ceremony – Leo Amery, Lady Milner, Mr and Mrs W.E.Prosser

The Sturry Flood I
Mrs Florence Emily Maud Bouldin (née Lyons)
17 September 1915 - 18 July 2005

Interviewed by Heather Stennett
10th November, 2000

When did the flood actually start?

Boxing Day, 1927

Where were you living at the time?

Black Mill Cottage by the river – I'd been born there.

Can you tell me the first that your family knew of the flood?

Mother was preparing for supper and she found the kitchen floor was flooded. The kitchen was two steps down but we had time to gather enough food and firewood to tide us over.

You told me earlier about your brother and the water coming in the front door and when it got very deep he was paddling around the kitchen in a bath getting bits and pieces. How old was he then?

About 12 I would think.

You also told me about when the water came in the front door your father had to race to open the back door to let the water through.

That's right.

The flood lasted for 3 days, I believe, before you could go downstairs again.

Before we could start the cleaning up process, yes

Could you tell me how many people were in your family at that time?

There were seven of us, 4 girls, my brother, my dad and mother, Edward and Edith Lyons.

Where were you in the family?

I'm the oldest girl.

Were you just inside for those 3 days or did you venture out at all?

The Black Mill "A now demolished part of the Black Mill taken from a painting by an unknown artist on a glass lantern slide of about 1880"

Well, my dad had to go out but the only way he could get out was through the front room window. No other way of getting out because it was still getting this enormous flood flow of water from the river.

So he climbed out the window, to a boat outside or did he just wade?

No, he waded, waded through.

What was your father's occupation?

He was on the council and so they had to be on duty.

During that time did you hear any tales of anything happening to other families in the village?

No. It was very cold, you know, at the time of the flood and later when the water went down we were skating on the marshes and they reckoned you could skate from there, Sturry Road, to Grove Ferry and from Sturry into Canterbury.

Did it often freeze cold enough to skate?

Oh, no, not as a rule. Well, there wasn't usually the flood water. It was bitterly, bitterly cold then and afterwards we had our illness, diphtheria, after that, you know. I got that.

Was anyone in your family affected?

No. I was taken away for 3 weeks as carrier of diphtheria, a carrier. When we got back to school they took swabs. I was 3 weeks away.

You went off to an isolation hospital did you, where was that?

It was at Eddington, Herne Bay. [It was almost certainly the Blean Rural District Council one on Thornden Wood Road, Herne, since converted into houses.]

Had you ever been away from home before?

No

So it must have been a very worrying experience.

Yes

Can I ask you your memories of your home life and your daily routine, please.

Nothing changed very much from day to day you know. We went off to school and one thing and another.

Can you tell me a bit about washday?

Yes. Well, we didn't actually have water in the house in the early days - we had to fetch it, and my dad used to

do that early on Monday morning to fill up the copper which was in the kitchen. Then it was washday, all day.

About what time would your mother start?

Well, she was up very early in the morning - six o'clock. It was very, very hard work. There was also rinsing water. There were bucketfuls of that needed.

Where did the water come from? Was it from the river?

Oh no. There was a tap outside although the rest of the cottage was derelict, there was a tap there.

So he didn't have to go far to get the water.

It was a tap, not a pump.

Tell me about the shops in Sturry. Any particular characters who you can remember?

Well, I think the Corks were the chief characters in the village. They had the newsagents and tobacconists' shop before the bombing.

Where was that?

Difficult to say exactly now, in the centre of the High Street. We had a lot of shops then, you know. We had 2 butchers, 5 grocers and I think 3 bakers in the village and two banks. The first Mrs Cork, well, her wig was

View of the Leopard's Head and Bridge House on 28th December, 1927. Mrs Bouldin's house is just out of the picture on the right.

often askew. She got up late, I suppose, and didn't look in the glass.

And you have previously told me about Lavender Bill and the Honey Wagon

Well, Lavender Bill used to go around emptying the slops and toilets. We children always enjoyed watching him sitting on the top of his cart having his lunch. [Main drainage did not come to Sturry until 1959/60!]

Did you stay at the Mill Cottage until you were married?

Oh, yes.

Where did you move to?

Deansway Avenue – that was early in 1939

Were you the first owners of the house?

There had been somebody in there for 2 months and they moved out on Christmas Eve and 1938 was a white Christmas. They were moved out in the snow and they were miners and they had coal in the cupboards over there. So we had the coal dust to clean up when we came in.

It must have been a big contrast to your previous house.

Having hot water and a bath, of course. We didn't have that luxury before.

At Mill Cottage did you have an indoor flush toilet or was it out of doors?

An outdoor one.

So an indoor flushing toilet would really be a luxury ...

Yes

When you moved in here to Deansway Avenue, was the street complete or was it still being built?

No, there was a gap in the middle and the houses on the front on Sturry Hill hadn't all been finished.

And between here and McCarthy Avenue?

Yes, there were allotments over there.

Did you have any 'modern' gadgets to go with your new house.

I had a wringer and a gas boiler.

Your husband was in the Home Guard during the war so on the night of the bombing of Sturry could you just recollect what happened.

Well, he went down on duty and I didn't know what had happened although I thought something must have done because the lights all went out and I was here in candlelight, so I didn't know what had happened until he came back. Awful, really, to think that the village had gone.

Sturry children Hop picking including Florence, Vera, Maud and Mildred Lyons and Carrie Moore.
(Carrie Moore was teased at school with the chant "Carrie couldn't carry any more")

During the raid you said that you stood and watched the searchlights.

We stood on our steps out there and watched, because you could hear something going around here and we went outside to see what it was. We could see this plane and the searchlights had got it trapped and I think that's what happened so he suddenly made a dive out of it because he was trapped. Each move he made, of course, they followed him with the searchlights, and he made a dive to escape. I don't think it was intentional. I don't think he had anything in mind. I think it was just to get rid of his bomb load.

Yes, the weight of the bombs would slow him down. [They were landmines]

And, you see, if he had been a couple of minutes longer over Sturry they would have been in the marshes, wouldn't they? The best thing was that they didn't go on the school down there because there were lots of troops billeted there.

The King's School was used as a billet, was anywhere else in the village?

No. That was the main place. It was full of soldiers.

What are your memories of the games you played?

Hopscotch and skips, all sorts of things like that. Altogether, we used to play altogether. We used to play down in the Hammels by the Church down there. The whole village of us used to go there.

Any particular songs?

Well, usually to go with things, I suppose, things with the balls. Two balls up the wall. . .

So what is the biggest change in Sturry – the Sturry of your childhood to Sturry now?

The Parish Hall, we had a huge Christmas tree, fairy lights. That went in the bombing.

Where was that?

Church Lane and we had a party there at Christmas

Who organised the children's party?

I think it was given by Mr. Prosser, he owned the mills... [William E. Prosser of Mill House, Mill Road.]

Was it a party just for the children whose parents worked at the mills?

Oh no, it was for all the children.

How many people were working in the mill?

Not so many because it was going into decline, very much so... When Dad came out of the army there wasn't a job for him there any longer. It was pulled down later. And since the previous floods they have built a wall up a couple of courses and this has protected them from flooding.

So far!

The Sturry Flood II
Mrs Ivy Holmes (née Giles)
3rd March 1919 - 1st August 2004

Interviewed by Heather Stennett on 13th September, 1999

How old would you say you were in that picture over there? About nine-ish?

No. I'd come out the infants' class. We had two classes in the infants. Mrs. Peel and, oh, Miss Middleton, that's right. There was a teacher, I don't know if this it was

this one, Mum said always used to smell of violet soap. Oh that was Miss Ravine. Yes, oh yes. She was very nice.

So was she the teacher after her?

No, she was on the other side of the curtain, because that was one long room and there were blue curtains that they pulled across to divide Standard One and Standard

Two, and then out in the middle lobby, in the next place was where Arthur Bournes was teaching. And then from there we went through to Mrs Reed, who was our, well, she mainly took needlework and while she took us for needlework, Mrs Reed, the boys used to have to go into Captain Riley.

So you could hear everything that was going on in the classroom.

Yes, it was a job sometimes, you know, with a bit of a noise going on, we used to be listening. "Come along, pay attention to what I am talking to you about." But yes, it was a bit awkward to have to share a room, well, just share one big room.

So what age were you when you became monitors? Did you sort of...

Er, I don't know if we did in that class, I rather think it was in Miss Ravine's, the second one up as far as I'm concerned and then there were monitors in all the rooms after that. Joan Stewart was sitting next to me, she had a brother, Sid, and I rather liked Sid, because he started to work with my father afterwards. My central heating flicked just now. It's not working, but...

No, it's just the boiler goes.

And he used to have to come along to talk to my Dad about work, but we had a little chat, too. We was quite pally, and it was when I was in Miss Ravine's class and we were sitting there as one does, and we were supposed to be up to... and suddenly a piece of wet blotting paper went zoom past me. Then a bit landed in my hair. Where's that coming from? One or two others had these bits of wet blotting paper on their books and that. Where's it coming from? Don't know. And do you know, it was not until we were actually living here, because I used to see Sid come up and you know the seat by the loos, just here, well he used to come and sit there. If I went down the village, he used to come and sit there so that he could have a natter when I came back from the village. And I introduced him to Bill and Bill and he always used to go to the sports over the road, the football, or cricket, or whatever, because Bill used to go down and, he said, "But I'll go and tap on old Sid's window," and, you know, they used to go off together. Anyway, it was not until them days after all those years – sixty at least, I was sitting talking to Sid one day and I said, "You know, there was always a mystery when I was in Miss Ravine's class," and he said, "Oh, yes?" I said, "Yes," I said. "Never did know who flicked wet blotting paper." And he collapsed with laughing. He said, "Well, I confess now," he said, "it was me." He went in a little stockroom. It was the room where they had the war, the war memorial, the brass plaque, you know, over the fireplace. Do you remember that?

That wasn't there when I was there, not that I can remember, anyway.

Oh, yes, they had the names done on this big brass thing, because that was one of the things they pinched first of all when they decided to pull the school. They first had, well, they broke in and they pinched the brass war memorial, a dreadful thing to do. Then they pinched the big brass bell, can you remember that? Was that there when you were there? They had that. Then they took all the lead off the roofs and it was in such a bad state that they had to, you know, they pulled it down. I always felt sorry because they were planning on having a reunion of all the old people. I was quite looking forward to that now we are all living back here, but that wasn't to be, before we knew it the school, they said, well the school will have to be demolished.

I think was the hurricane as well, combined with the damage that they had done with things, and then they had to do it.

They had to pull it down, yes. It was a shame, that.

I'd like to ask you, Ivy, but where did you live when you were a child.

Along Providence Place, you know, where there were those nurseries, well, I was actually born – there are three cottages there, still there, still the same, still called Providence Place. Well, I was born in the middle one there and that's where your Mum used to come weekends with me.

She used to look forward to coming and staying with you.

And so did I. Good old natter in bed night-times. My father used to say, when my grandfather died, you know, Dad used to say, "Oh, let's have Amy here more," I don't know whether he called her May or not, but I always called her Amy and I think all of the village girls there called her Amy.

She was Amy until, I suppose, she left work and went into service, she was still known to some of those, like Elsie and that, as Amy, but I think it suddenly became more sophisticated to be called May, and so she grew up and called herself May. [the interviewer's mother, May Bacon, later Mrs Philip Stennett]

Yes, yes. Well, Dad used to say, "We'll have Amy this weekend. Don't forget to tell her." So she used to come home from school with me Friday nights, and we used to play hopscotch, have a skip, you know, skipping ropes, and always go fishing for tiddlers, that was a laugh, that was. We used to go down Fordwich, but Amy wasn't with me that particular weekend. I think it was Lily with me, yes,

Photograph of Arthur Bournes, school teacher

Lily Bubb. She was with me, and we went, you know the King's School landing stages, it's still in the same place, and we had a jam jar with a bit of string round it and we was fishing for these tiddlers. You never see these tiddlers now, you know. I suppose all the big fish just eat them up. And I suppose they've just gone. But we used to have our jam jar and try and get a tiddler to take home and then Lily said to me, "Oh there is a big one gone underneath."

I said, "Where?" I leaned forward on this here rest and I went in head first, head over heels. And it is a memory I will never forget. I can always remember Lily grabbing my shoulder, saying, "Don't go, Ivy. Don't go, don't go, don't go", and she was grabbing my shoulder, and of course the current was strong in them days. She couldn't grab me. And then I know I was coughing and spluttering about, I was gobbling all this water down, and then a great big hand came and grabbed me up and said, "You silly kids," chucked me on the bank and cleared off. And do you know, there again, I never knew who rescued me. And it was George Robey from Fordwich. That was a name, you know, your Mum would know.

Oh, yes, I know George Robey.

You did, yes. And you knew his wife then, Norah. She was Norah Collard and she only died two or three weeks ago, Norah did, yes. And it was, when we came back to live, we'd done all our moving around all over the years, and when we came back to live here we hadn't got a thing, because we had got old Mum living with us and she was very poorly and we used to shove the joint in, it was the usual thing Sunday, shove the joint in and we would say to Mum, "Don't worry. Don't go to the oven. Don't worry. It will be all right till we get back." And we always went down Fordwich, up one hill and down the other and back, and by the time we had got back it was time to put the veg on. It was, you know, a regular thing. And we used to meet George Robey sometimes coming up from Fordwich and we used to have a bit of cheek, and I used to cheek him back.

So one day he was cheeky to me and I cheeked him back and he said, "'Ere, now listen." He said, "Now look

here, I don't want no more cheek from you. If it wasn't for me," he said, "you wouldn't be here." I said, "What do you mean I wouldn't be here?" He said, "Well, I pulled you out the river. Remember when you went in the river?" I never knew that until all those years later, so that was two things. What with George Robey and poor old Sid lobbing the wet blotting paper at me when I was at school and me not finding out until he was an old man and confessed.

At least two mysteries were cleared up, then.

Well, I didn't half get into trouble, you can bet your life. Mum said "Now you'll go to bed without any tea." So up I went to bed, no tea, and in the evening, I don't know what our Mum did, I think, she had gone down the garden or something, but up come my old Dad with a bun and a bit of sandwich. "'Ere, quick, eat it before your Mum sees." So I did have something to eat.

Washing day, was it always a Monday?

It was a Monday, yes, always, yes. And of course there is a bit of history attached to that because when the Holmes's come to live next door I was still going to school and Bill and his brother came and lived next door.

You married the boy next door then?

Yes, I know, the boy next door, yes, yes. And my Gran used to wear – I don't know if you have ever seen them, but they was called bloomers in them days. They had a white band round the waist and a big button at the back to fasten them up. Well, they was like miniature barrage balloons. Really. Because they went below the knee and there was another band below the knee. They had no elastic in them days. And if you wanted to go to the loo, see, you just pulled the back open and then you had to tuck it back in. That was the only fastening at the back, like. Old Gran used to say, "I can't make it out. Look at this dirty mark on my bloomers. How can that get there? It has been boiled and it's been rinsed and it's been put in the blue water – you know, they used to use them little squares, blue squares. [This was before Dolly bags] How did that get dirty like that?"

Well, I never did know. And it was only when Bill and I were courting that he said to me, "Oh, we used to have some fun when you old Gran's got her knickers, or whatever you'd call them, on the line." I said, "Now what do you know about that?" He said, Well, Ernie, him and his brother, used to stand at the back door. It appeared that old Gran always put sheets along first, and then some towels, they knew exactly where she'd put them, and right opposite their back door she used to put this pair of bloomers. So of course Ern and Bill had a little patch of stones beside the back door, beside the step, and they used to say "Got it!," if it went right through, "Got it! That's one to me." "Got it through." "Oh, that's two to you," you know. They used to lob these stones, so of course that's how Gran's knicks got muddy and dirty patches. And she never did know because by then, you see, we were courting and we were, I forget what happened, I didn't go in there like I used to as a nipper, you know, because I was in service and the time out of service was pretty limited, at least it was when I worked down in Brooklands in the Fordwich Road.

I know. So when you were younger, how many of you were actually living at home?

Only me.

Oh, you were the only child?

Oh yes, yes, that's why I'm so good. So Amy used to say, "Aren't you lucky, you've got no one to fight with."

And your grandparents lived next door?

Yes, the first house. It was to the left, nearest to Setterfields. There was Gran, then there was us, and then the other side was a Mr Spindler. I was twelve when Bill came and lived next door to me, so it was somewhere about that age.

And that was the house that they moved into, was it?

Yes, the Holmes moved into where Spindler lived, yes. So I always used to pull Bill's leg. I'd say: "Couldn't get away from you, could I? Come and live next door to me." Yes, there was him and his brother, he was aged 24, that's him up there in that photo on the mantelpiece. We then moved on to Brook. We were just outside of Wye, outside of Ashford, you know, there's just a little village, we then moved out there and one night Ern came knocking on the door. He used to pop in from time to time to see us. Because they had a stepmother, see, and life wasn't very good, and he was in digs, Ern was. So one night, a knock on the door, I went and there stood Ern with a little bag, all his worldly possessions. "Is Bill there?" I said, "Yes. Come in" So he said, "Do you think I could have a lodgings here," he said. "I've been kicked out." It was New Year' Eve and he'd had a bit too much to drink, so he got kicked out of his digs. So he came and spent the night in our spare room and then he didn't go. He stayed. Bill said, "Oh you might as well dig in with us." So he stayed until, that was I suppose it was about, I know I was expecting Les, it must have been about, well, it was New Year's time and Les was born in August and he stayed with us and he said to us, when he was sort of, well we thought it was in then, that war would be declared, Ern said to me, "Well, I filled in the coupon in the paper," he said, "and if war's declared tomorrow," he said, "I'm volunteering," and Bill said, "You don't do that, you are in a reserved

occupation," because he was cowman, same as Bill. "You don't do that." He said, "Yes, I'm going to," he said. "How I look at it," he said, "There's plenty of us young chaps around, hopefully it will leave you to look after Ivy and the baby, because Les was then born and a few weeks old, and he said, "If I volunteer then hopefully they won't want any new married chaps." So he volunteered. Never saw him again. [Sgt E.E.C. Holmes RAFVR, died 24 Oct 1942]

That must have been tragic that, I mean,

Only 24.

I haven't personally experienced the loss of somebody like that, I mean, it's one thing for somebody to die of old age, isn't it? But at 24 it's tragic.

That's right, yes, but at 24, yes. Yes, I never saw him again. Bill told him the morning he joined up, because they called them up ever so quick, within about receiving his coupon, like, that he'd filled in. We posted it in the afternoon, Sunday afternoon, because we walked along to the little post box, the three of us walked along. He posted his coupon and I know Bill said, "Oh, you are silly to do it." He said, "I'm going to" and that was it. He'd made up his mind and I think about a week later he had notice to go up to London and he was gone in three weeks. And he said to me, "What I'd like you to do," the farm fields were out the back of our cottage and there was three stiles, he said, "When I get on the third stile," he said, "I'll wave to you." So he said, "Put a towel out the window so I know you're there," and he had got an arrangement with Bill somewhere that Bill would, you know, give him away, send-off, and it was the last I saw of him. He got right up on top of the stile and waved me three times and that was it. Yes, sad at 24. Yes.

Had your father been in the First World War?

He was called up and he was in it, I've got his photo here, he got invalided out with his eyesight. There has always been bad eyesight in our family, and I consider myself lucky, because although I'm treated at the hospital every six months for glaucoma, thank goodness I didn't wear glasses until I was working in the Pedigree Toy Factory. That's my Dad.

Oh, gracious, yes. Looking very proud there.

Oh yes. Yes, it was in, what was it? He used to ride the horses.

He was in the cavalry, was he?

Yes, I suppose so, yes. I can't think what it was now.

Was he based locally when he was in the war?

Flood looking towards Canterbury

Yes, in the barracks at Canterbury, yes. Yes, (pointing to a brass vase) that was one of Mother's little treasures, only Ivy hasn't polished it round like Mother would have done, has she? I'll do it tomorrow, that's what I am always going to do. Do it tomorrow.

What did your Dad actually do when you were living down there? What job did he do?

When he came out, when he was invalided out of the army, he didn't know what to do and he went down, he used to be a bell-ringer in Sturry Church and he started to ring the bells when he was up at Broad Oak, so he used to run down through the woods and he used to have to stand on a box to learn to ring so, you know, he could ring the bells then.

But where were they living then when they were in Broad Oak?

In that house next to the chapel. Yes, next to the chapel he lived, yes. And there was a builder - I don't know if you have heard of Slingsby, the local builder?

It is a name I've heard of, but I didn't personally know him.

You must have done. I'll tell you a lady who would know, because Paul File, our local plumber, he is always up and down here with P C File on his van, he has a yellowy colour van with green letters, well that

was his father-in-law and because Dad being a bell-ringer, and he was head, well captain of the Sturry bell-ringers group, like, and he, Dad said, you know, he didn't know what he was going to do and he said, "Well, perhaps I could have you, but you don't know anything about it, do you?" and Dad said, "No." So Dad came down the colliery, went down the colliery, and he was not down there long. He managed to get a job straight away at the Chislet Colliery, so he went down there. Then one night, Mum called me up, "Dad's late coming home. Dad's late coming home." And when Dad did come home, there he was, head all bandaged, chest all bandaged. They'd had a fall of coal and they got him out, but it fell right down on him. See, that used to happen in them days, and because he was a bit worried and Mum said, "Oh, don't go down there again, don't go down that mine again," and of course he didn't go and ring the bells, so old Mr Slingsby came along to see where he was, you know. "Why didn't you come to ring on Sunday," because apparently they were very short numbered and when one was missing it was a bit difficult, in fact they couldn't always ring at all if there wasn't enough. So he said, "Oh, I can find you a job if you don't mind doing the rough work." So he put him on, and he stayed there until he died, because he was only 47 when he died, and that was heart problems, Yes. Yes, he looks very smart there, doesn't he?

So when did you come back to Sturry?

When Bill was, let me see - he retired at 65, so he was 59 when we came back to Sturry. We came back to live with Mum at 2 Church Lane. Because my Dad had died and Mum married her old school pal, old Charlie Impett.

Right.

So there was just us two left and so Mum said, "Oh, come and live with me." She'd been itching for a long time for us to go and live with her so we packed up and came and lived with Mum. We said, "Well, it's only temporary because we are looking for somewhere to live in Sturry." We thought we'd have to rent somewhere. But it so happened that we had bought Mum's house and we thought, well, we put on a bathroom, well she never had a bathroom, and we thought, well, she wouldn't move out of there. Anyway, we said we were looking for somewhere to live. She said, "Oh, sell this thing," she said. "Sell this, I'll come with you." So we were never more pleased. So of course we sold that, so then we had the money for this, which was quite good in them days, you know. And they wanted to get rid of this place quickly because, you know, Finns had it, you know, down Fordwich Road, they had it and it wanted a lot doing to it inside because there was no central heating, no double glazing, no nothing. Bill said, "Oh, that's all right, I'll do that, I'll do that." He was very happy. He didn't do the double glazing but he done all the central heating, put the radiators and that in. So, well, we sold

Mother's place and she came up here with us and she was with us for three years before we lost her.

Oh, good, you had a lot of time with her, then. It is nice when you have got a house where you have got memories.

Well, she always used to say it was really her happiest place, because she said it was so modern. It was so modern. Because she had the spare bedroom, she used to come out of her bedroom door into the bathroom. She said, "Oh it is wonderful to have to do that."

So what were the toilets like when you were younger?

Oh, the old buckets. We had the old buckets. Well, even when we were going up to school, I mean, Amy would remember this, it was buckets. Toilets of wood all the way through the village and the houses what didn't have a back way, they used to have to go out the back When they didn't have a side entrance, or back entrance of any sort, they used to have to take a big bucket in from an old cart [popularly known as the honey wagon] and empty it in the garden, like, and then bring the bucket right through the house. It must have been terrible.

What did you do of a night time if you wanted to have a wee in the night?

We used the undertaker. Under the bed. We always called it the 'the undertaker'. Oh yes, that was the thing in them days, yes. But we had to share wash-houses and taps with my Gran along Providence Place, and one copper to share between Gran and Mum and it was light the old faggots and shove underneath, get the water boiling, to get enough hot water to start washing. Then when you'd done your washing you filled it up. There was a tap luckily out near our washer, it was the only tap we had. Mum's last job at night, or Dad, whichever, was to go out and fill up the kettles and stand on the stove to warm up overnight, because we let the fire out. The water used to be warm. But that was the situation in them days.

What would happen if like today when it was absolutely teeming down. Did you stop the washing on a Monday and wait for fine weather, or did the washing go ahead, whatever?

Oh, no. It was Gran's washing day Monday, Mum's washing day Tuesday and that was it. You didn't step out of line. You had your own days.

I remember helping my Gran. She used to do the washing. In those days she still used a copper and a mangle.

That's right.

A big old mangle, and turning the handle, for the washing. Didn't iron towels. Used to have to iron quite a lot, well sheets had to be ironed. And of course they were then, big old cotton ones, they wanted a lot of ironing and pillowcases the same. Yes.

Have you any memories of the Sturry flood?

Oh yes.

Because you would have been affected where you were living.

We were three stairs up. The water came up three stairs. Yes, it came in Boxing Day, 1927. We had these friends, like Mum and Dad's friends, the Banks's and he was the first, I think he was the first man in Sturry to sort of have a van for his business. He used to travel, I don't know how the miners used to get up from Sturry if they hadn't got a bike. Used to bike from here up to the Chislet Colliery or walk and he had got this, well van I suppose you'd call it, and it just had two wooden columns each side, tied to, you know, the side of the float, you wouldn't be allowed to do it nowadays because they used to rock about a bit and he used to take the Sturry miners up to the colliery. And he had just bought this van and he'd got his first removal van, removal job, and he went off the week of Christmas to take furniture from Canterbury up to Sheffield. Well, in the meantime the weather got terrible and there was so much snow he couldn't get back. So we had invited like Mrs Banks and Muriel to come and have tea, I suppose that would have been Christmas Eve. And then it snowed so bad that we said, "Stay with us," because Ern hadn't got back and of course she was worried because no means of letting her know where, she didn't know where he was. So they stayed with us, and there we was, next morning on Boxing Day, we had the old white hearths, you know, you wouldn't know them but you had to whiten the lump of white hearth stone to make them nice and white, and Mum said, "Oh, we must have got a crack in the hearth." She said. "The water's coming through." I mean it was all round, but we just didn't dream it was going to come indoors. And it was starting to bubble up and I always remember we just grabbed our breakfast and tore off upstairs. And there we were over three days until Ernie Banks got back, and he was a fireman.

So he's the Banks on the photograph?

Yes, that's Ernie Banks, yes. So he had the long waders for being a fire officer, like. So he came along and well he went home and he found Muriel and his wife wasn't there so, of course he guessed they'd be with us, so he came back and he said, "Oh, I'll take you out." And he piggy-backed us out. And it was pretty well up to his knees, and I know when it come to my Dad, he got us out, all of us out. Must have been, I mean, he was only a slight chap, must have been awful for him, because my Dad was a little bit more heavier than him and as he came across in from our front door, he kind of rocked a bit and we thought any minute they would both go over in the water, but anyway, he got Dad safely out, all dry.

And then we stayed down there for about a week or more, because that was a terrible do. No, we must have stayed a fortnight, because that was a terrible do, because, you see, just along the road was sewage works, and having the door open to get us out, we didn't realise, but when the water went down there was all that all over the floor. It was appalling.

So what had happened? Had it snowed and melted quickly?

Yes. And what had happened, it had been a very, very bad frost, and the sluice gates at the mill, they had froze. Being over the Christmas holiday they were supposed to have gone and moved them up so the water could flow through, but being the Christmas holiday I suppose they thought, 'Oh, blow it,' you know. They didn't do it. So the sluice gates were frozen, so, I don't know whether it would be up or down.

Milk delivery to Providence Place by James Peel

Well, frozen so that you couldn't let the backlog of water through it.

And it just flowed through and then it just went through over the churchyard and went all over the village and plus the fact that it had frozen in other places, I can remember when we got out from, after Ernie Banks had rescued us, there was Muriel Banks, the daughter, me, who was there, two other girls, who you wouldn't know, me Mum would remember them, and the four of us, it was just frozen solid from Brooklands, where the water had flowed over, like, from the rivers, and we actually walked from Fordwich up level with Chislet Colliery on the ice.

Gracious!

Yes, we linked arms and then if one fell down, of course we all fell down, but we actually walked from Fordwich to Chislet Colliery. Yes. And opposite, I can remember they wanted, of course it was the field opposite, there is still a field now. They came along with their skates, one or two people in the village who had got skates, like, they came along and they couldn't skate on it. They thought they were going to, because as the wind blew, it was a terrible spell of weather, as the wind blew, the ice, it froze in ripples, so they couldn't skate. And of course that's where we come to fall down, going up to Chislet, because occasionally we met a bit where it was rippled, where the wind had blown up some of the dykes.

Gracious.

Down we went. I've actually got a photo, I have got an original copy. It's a bit tatty, but I've actually got a copy of the Daily Sketch that came out that week.

Let me see. Well, 'Arctic Adventures in the English Iceland". Gracious me. December 29th, 1927. So it was obviously all over the country that it was bad weather at that time?

Yes, it was terrible weather. It started, well I think it started in some places at Christmas time and then it went on into the New Year. I don't know if there is any photos inside. Actually, some of them, now there's the...

That's Sturry.

That's right. There's the Leopard's Head. It's Vikings garage now here and the house where the people there, opposite was the Lyons family and then that actually is Canterbury. Now that's a long hoe. Now that's my Mum out the window. We tied scarves together, and we had to empty the bucket, we'd got just a few lumps of coal that old Dad managed to rescue for us, and we lowered a jug down in the bucket, you know, stood the jug up in the bucket, and that's one of the Peels. He came and tipped the pan – because they used to deliver the milk in those measures, no bottles in them days – and that was Mum, and I think that's me poking my nose over the top and I think it's Muriel, but that's my Mum.

Gracious me, what a picture to have. Ah, that's somewhere else. There are some photographs here from various places in Kent. But that one, definitely, that's wonderful. So that was down at Providence Place?

That's right, yes. The middle one, yes.

So did you take the furniture upstairs when you saw the water coming in?

Well, we took up what we could. You see, the rooms were so tiny, we didn't have much room. They just had to stop there really and take pot luck.

That's a wonderful photo.

Yes, that's right. Is that Sturry Fire Brigade? No, it's not, is it.

It does say that fire engines from Herne Bay, Sturry pumping water out of the cellars of somewhere.

Yes.

It's lovely that you've kept these. Now tell me about your mother.

Mum went in service in the village for her first job.

Did she?

She worked for the Hoares, Jack Hoare. Fred Whittaker also worked there.

Did you go into service locally?

Yes, I went down Brooklands, in the Fordwich Road, where Finn's are now.

Ah.

I was in, and then Lily worked with me, my sort of friend, and I don't know, I can never remember what it was, but there was a very serious crash in the banks. Did they call it the Wall Street Crash? Something like that. And I know old Mrs Bird lost all her money and she said, "I can't afford to keep both you girls." So I said, "Well, I'll go," because Lily was there before me, and she said, "No you won't. I have to pay Lily sixpence a week more than you." And they sacked poor Lily. And I was so miserable about it, because I thought it was such an unfair way of doing it. So I said to my Mum, "I'm not stopping there." So Ivy hopped off and got herself a job in Canterbury, up the Dover Road. Oh, she was an old cat there, but I stuck it out until we got married. It was nothing like as nice as with Lily at the Birds down Fordwich. I got sixpence a week more than what I did down Brooklands. I suppose you can't sit up there comfortably, the cushion's not right, is it?

Ernest Banks and Arthur Bournes and the Sturry Fire Brigade pumping out water in St Peter's Street, Canterbury in December, 1927.

Sturry and How It Has Changed

by Dorothy Weal
born 1904, died 6 April, 1994

I hope to give you a picture of my life of 54 years in the village. I was not keen to come here at all! My husband and I were both born in Dover – I remember my Mother waking me up at five o'clock in the morning at the age of 5 to see Bleriot land. Although we experienced the horrors of the First World War with bombing and shelling from the sea, we managed to enjoy life very much as the young do. My husband started work at Dover Harbour in 1913 as a Morse boy, the railway then being South Eastern and Chatham – steam, of course. As was usual he progressed to office staff, serving at several stations before being appointed to Sturry in about 1922.

The station in those days was a very busy place. It had a stationmaster who was in charge of Sturry, Chislet Halt and Grove Ferry, two full time clerks, one learner, two porters and three signalmen whose duty was to open the gates for the trains. I can never remember seeing them walk down the steps - they always slid on their hands down rails polished like glass from years of like treatment. All hours were covered by the signalmen. Night as well as day. As well as many passengers in those days, there was much parcel traffic, farm produce and movements of farm animals. All the office work of the Chislet Colliery Halt was also done at the Sturry office. Stationmasters I can remember include Messrs White, Haydon, Stanbridge and Post.

We decided to marry in 1926, the year of the general strike, I can't remember that it worried me very much as we couldn't find anywhere to live and up to a fortnight before our wedding we were still seeking somewhere. There were no building societies as we know them today and with our wages could never have committed ourselves. Anyway, we then managed to get a flat in Canterbury for 18/- a week. After a couple of months we heard about Orchard View, in Mill Road, to rent for 12/- a week. We felt rich with 6/- extra to spend. It was not the Orchard View you see now. Some years later, after we had left, the house was demolished by a bus, the driver having had a heart attack.

I had seen Sturry before we moved, of course, and thought the village reasonable but had no idea of what it would be like to live in it. I was not really fond of the country and when, soon after I came, I met Mr. Peel's cows from the farm going down to graze by the river, I was terrified! When it was time they would often start out to amble down before Mr. Peel was ready. And he would come flying after them on his bicycle.

The house I came to was two-up and two-down with a wash house and one tap. We had a cesspool for waste water but no drainage, so had a bucket for our lavatory, which was emptied twice a week. The cart for this started about four in the morning, it was later for some people of course. Strangely, some of the village properties had to have their bucket taken through their houses which sometimes happened to be at breakfast time. And if you ever met Mr Frank Johnson, who lived in Fordwich Road, he would tell you how he and his brother, as soon as they heard the cart stop, would grab their breakfasts and run upstairs!

There was no street lighting and most houses were lit by gas. For cooking I had an open fire with an oven at the side and a gas ring. In 1946 I had a new fire put in the house where I live now and the man who came to do it was of the old school. He sent the boy to the farm for two buckets of dung for making cement and said that it would never crack and I would never get a nail in it, and he was right.

It is difficult to realise how well we were served by our trades people then. The baker, Mrs. Ryan's, is the only shop still the same. The chemist was where Mr. Nye, the butcher, now is next to the Post Office, which had the post box in the building. Mrs. Baines [the postmistress] once told me that when they were manning the exchange in the room behind, it was quite common for people to post letters during the night for delivery next day. All sorting was done at Sturry for all the villages round the area. The greengrocer was still there - with this difference. Wyborn's, who kept it, also kept pigs on the allotment next to the cricket field. When a pig was killed it was sold in the shop and you always had to order the sausages. They were so tasty. Of course, this could not happen today. Mr. Brooker's, the butcher further down the village, had one of those meat blocks which were common in those days it being the trunk of a tree. I expect you remember how they used to scrub this every day. After the bombing it was found in the allotments where it had been thrown by blast.

The drapers-cum-shoe shop, etc., was run by the Tharps, who had a niece living there named Joy Skyrme, who opened a shop in Canterbury in Castle Street afterwards which is still there. The most important shop in the village was Cork's, the paper shop which sold everything. It was Mrs. Cork's proud boast she had opened every day since coming there. Should you run out of anything when she was closed, you could always ring the side bell. It was affectionately known as the Ducky & Dear shop, oh, happy days!

In all there was a forge halfway up the village street, four bakers, one in the Island Road, three grocers, one draper's shop, one chemist, two butchers, one tea importers, one bicycle shop, two greengrocers, and a barber's which was kept by Percy Tuff. The farm which supplied our milk and cream and eggs, when plentiful, I always brought 12 doz. @ 1d each to preserve, with a dozen thrown in. There was a bank where the carpet shop is now. The WI has tried several times to persuade the bank to open again but with no success. I understand that just before I came there was also a bank in Mr. Nye's shop and apparently his shop is still called Bank House. The lady who did dressmaking was in one of the houses and on the corner where the public lavatories are going up was a large house with a baby linen and wool shop next to it. They were there until 1963. When my husband was alive he rented the allotment next to it.

In the Island Road there were two flourishing gate and hurdle making businesses owned by Mr. Arthur Homersham and Mr. William Homersham for whom Mr. Cyril Homersham worked. The wood was transported by horse and cart from Trenley Woods until 1941 when all work was transferred to the woods. Mrs Louisa Homersham told me that they were paid 9d to make a sheep's hurdle, and 10½d for a pig's hurdle.

We had a good doctor by the name of Ince, [Dr A. Godfey Ince, F.R.C.S.] and a marvellous nurse who went everywhere on her bicycle. Her area covered all the villages around - she delivered babies, looked after the sick and attended the dying. Nurse Mollie McCormick was followed by Nurse Payne and Nurse Gladys Saul. They were paid by the Nursing Association. This was a voluntary association for which we collected 12/- per year for the master class, 10/- per year artisan class, to which I belonged, and 8/- for the labouring class, such as farm-workers, etc. You called her for any medical reason and she would decide if you needed the doctor. Even if you were having a baby she would decide if a doctor was needed. They were very poorly paid, and Nurse Saul told me that after the new Insurance Act in 1948, it was the first time they could not attend anyone without a doctor's consent.

In 1928 the baby clinic was formed. Nurse McCormick still delivered the babies but also attended the clinic which then had a country nurse for aftercare, etc. Mothers attended to see the doctor free and to buy food for the babies. This was a great benefit for mothers and babies and when the hall was destroyed in the bombing a room was found in the Island Road, with only a break of one week. It was a most hair-raising time during the war with German bombers overhead and screaming fighters trying to stop them. We always wondered what we would do should anything happen while the babies were all undressed.

The Christmas of 1927/28 saw the flooding through a combination of circumstances, much rain, tides and winds, etc. caused the river to burst its banks. Fordwich was cut off and the whole of this part of the village was underwater. Hassocks were floating in the church,

wreaths floating up the High Street and houses at ground level, or below, had water pouring through them. Only the cellar of my house was flooded because we were up a step. The cottages on each side, three on one side and the two still there, Mrs. Brenchley's and Mr. Oaks, homes were flooded right through. The day after Boxing Day it froze and the fields were lovely to look at. With the waves sparkling in the ice, it was said that you could have skated from Fordwich to Sandwich. The poor chickens were left on their perches with nothing to eat.

There were no street lights during my early days here but some gas lamps were placed in the village itself with a man, Mr Tyler, to light them each evening and extinguish them each morning. Since then we have become very well-lit compared with some villages after pressure from our Parish Council. After the two buses a day when I first came here, road traffic continually increased and a bypass for the village was proposed. Many ideas were suggested to overcome the hold-ups by the crossing. In fact, when the Westbere Butts was built it was facing Herne Bay where they thought the road would be, with the back of the pub on the Island Road. It is still like that, no road yet, but they expected one to be built then in 1928. Four different roads had been proposed and still traffic has to go over the crossing, although the High Street bypass of 1962 has helped a little. The wooden houses on that road did face onto a lane on the other side of which were the allotments and the cricket field. It was called Sporting Place and I understand that years and years ago it was called that because it was where the cock-fighting was held. There has been a cricket club since 1863. [This ground was sold in 2004, leaving the Club homeless. Since then they have had to play wherever they could hire a pitch.]

Our spiritual needs were very well served. We had our church, the Baptist Chapel in the village, the Methodist Hall and the Gospel Hall in the Island Road. The Convent was also in the same place as it is now. We also had our Parish Hall which was next to the Church. It was quite large, it had a stage with dressing-rooms behind, as well as a kitchen. And in this hall were held all meetings, dances, whist drives and parties etc. I think a branch of every association possible met there and there was even a concert party.

Sturry Station facing Ramsgate, June 1958

The village was growing all the time and education was becoming a problem. The Primary School was overcrowded and the new senior school was opened in 1935 for 170 children. Now there are well over 800 there. The Junior School was opened in 1967 at a cost of £70,000. But when the primary school was built it cost £200. Somewhat different! And we still have to have extra classrooms in all three schools. Then came the war. It was thought that the Medway towns would be bombed. So the children from Gillingham were evacuated here. They also had to be squeezed into the schools, but not for long. Nothing seemed to happen and the children did not like it in the country. There were no fish and chip shops.

When the war did hot up we in Bridge-Blean Rural District Council were in direct line from the continent for the bombers. We were really in the front line. We were having air raids all the time, day and night, but the most devastating were the land mines dropped in the heart of the village in 1941. Fifteen people were killed and we knew them all. The village was wiped out and the damage to houses was over a large area. There were 76 high explosive bombs, and 1000 incendiaries dropped in our village. The Junior Kings School and the Barn were full of troops but we never knew of any of them killed. But the war is a story in itself.

So we pass on to the loss of the hall and how all associations, meetings, etc., came to an end. Special events were held where we could rent a hall. The Wesleyan Methodist chapel had by then ceased to be used and a move was made by Sir Arthur Pugh and others,

including the Revd. W.H.Oldaker, Mr.B.R.Raffety, Major C.H.H.Kenworthy and Dr R.A.C.McIntosh, to buy it for our use. With alterations, etc., this was going to cost £1,500. Shares of £5 each were offered to all associations and the general public. A grand total of £1,040 was raised and with other efforts by 1954 was completely paid off. The Social Centre opened in 1948 but during the following two months there were only 11 bookings, rather different from today. Special efforts, through the years, have been made for curtains, tables and so on. Then in 1972 it was reconstructed, as you know. The stage was always considered a must, but so far costs have ruled that out. After we opened where the car park is now, was a cottage and garden and this was occupied by Mr and Mrs William Cole. Cars were not the problem, as now. It was hoped in time that we could extend the hall as the two cottages behind were then condemned. But as you know also, they have been restored.

All through the years pressure was put on the council for mains drainage. There was never any money, or it wasn't the right time. And then the war came. But then at last we managed it and they started rebuilding the village. It was quite a long time before we were all connected and in spite of grants there were still a number of houses without bathrooms.

From my window I could once see woods, fields and a path leading to the Humps. I need not tell you how fast the new estate has grown, we knew it would happen but never thought that such a large area would be covered. Where I once only saw fields and trees are

The old hand-operated wooden gates

Sonnanurg, now 2 Sturry Hill, once the home of Lieut-Colonel Bredin and his family

now houses. It is sad to see trees destroyed. Where Mr Brett's gravel pits and lakes are now, we once roamed over fields in the early morning gathering mushrooms and the delight of my younger brother when he came to stay with me, was to go out and gather these mushrooms for his breakfast. You couldn't buy them in the shops then, as you can do today.

There have been many changes - some sadden me - but there are some good things. One is our lovely library that we started in the 1920's with a cupboard in the Primary School. Numbers of borrowers grew so fast in 1937 we came to a room in the village. It was open three afternoons a week, and was staffed by volunteers. To quite a lot of people to go to the library was a social occasion and the late Bishop and Mrs. Rose always came to us for their books as they said that it was too impersonal in Canterbury. When the new library opened in 1970 full-time staff were appointed. We miss seeing our volunteer friends but it had to come.

There never seemed to be any difficulty in recruiting helpers for all the activities - even the first fire engine was bought and operated by volunteers. This was housed in a shed behind the Rose Inn. It later went to Fordwich road. At night a call boy roused the firemen, at other times they were called out by a maroon. This went on until the Fire Brigades Act in 1938, then when men were on duty at a Fire, they could claim a fee. Until then if buildings were not insured, the firemen would have nothing even if they were on duty when they should have been at work. They competed in all the fire brigade competitions and won many shields. The volunteer brigade went on until 1941, then became part of the National Fire Service, with the new Fire Station built in 1961. I have mentioned Milner Court. When I came, all land on the right side as you approach the church was called the Hamels, and was the village playground. The barn was considered to be for our use and at one time there was a Barn Restoration Fund, for which we in the village worked. The right of way through the Hamels is still honoured but a public footpath across it has been closed.

The purchase of the Social Centre meant that many associations and societies, etc. could reform after the war. With such a growing population different interests and pleasures also meant the village as we had known it had gone. A clinic, gardeners' society, WI etc. have continued through the years, but many have fallen by the wayside. Others such as this club have been formed. For me I have enjoyed meeting all the strangers coming to our village, both young and not so young. I hope that at some time in the future littered streets and vandalism will pass, and we will have pride in our village once again, but sadly I feel sure that we will one day become a suburb of Canterbury and who knows what will happen to us?

The former Sporting Place allotments before the new road was built

Coming to Hersden in 1930

Charlie Baillie

In conversation with Ross Llewellyn at an unknown date

When we first came to the village [of Hersden] we moved into rooms with somebody. My mother and my father with three children. They were just living in one room until they got fixed up with a house. This is what used to happen then. So they could get the people who was coming in – get them established.

Houses were being built at that time. My father was waiting for this house to go and one came up because this chap who was in this house – Tommy Hughes - they built a new Social Club and he and his wife went in to be the steward and stewardess. So my father moved in to number 8 The Firs. We stayed there right up until mother moved out – that was in the 1980's. I think that we came in about 1930.

My father went watchman then on the building site – night watchman for a while, then this job came up for a storeman/storekeeper for the new Home Guard that was being formed – a full time job, something like the Terriers [Territorials]. I don't know what the reason for it was, just establishing a force. That was in the hut down the pit lane. Lots of them had come out of the army, some went down the pits and joined the Home Guard. An influx of all the troops that came out made up this second Home Guard. It was quite a good life – all right. The chap who was in charge of it, Major Curtis, he was made up, he was working in the pit, he was a natural person to take charge. He wasn't big-headed or nothing. He could put Major in front of his name all the time, Major Curtis, Major David Curtis.

We went to the Black Hut down the bottom of the village, the primary school.[1] Right from when I was five-year-old. It started off when I was a 3½ year-old and my mother sent me to the Convent, because my sister was going to the Convent at the time. You know what women are like, give him a bit of education, she said. In the Convent they take young children like that. But as soon as I became 5, I wanted to go with the lads to the primary school. They called me sissy. The first day I went to school my mother dressed me in these little patent leather shoes and I got into more fights that day over them patent shoes. Anyway, I enjoyed my schooling down there really. I was there 'til I was 11 years old then went to Sturry Central, stayed there 'til I was 14. You left school at 14 then. I left school on the Friday and started in the pit on the Monday. My mother had gone there, the women used to sort the kids out, and sorted me a job out in the lamp room, so that's where I worked for about 6 months. Then I got a job in the engineering shops as

a blacksmith's mate. I was that until I was about 18, blacksmith's striker. The engineer came round one day and said "We're short of a tool smith. Do you mind taking the job?" Of course I was over the moon really. So I took that job on, I was on that for about a year. Then I had my call- up papers, for a medical for National Service.

So I went and had an examination for that and I was waiting for my papers to come. They said it would come within a couple of months. I went to see the engineer to see if I could get a job shunting engines about. Because it was more money, you always go for more money. I said it's only for 2/3 months before I go in the Army. He said as soon as you get your papers to go come and see me and I'll get you a reference to get in the REME. I was waiting for the call-up papers but they didn't come. I was waiting 6 months, a long time. I went to see the manager to find out what had happened. I think it was John Shaw then, he said that I'd been deferred. I couldn't do nothing about it, this was after the war - about 1948 when they were calling up people for National Service. I didn't know pit workers were exempt, I expected to go. I wanted to go, another experience. One of my mates, Herbie Waite, he went in. He was killed in Palestine. I ended up driving one of the little shunting engines. Of course I wanted to go down underground, to get more money again. So I went and done my training to go underground.

You had to do 2 years on the coal to become a fully-fledged collier. When you had a rise then it went from 27s 6d to 35 shillings – a big jump in your wages – and if you weren't doing your work you were out. There was the "butty" system then, of course, when the man at the top was given all the money and paid the men out of it. I seen some of that when I was a boy. When you was a boy 9, 10 and 11 you were running round the pits especially on a Friday. The butty system then was they'd all sit round in gangs and the ganger would have the wages for that face for that particular week. That was shared out into the shifts. Perhaps they had done two shifts with one gang and two shifts with another gang and they had to go round hunting for their money. This was where you got a lot of trouble. I've seen lots of fights. Terrible fights where men have gone up and they've been paid short. They've had to fight for their money which is very unfair. Different men coming up from different areas and they were tough. Specially the men from Lancashire. They'd have them clogs on. They'd say "do you want an up and downer?". If you said "yes" you were in trouble. They'd kick lumps out of each other. It changed from that over to the system, a proper way of paying. The management said rather than a particular boss and that was better then. When I started work there it was normal. The market system was if you weren't in a regular gang you were on the market and when they made up the gangs in the morning, the overman would came along an sort out all the spare men. Perhaps men were off for medical reasons. He would just fill in with these extra men. Sometimes it was a good thing to run the market because you got to know all the situations. When we finished in Chislet and I went over to Snowdown, I run the market for about 6 months. It was really good. I went to work with a different gang every day and that was on ripping and on the faces. So you got to know all the men in the pit. In this pit I worked on ripping and reel cutters. You had three men to the cutter and I went through as representing the cutter men for a new contract with the union. To finalise a new contract to the new system it wasn't based on the men. But it was still the same, they split the wage into two or three and timbermen got the same. Much the same, you know, Ross.

Then I worked on opening faces. We opened different roadways through – between faces - down the rear drift from the bottom of tension gauge into the main gate. The gangs we worked was pretty good. Nice chaps. We all know each other. Us kids grew up knowing all the men who worked in the pits – what jobs they worked on. They knew us and all. If you did anything wrong you'd get a clip round the ear and I didn't interfere with people or become a nuisance.

I've said that we were very lucky because this area, great social life and with the management in power then you had a great welfare system. 1st class welfare, best in England I suppose. When you say that the Davis cup team came here to train you can tell the facilities that we had. Courts – bowling green, the lot. We were very lucky to have all them facilities. I've said to these people, you'd have different managers working the pits; if they had a good rugby man down there and a rugby team, he'd offer him a job in the pit.

I think it was Dan Evans, all that lot came up that way. And you had all the top bandsmen from Durham playing in the band down here. It doesn't seem much now but when you look back at all the top sportsmen that's come to this area for jobs and then settled down. Their offspring, you're getting all these genes coming to these children. You have more of a chance getting a good sportsman out of that lot. I've had a marvellous life in this village. Good childhood, good teenage years. Country dancing. We'd go to a dance nearly every week. You didn't have to travel about then like you do now. No drugs. A certain amount of beer when you were a teenager. You wouldn't have the fighting like you have now because most of the people had gone through the army. They'd had enough fighting. They just wanted to live in peace and harmony.

You just went out, had a good drink and enjoyed yourself. The boys and girls used to mix at that particular time we used to. We went to the same places and mixed with our girls. I was made redundant when Snowdown shut. I accepted early redundancy – that's what it was. 1985, wasn't it? You couldn't refuse. You knew what payments you were going to get. It was very fair really – can't grumble. We would still get coal. It's worth quite a lot of money really. It doesn't cost us anything for heating. When you look back it was a happy existence really. Most people were pleasant to each other. Everybody accepted each other.

I've always been interested in painting. I've always done a little bit. I never had time to take it up. When you are a teenager and then you are married you haven't got time for anything like that. As soon as I finished I went into the adult studies in Canterbury. You only went in there for 2 hours a week. Studying painting and drawing. I went in there to learn how to use different materials and different papers. I quite enjoy that part of it. That's really interesting once you get into it. You could get the clay in there and bring it home and do some of your modelling there. Oils, acrylics, water colours, pastels - I've got it all there. [2]

There's been big changes here, of course. We used to take the accumulator up to the garage on the Island Road to get it re-charged. That's before we had the new fangled electric radios. I can remember the Blacksmith's shop working in Sturry. Before they built the new road there used to go right round that corner. Beside the Rose Inn. Of course there wasn't the traffic on the road in the late thirties. So you'd have the chap with the horses just outside and he'd be shoeing them. You wouldn't be able to do that now. Before the Rose closed it was difficult to get across the road to get into the pub. You can't imagine East Kent Buses and all that traffic going round the little roads in Sturry. Imagine, the army convoys had to go through there during the war time, and tanks. The night that Sturry was bombed there was lads going to school and our right winger, he was killed that night. I used to go round the shop here to do my mum's shopping. I knew them in the shop. We had three shops in the village then and Rosie Davis'. All the kids got their shoes in Rosie Davis's shop. You'll remember her, Ross, won't you?

[1] Muriel Thomas FIFTY YEARS OF METHODISM IN A KENTISH MINING VILLAGE – Hersden 1929-1979 (1979)
[2] Ross Llewellyn - HERSDEN - Chislet Colliery Village (2003). The cover was painted by Charlie Baille.

The Silver Jubilee of 1935

Betty Marsh (née Bull)

Sturry High Street before the war, looking south

Interviewed by Heather Stennett on 3rd April, 2000

The first place I remember is Westbere because I went to school there. We had moved from Sturry to Westbere when I was about 4 and were there until I was 8 and then we moved back down to Sturry. My sister was born there in 1936, with Dr. Ince and Nurse McCormick in attendance. I particularly remember Nurse McCormick on her bike, rushing up and down with a bag on the back in which, of course, we were told all the babies were.

We were living there in 1935 when we had the Silver Jubilee and I remember that we had lots of red, white and blue all around the window, flags and, of course, fancy dress. We always had fancy dress. I know that one time my brother [Douglas Bull] was in fancy dress as a judge, (I don't know if it was then). My mother [Nancy (Annie) nee Bellingham] had a lot of fun making his wig, which was of cardboard with all these white sausages all over it, and a long gown. She said to him that he should look very straight and not smile and so, of course, we stalked around and all of the children were running round trying to make him laugh.

I went as a Victorian child and we always seemed to have dresses with flounces on them in those days, and I wore pantalettes which were really like a pair of white

pyjamas with lace round the ankles, and naturally the kids all thought that was funny, how they could see my drawers. I had a bonnet and my friend, Irene Webb, had a very pretty orange and yellow dress and it was covered in streamers and balloons. She had a hat with tassels on it and she looked very good. She went as Carnival. Well, we were over in the field next to the railway line, the King's School field. That's where we had the proceedings and we had to walk through the Hamels to the old hall, the old parish hall, [destroyed in 1941] and in the hall there were people having a meal. I think they were probably having tea, and we paraded right round the room so that they could all see our fancy dress. Well, behind us there was a very large clown waving a beer bottle. I don't think that would be allowed now - he was acting as a drunken clown, you see. And he kept bumping into us - in fact he broke two of my friends' balloons and we detested him so we moved up about four places to get away from him. I remember that very well, but I liked him enough later because I married him in 1951! That was Peter Marsh.

Are there any photographs in existence of these fancy dress parades?

No, I don't think there are.

What else did you do?

High Street looking north

Well, there was Sunday School and going to Church and fruit picking at Mr. P.T.S. Brook's farm.[1] We always went there to pick red, black, white currants, raspberries and also hop picking and we went blackberrying and picking up bits of wood in the woods with my mother, for heating the copper, because we only had a cold water tap.

What about village characters?

There were several people I remember well. There was a gentleman called Mr. Easterbrook, Jimmy, and he was very enterprising because in those days in the summer you would have all the charabancs, mostly from London, going down to Margate. They would be stopped along by the Mill Pool, waiting right along the street queuing for the railway gates to open [and right up beyond the Four Vents crossing at Westbere, too] . There were more trains, I think, in those days than there are now because they would be blocked right along. He would get in a coach nearest to the Mill Pool with ice cream and he would sell as many cornets as he could by the time the coach got to the station where he would get out and go back down and do the same thing again. The other man that I remember particularly was Charlie Neaves. Then the war started and I had just left school. I was fourteen that year.

We are talking about the 2nd World War?

Yes, that's right. 1939. My mother woke up one morning and she thought we won't be going hop picking because it was raining. She could hear a lot of noise but when she got up she found there was a fire nearby and the street was full of people. And we all got up quickly because

our house and the adjoining ones were all, as she called it, wooden clad. They had that wooden clapboarding outside. It was a very ancient house - it was a Queen Anne House and my mother was very proud of it.

When you looked up the chimney there were rods and hooks where they used to hang the pots and little cupboards on each side of the fireplace with a long brick seat inside. It had once been very large but had been altered a lot. My mother always insisted that it was haunted.

Whereabouts was it exactly?

Number 20 High Street, where the Fire Station is now. We went round the back where the library is now and it was a lock-up garage on fire. Charlie Neaves lived in the house behind where the dentist is now. Charlie was a fireman but the fire engine was out at a grass fire and I believe the thing burnt down before they got back. I remember he got off the fire engine and ran over to the house because his father lived there and I think the place had practically burnt down. We were throwing buckets of water on our houses because the paint was all starting to bubble and it was getting very, very hot inside. And standing in the crowd was a small boy called Jimmy Phillips, [Percival James Phillips killed 18th November, 1941, aged 6] and he said several times "poor Chartie" (he meant Charlie).

When we went hop picking Charlie Neaves used to drive the buses for Mr Ernie Banks. And he used to tear down Well Lane, down the road to Fordwich Lane, without stopping and we used to hang onto the seats for our dear lives. And when we got back to Mr Bank's yard

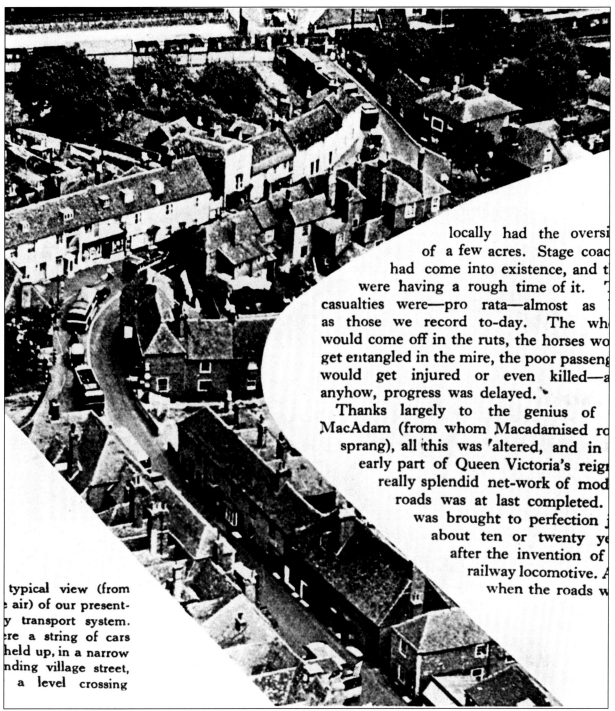

locally had the oversi
of a few acres. Stage coac
had come into existence, and t
were having a rough time of it.
casualties were—pro rata—almost as
as those we record to-day. The wh
would come off in the ruts, the horses wo
get entangled in the mire, the poor passeng
would get injured or even killed—a
anyhow, progress was delayed.

Thanks largely to the genius of
MacAdam (from whom Macadamised ro
sprang), all this was altered, and in
early part of Queen Victoria's reigr
really splendid net-work of mod
roads was at last completed.
was brought to perfection
about ten or twenty y
after the invention of
railway locomotive.
when the roads w

typical view (from
air) of our present-
y transport system.
re a string of cars
held up, in a narrow
nding village street,
a level crossing

Aerial view of Sturry in 1934 (note traffic jam and goods train on level crossing)

we used to sing "Here we are again". I think we were always relieved that we had got there in one bit. He was a bit of a character. I think that he did it on purpose. He used to go "Wheee. . . here we go!" You must know Well Lane, how very narrow it is. If anything was coming up – well, hard luck - because, of course, people could go up and down there in those days. Come straight down, he did. And at speed.

Dangerous!

I'll say. I do remember the cows going up and down the street because they were along in the field between the two bridges. Mr. Peel's farm being at the bottom of Sturry Hill, they had to go up to be milked. I think they came down from the farm in the morning and they went back up in the evening. Then, of course, there was Mr. Robinson and the lavender wagon. He used to go around emptying all the buckets of sewage. It was all cold taps, and we always had a tin bath in front of the fire. Nice bath, but the water had to be heated in the copper, of course. It was pretty hard work for our mothers. Also several times I remember the sheep going to market and they completely filled the whole High Street, as they walked there. Can you imagine it?

Was your house one of the ones that were affected by the bombing of Sturry?

59

Yes, but it wasn't hit directly. The bomb dropped where Franklyn House is now and where the pub was. But every house was completely shattered and we lost most of our things really. When that happened I wasn't at home. I left home at 14. I went hop picking and what have you, and after the Christmas I started working in a girls' boarding school. So I was away from the village. Then I went on to the King's School because they were evacuated to Cornwall, (both schools were evacuated) [2] and I worked down there and while I was down there Sturry got its mines and I wasn't able to come home. I had to stay there in that empty school with my friend for Christmas. That's one Christmas I will never forget. We didn't have a home, either of us. Her little brother Jimmy Phillips was killed in the bombing. She came home the following year and she was killed at "Claremont" on the Island Road by shrapnel. Her name was Ivy Smith. [Ivy Ethel Smith, killed 7th June, 1942, aged 17]. Her poor mother lost two children in 2 years.

What a sad time.

So I was away from the village when all that happened and when I left the King's School I went into the Women's Royal Air Force and when I left that I was nursing at Canterbury Hospital and only came home on my days off. I wasn't living in the village for quite a few years.

I see.

My brother used to take his truck up and get logs from Mr. Homersham's woodyard. That was his Saturday morning job. Mine was getting people's shopping. I used to get a few pennies for doing it. Go to Mrs. Cork's and get all your sweeties. She had everything in that shop. . . We used to go up by the railway to the Forge beside The Rose Inn and watch all the horses getting shod and smell that particular smell that you get off the hot hooves. Alf Robinson brought horses up to the forge during the war to be shod, from Fordwich. It was certainly in use part of that time but not now, of course.

I can't remember it, of course.

We used to collect the chippings from the woods, too. Go up there with my Mum with a bottle of Bing [a local lemonade] and a sticky bun. There was a bank up there that grew white violets. Looked down over the field towards the railway line and that bank was chopped away some years ago. We used to take up a tin with cotton wool in it and take home white violets for my mother. Beautiful perfume. Poppies in the corn, lots of wild flowers. Mushrooms by the cricket field. Blackberries. Good memories.

[1] H.Stennett and K.H.McIntosh, eds BROAK OAK – A Kentish Village Reconsidered (2006)
[2] Robin Q.Edmonds THE HISTORY OF THE JUNIOR KING'S SCHOOL 1879-1956 (2008)

A Fruit Farming Year

Kath Thompson at Work

by Linda Lodge

Kathleen (Kath) Thompson moved to Broad Oak with her husband, Bill, in the summer of 1940. Bill was already working at Broad Oak Farm, which was owned by Mr P.T.S.Brook, and Kath joined the "Summer Gang" of local women who were employed to pick fruit. This then included blackcurrants, plums, pears and apples. Before long she was working full-time at the farm.

Once the leaves had fallen in the autumn the men began pruning and the women cleared up behind them, burning every last twig to prevent disease. Another job in the autumn and winter months for both men and women was washing and grading the apple and pear harvest which was stored in boxes. In later years a cold store was built until Mr Brook and several other enterprising farmers established Sandwich District Growers at Preston and the farm's fruit was taken directly there to be processed.

In early May the women would begin "blossoming", that is removing excess flowers to space out the pear and apple crop. During the Spring of 1944 Mr Brook called the women together and warned them of the danger posed by Germany's latest weapon – the VI Flying bombs, nick-named Doodlebugs. He urged the women to take cover the instant they heard the missile's tell-tale drone. Kath vividly remembered the first time a doodlebug was heard while the women were "blossoming". Far from seeking shelter, every woman scrambled up her ladder to get a better view.

Whilst German bombs did fall on the village and a low-flying bomber peppered holes in Kath's sheets on the washing-line, there was more danger, albeit less life-threatening, flying around the orchards each Spring. A local bee-keeper placed hives there to assist with pollination and some small black bees, possibly Italian in origin, proved very aggressive during the removal of blossom, especially when it disturbed them during foraging.

By June the women began "thinning" – that is removing developing fruit to leave room for the rest to form perfectly.

Blackcurrant picking began in July and lasted from three to four weeks with extra casual labour brought in by bus. This work was paid at "piece work" rates, i.e. for every tray of fruit picked. Picking currants was Kath's especial forte and in some weeks she could earn more than the men on the farm.

A blackcurrant picking machine was trialled in later years but Mr Brook was unimpressed by the amount of fruit left on the bushes and the damage done to them. Eventually in the 1970's when the market slumped the blackcurrants were grubbed out.

In the late 1940's strawberries had been extensively planted on the farm and Kath returned to work hoeing them in June 1951 after the birth of her second child in February that year.

The first apples to be picked in August were Beauty of Bath and Miller's Seedlings, both early varieties of eating apples which could not be stored. They were also easily bruised whilst on the trees and in general handling. Although Mr Brook was a gentleman farmer, employing a forelady, foreman, and in the 1950's, a manager, Mr Wild, he was always involved in the day-to-day running of the farm. So when the Millers showed excessive bruising one year he came to demonstrate how to pick them correctly. Having carefully collected a bucketful,

he then managed to drop the contents whilst descending the ladder – much to the amusement of the assembled women. Undeterred, he picked a whole tray but was forced to concede that that these, too, were marked and bruised despite his being extra careful.

Before the introduction of dwarfing rootstock the apple trees were tall and 30 stile ladders were required to pick the fruit. Two of these ladders would be locked together in an "A" shape and a degree of safety and balance was achieved by the heavier woman climbing higher than her lighter partner. Apple picking continued through to November with varieties including early and late Worcesters, Laxton's Superb, Lord Derby, James Grieve, Cox's Orange Pippin and Bramley.

The farm's plum trees were later removed and an orchard of French Morello cherries planted. Kath remembers having to use scissors to cut these the first year they cropped. Another year the day's picked crop vanished after the women left the orchard and before the tractor arrived to collect them!

Until the Land Army girls began to wear "Bib and Brace" overalls during the Second World War, none of the women on the farm wore trousers. Even after this more practical apparel became widely available many of the older women continued to wear dresses or skirts and tops.

Kath continued working on the farm after it was sold to F.W.Mansfield. By the early 1990's she was only working in the summer months with Pearl Castle, picking raspberries and runner beans. She finally retired in 1993 at the age of 80 with some reluctance but a lifetime of memories which, at the age of 97, she can still recall with consummate ease.

Apple Picking 1964/5 Forefront L to R Dot Gammon, Ella Gammon and Rose Chaplin. In the background Kay Keem with Sharon and Gay, Kath Thompson with Wendy, Brian, Liz and Michael Moran, Sheila Moran and many others.

Filming in Fordwich

Roy Thomas Edward Morris (born in Fordwich, June 1931, at 3 Ivy Cottages) and his sister, Betty Dorothy Todd (nee Morris), (born in Dartford, January, 1928) interviewed by Monica Headley on 3rd March 2010.

Betty: During the early 1940's a film called THE CANTERBURY TALES was made in Fordwich, but also in the surrounding villages and all of us children watched, saw all the film stars and took part. Some of the village boys had parts – Lenny Smith, Ron Murray, the Tamsitt brothers, Terry Pickford and my own brother-in-law, David Todd. We all watched the film being made and I think some of us were in it but we hit the cutting- room floor later on. But we were all invited to the premiere in Canterbury. Most of us have copies of the film. A lot of it was shot on the landing stage at the Fordwich Arms and in the High Street, and of course in the George and Dragon pub. Mrs Gertrude Line was in it and the shot of Lenny Smith on top of the hay waggon was taken from the window of the George and Dragon, Mrs Line, I think, leading the horse. Some scenes, too, were filmed in an upstairs room inside the Manor House. [1]

They needed to do some shots in the studios in London so some of the cast went up there. They wanted to have 4 year old David Todd. At first his mother didn't want him to go but in the end he did go.

They have a reunion of this film every so often and then the crew and the stars walk round the various villages. About 5 or 6 years ago I attended one in Fordwich, where we all met and walked all round the village and remembered all the shots that were made in the film. I think that last year the village chosen was Chilham, where they all walked round.

Roy: To carry on the film theme, I did go to the premiere at what would be the Friars cinema, which of course is now – and will be - the Marlowe Theatre, and being a premiere, all the stars came, including Richard Attenborough and his wife (Sheila Sim) and Eric Portman and it was a very good occasion. [2]

Betty: During our time as children there were no hops growing in Fordwich so our aunt, Miss Jane Morris, used to go hop-picking for Mr John Holdstock at Elbridge Farm. She used to go and pick for him, as I think, did other members of the village, but the Fordwich hops

Early View of George and Dragon by Alfred Palmer, R.O.I, painted from the old Parish Pound

had long gone by then although the poplar trees surrounding the hop fields – some of them are still there at the Fordwich end of the Old Park. They were planted by our grandfather, Thomas Morris, when he worked on the farm. During our time the farm was mainly a fruit farm. The farmer grew gooseberries, blackcurrants, apples, plums and cherries. And the women in the village, of course, all worked in those fields and orchards, picking the fruit. Children would join their mothers during the holidays and after school. All the orchards had different names and us kids knew them all. Mr Ernest Cannon worked on the farm with the horses as a wagoner and his assistant was Mr Alf Robinson.

We had two shops in the village, one a post office –cum – general store run by Mr and Mrs Arthur Taylor and one a sweet shop, kept by Mr Arthur Boys. We were all very poor except the farmer, Mr Daniel Brice, who lived at By The Way House. Our family house was 5 Brown's Cottages, now The Maltings.

Our Mother [Dorothy Louise, nee Ladd] was a registered foster mother and, that despite living in a 2 up, 2 down cottage, with an outside loo and water tap shared with 2 other houses and no bathroom. Cooking was done on the kitchen range – there was great excitement when a gas ring was installed! Lighting was by gas or oil lamp.

As a foster mother, one or two children would arrive in April and stay until June, and then one or two more would arrive and stay until September. We were always brought up with other children. As our Mother was a

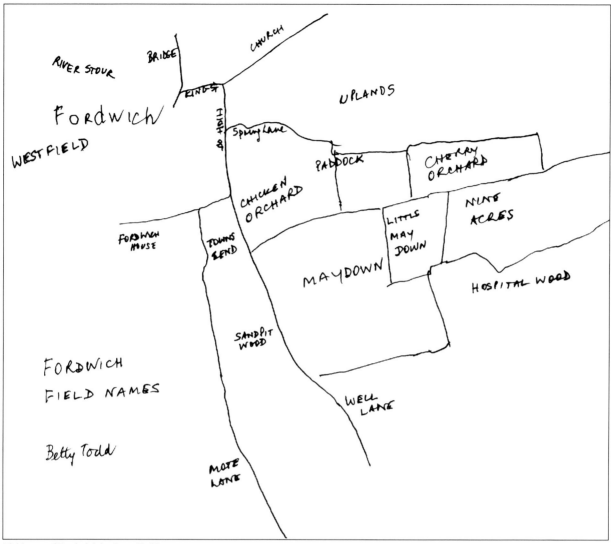

Field map of Fordwich by Betty Todd

Beating of the Bounds in Fordwich in 1922 thought to include Elsie and May Spratt, George Bowman, William Joiner, snr, Jane Morris, and some of the family of Hettie and Richard Swain, Dolly, Alec, Alan and Joan.

Londoner, she took children from the poorer parts and gave them three months in the country. I believe it has something to do with the Lord Mayor of London's Fund for Children.

Roy: My childhood memories are mainly of visiting the many uncles and aunts we had in the village. There was no restriction set on playing. We were over the fields for hours on end, on our own, mainly with the cattle as well. We'd even walk to Trenley Park – as far as that – and, of course, the marshes to the south of the river were never flooded in those days, as we could walk over the marshes, and up through the woods to Stodmarsh Road, and back through the orchards or Well Lane and that was mainly our childhood.

One uncle particularly was well known in the village was Mr Bill Joiner, driver for the Kent County Council. He swept chimneys in his spare time for a few pence. Most evenings you would see him with his sack and his brush. For about sixpence he'd sweep out a chimney and really clean out the kitchen range which was a work of art. Another chimney sweep was Mr Nelson Knight.

That's my main memories as a child.

Of course, there was Mrs [Edith Maud] Brice, the farmer's wife, with her enormous hats. She never walked on the path. She always walked down the centre of the road, particularly on Sundays when she went to church, which she couldn't do now! Not with the traffic being what it is these days. I don't think Mr Brice could have gone with her that much, she'd have gone on her own.

Very pleasant memories, really, as a child we had no worries but we had no money so we didn't know what it was like to have it. But happy times really!

Betty: We always went to church on Sunday and Sunday School and I usually had to go to Sturry Chapel as well because our father was brought up as a Methodist so we had two religions. [This was the Wesleyan Chapel in Chapel Lane, attached to St Peter's Church in Canterbury, and now the Sturry Social Centre.] I remember one Sunday in particular [August, 1939] when the submarine THETIS went down. The church was full and we sang "Eternal father, strong to save..." and everyone, I think, cried. I'm sure only three men were saved from the submarine and 99 lost. I do remember that.

During the war our father [Albert Morris] was a volunteer fireman and, as such, we had a bell in the front room, and when there was a raid, or the Fire Brigade was

Apple-picking team at Fordwich Left to right: Mrs Dolly Robinson, unknown, Mrs Mary Ovenden (nee Homersham), Mrs Molly Butterworth, Mrs Kathleen Murray and Mrs Brain.

needed, the bell used to ring and nearly take the roof off! My job when it rang (while my father was getting ready in his fireman's gear) was to run round the village at any time of night and knock up other families or other men. I used to knock up my uncle, Mr Bill Joiner, who was also a fireman. I'd bang on Mr Percy Whittaker's door, just to let him know. Then I'd run up the street to Uncle Ethelbert (who was always called Mike), my father's older brother, who was head of the Home Guard in the village and on the way up, I would knock on the door of Luke Castle, the gamekeeper, to inform him. I'd just knock, you know. We were frightened of him because of course he always had a gun with him.

Roy: I think one of the main differences in the village of today is that in our day it was mainly the church. We had a large choir, eight male voices, then we had the women, the boys and girls. We all had our stuff to wear at Church. It was a big part of the village. Perhaps Betty remembers more than I do?

Betty: I do remember that at least the men's part of the choir made a record – obviously of hymns and it was very well received. Mr David Vidler was the organist and choirmaster. I've never forgotten either the time when a very low-flying German plane came over Fordwich after being attacked. Unbelievably, we all rushed out of the church, including the Rector, and ran after it down the Drove as it lost height. Obviously it went faster than we did and by the time we got to the marshes it had already sunk into the wet ground out of sight.

[1] Paul Tritton A CANTERBURY TALE Memories of a Classic Movie (2000)
[2] Paul Tritton MICHAEL POWELL'S CANTERBURY TALES Setting the Scene for a Classic Wartime Movie (Parkers Print on Demand, Canterbury, 2010)

A Woman of Parts

Sylvia Constance Cox
1st October 1919 - 10th January 2002

Interviewed by John Line on 10/11/1999

May I call you Sylvia?

Of course. Yes

When did you arrive down here in Sturry?

I came to an interview in April, I think it was, 1940

That was to the Frank Montgomery School

Yes. It wasn't called that then - just Sturry Central. It was called that because all the children were brought in from the surrounding villages and it was the only school of its type in the area. I had stayed at College for a third year to do intensive PE training and I wanted to know whether we were going to stay there in the school in no man's land or be rushed off to evacuation. Every holiday from College we had to volunteer to take groups of children with the ordinary staff to the places where they were going to live during the war. As I have

an older sister who was already a deputy head in London she said "You'll come with me, won't you?" When it happened we enjoyed it so much we did it time and time again.

Did you just go to the one place?

No, the place we liked best was the first one we went to - something beginning with W - I'll think about its name later. It was near Salisbury Plain because we were having some hectic nights over here. When we went to our school even the train drivers didn't know where to stop. All the children had a flash on their shoulder to indicate which school they came from. I had my 10 given to me that I had to look after. A big burly man came up and said stop. I saw to my horror that half my children's brothers and sisters were in that group in front. I said I'm not really a qualified teacher but I thought that wasn't right and said so.

At my interview I was quizzed by the Board of Governors who had come to do the interview and they asked me if I had any questions and I said is this school in no man's

Sturry High Street after the bombing in November, 1941

land because if it is it will make a lot of difference. I can use the experience I gained in London with the children that are here, if not we'll be on the move just as the London children were. The Headmaster, Mr G.E.Draper Hunt said "Well, that's ruled out because this is no man's land and nobody will remove us from here except Hitler and his tanks". So I said I have another 3 interviews to go to. "Oh", said Harry Young, another Governor, "in which case we will have to meet again. We don't like doing that - can't you make your mind up this afternoon, so go outside and think about it while we interview the other candidate, Miss Dickinson [later Mrs Percy Amos]". So I walked around and thought about it and it looked rather good. There was a lot of new paint and the children were in uniform which was quite impressive in those days so I said yes and that's how I got here in 1940.

What subjects did you take?

I started off with my proper subject, PE, [physical education] but every time someone was called up the subjects had to be covered because you would not get any men to cover them so I taught all sorts of things, including needlework. Mr Blake who lived just down the road from here who taught woodwork and because he was 40, that felt awfully old then (it doesn't now!), he was left to one of the last and then he had to go to the north of Scotland to help build a tiny boat ready for the invasion. What upset him most was they hammered in the screws and didn't do the job in the right way. Mr Blake, we had for a long time and poor old Mr Bournes. He kept leaving school and then being asked to come back for another term. He was also in the Fire Brigade and on one occasion he was attending a fire on a tall building and he was up a ladder holding a hosepipe and when the water was turned on it shot him off the ladder and next day at school he was covered in bruises black and blue down one side. It was quite an exciting time – I used to have to ride with the children on the school buses in case of air raids and once we were machine-gunned when crossing the playground to the shelters.

What did your mum and dad do?

My dad was in the Navy for 22 years. He had 4 daughters, and was disgusted that he didn't have a son to follow him into the Navy, so my youngest sister joined the Wrens and she was having such a good time of it because she was in the Met department - very few people were taken for that as you had to have 3 Higher exam levels at certain degrees, Maths, Physics and something else. She did a lot of her training in Ireland. So I said when I started teaching here it would only take me about 2 years to pay off my loan because you had to borrow half the money to pay for training in those days from Kent County Council. This only left me £8 per month to live on. It doesn't sound much but I

had my bike, you didn't go anywhere on the train or the buses. My dad said when he was home on a short furlough why do you cycle up from Sturry and I said for several reasons – firstly, I don't like standing on a platform and being a target for someone to do the machine gunning at, because that sort of thing happens also if I am on a bike I'm a small target and they are sure to miss me. He said if it's because you haven't got the bus fare or train fare I would have given it to you. I don't think he would have done! Anyway I had my £8 and I had saved £10 in my Post Office savings book. I said I'm alright and I might be joining the Wrens in 2 years time. After 2 years I had paid my loan off and then a decree came out that no more women staff were allowed to join the Wrens and things like that.

You have had a very varied life in Sturry . Did you buy this bungalow on Babs Oak Hill straight away?

No, Mrs. Brickwood lived here. Her husband had been killed at Dunkirk when her daughter Margaret was only 10 and I very soon became part of the family as a sort of elder daughter. Soon afterwards Mrs Brickwood was offered the chance of buying the house but I bought it as a sort of sitting tenant with a loan from the bank. When you compare the money it cost me just under £500. Of course during the war ceilings fell down and other slight damage was done to the house.

Tell me about your war. I know that there were the 2 landmines dropped on the village and a lady was injured in Hersden when a convoy was shot up, and there were other bombs falling on Hawe Lane because of the military stationed there and in the area known as the Camp situated between Babs Oak Hill and the Westbere Butts. Also several planes were shot down in the area - both British and German.

And there were bad attacks on two East Kent buses on the same day. Don't you remember the time when Doreen - was her surname Collins? I forget - who was brought up by her Grandma because her parents were killed in London and she was as deaf as a post. She was on the top deck of one of the buses that were shot up and she just sat there and didn't get up at all even though the planes were circling and shooting up the public transport to lower morale because she hadn't heard them.

There was a lot more to the war round this area than people realise. So whereabouts in the village were you when the landmines came down?

Bang in the middle of the High Street. Someone in the village was a Guide Captain, I can't remember her name [Miss Margaret Newman] and so I said to Violet Hammond who taught History here, instead of going to the pictures tonight we should go and see if she's alright to show goodwill. We went and knocked dutifully on the door - said we don't want to come in but we were sorry she was ill and did she want us to take Guides this week. We said we would. We went along the street to the Red Lion. We could hear the planes buzzing around and there was one house that had a doorknob which could be opened from the outside so we went in luckily and a women was at the ironing board and her son was next to her, a nice lad from school. When the explosion went off the force was so great that the iron flew out of her hand and the coal from the fire and everything went black and shook up and down, up and down, and Violet lost her glasses and I dropped my torch with my concern with checking that I was all in one piece. I said if you don't move your feet we might find both glasses and torch. Meantime, some people were calling out for help from the other side of the road but we couldn't get out of the door so we went out of the window and there was a granny from London looking after twins for her daughter who was ill. While helping the children I put my foot in a chimney pot and fell over so the woman said "Give me the children. You're no good," so I handed them back. Then a young soldier said to me- "Would you mind looking at the back of my neck as I don't know if its bleeding much or not?" As I had lost my torch he gave me a box of matches so I could see and put my hankie on it and I said "It's not too bad - not spurting out or anything". So I told him to go to Milner Court where his unit was to be looked at. Then I thought it was time I went home as I wasn't doing very well there.

The next day I went up to Rainham to see my mother because we were all scattered over the place and it was better than writing. My mother didn't take the Daily Mirror but someone had shown her the back page which said " OK village is not OK " (Sturry) and commented that the raid was probably because they showed too many lights but a train came into the station which showed slit lights and probably attracted their attention. On the next day the nice lad brought the glasses and the torch back to us. Bobbington was his surname, I think. I don't know his Christian name as Draper Hunt didn't allow us to use them.

Draper Hunt was a bit of a disciplinarian

I think he was a little too fond of his cane.

It didn't do us any harm.

No, you are still all alive.

I think it improved our morals. I remember one day I was on the Island Road, just past this junction, and there was a little stream that came down from the woods. There were bars across it to stop you falling in. My friend Peter and I had just come out of the woods

and we were looking at the stream and we picked up some small stones and were plopping them in the water, not doing any harm, and Sergeant Fuller [Sgt W.F.Fuller] came down the road and saw us and bang bang round the ears and said if you block this stream up someone's house will flood - don't you do it. Because of that and Draper Hunt's cane it set me in the right direction. Having got roughly through the war and you are teaching all sorts of subjects at the school due to the shortage of teachers and you were also heavily involved with the Guides .

I started when the vicar, Rev T.G.Williams, asked me when Miss Newman (now I've remembered her name!) disappeared from the scene. [She got married.] I said I had someone to help so that should be alright. We used to practise camping in the vicar's garden before we went away to camp. We went on a weekend camp and one mealtime Mr and Mrs Draper Hunt visited us while they were collecting for the church roof fund and Mrs Draper Hunt told her husband not to eat too much bread because it was still rationed and didn't want the Guides to run short. They used to live on the Island Road but the lease ran out and they returned to Herne Bay.

As well as the Guides you were also involved with the church, weren't you?

As most of the Guides were in this area I moved from Westbere to Sturry church.

You were also in the choir and on the Parochial Church Council and you still are, aren't you?

Yes.

Are you enjoying it?

Living in Sturry, yes or I would have gone, wouldn't I? I had lots of different interests. If I had kept to school all the time that wouldn't have done. If you are connected to the Parish Council you get to know people,. They think you can do marvellous things but you can't. For instance one day I was walking home past the toilets when a person came up to me and said there is an overflow flowing can you do something about it, I said no but I know a man who can. I saw her later and she said I knew if I told you it would be fixed.

We were both Chairman of the Parish Council and had to get involved and if you said you would make the water stop you had to make sure it did stop! It was a very interesting job and you have got to be involved with the village.

You were on the Council when I left. I left because it is no good one person trying to do everything. It was a small village when I came here and now it's the largest parish in the area. When I was on the 11 plus panel and interviewing the doubtful children it was quite clear that Sturry and Blean were the best schools in the area and it didn't matter how big you were because per head capita governed how much money you had. You got so much for an infant, so much for a junior and so much for a senior. If you have a lot of children in the school you obviously get more money to use up. If you have got a big spread of children it helps those who are not so good, they get a bit more confidence and make more friends and the parents mix more too.

Things have changed and people have gone non-community putting up 6 foot fences and coming in and staying indoors.

Don't you think children spend too much time sitting in front of televisions and computers?

It is good for children to learn computers because they are the thing of the future.

Yes, but not to the extent that they do nothing else and it comes to something when pupils come to school and say they haven't done their A-level homework because they have been playing on a play station.

Golf?

Yes, 10 years as the secretary of the ladies section at Canterbury Golf Club. I was given honorary membership after that and I've only hit one ball since then. I injured my neck. I did it when I got terrible cramp in the middle of the night so I decided to get out of bed and walk round on it but I couldn't put it on the floor so I forced it and fell over. I tried to see if I could move,1 could so I crawled along to the light switch, put the light on and decided I wasn't too bad I could move my arms and shoulders alright but by the next morning I couldn't move my neck at all. I went to the doctor who said it is probably muscular and will probably be all right. It happened 3 years ago and is still not right.

Did you make Captain of the Ladies section?

Yes, I think it was in 1980.

What was your handicap?

It varied - up and down - not much cop really. It was 19 at one stage. I got more enjoyment from teaching beginners to play and going round with them and taking a pocket full of old balls which it didn't matter if they lost.

Were there any highlights in your life?

I think taking the children abroad for a holiday. We used to have about 6 staff which I insisted on, as you shouldn't go with just 2 staff and 22 children. We had some jolly good times. You also found out more about the children than you thought you knew. There was one girl who was quite unlikeable in school but coming down the chair lift for 20 minutes I learnt so much about her that I felt quite sorry for her and from then on we got on well.
Another achievement was that I was Chairman of the GCSE Board. At my first meeting I suggested that instead of making samplers we should teach the children to make a garment that they would be proud to wear down Canterbury High Street. This garment could be made over a period of 15 one hour lessons and could be judged on what has been achieved over that time and given a GCSE grade. This idea was accepted and called the Kent B experiment. At the end of the year we had to go to a Sheppey school to grade all the garments for the GCSE grades.

In 1957 I was appointed deputy head of the Archbishop's which was a much bigger school with Mr Ronald Ratledge as Head. It was hard work - no computers to do lesson schedules on and Mr Ratledge used to do most of that work but I had to look over it to check, as a trouble shooter, for any mistakes or double scheduling.

Thank you very much Miss Cox, it's been a pleasure talking to you - one of the stalwarts of the village over the last 60 years.

The Bombing of Sturry

Evelyn Mary Bates

Evelyn Bates and Sylvia Cox
Joint photo on the fiftieth anniversary of the bombing of Sturry 18th November, 1991

Interviewed 14th June 1997 by R.Q. Edmonds

Are you called Evie Bates or Eve?

They call me Eve. It's really Evelyn.

I see, yes.

Well, it used to be Evie, but it's now Eve.

And where were you born, then?

In this house, on June 14th 1910, [1, Chapel Lane, Sturry]

And you had a brother, didn't you?

I had a brother, yes. Stanley. He was eighty-three when he died. He lived here practically all his life; he was born over in the little cottage in the street where Mrs. Ramsey lived, that's where he was born. But I was born here.

And were your mum and dad here even longer than that?

No, they came with Stanley, but they were married at Sturry Church. They had a good bit of fun really, because my mother was nanny-housekeeper to the Fleets in the village, they were farmers at Hawcroft Farm. And there was a fete one year to get funds for the Parish Hall, which was in Church Lane, and Mrs. Wood, the pork-butcher's people, the old lady, she made a wedding cake, and they sold it for sixpence a slice, I think, and there was a little quill in it, and whoever got that could be married at Sturry Church free and have all the trimmings free and everything. Well, my mother was living at the farm, so she came down and she won it - but in those days, the elderly people, they were very funny if you'd lost anybody, weren't they? And Dad had just lost his one brother, and Mrs Wood wouldn't let him get married in the June as they were going to, so they had to wait for October. So they had this prize but she wouldn't let them have the bells, and they didn't have the choir, they didn't have all that. It was the Reverend Brewer [Revd. H.P.B.Brewer, Vicar of Sturry 1885-1914] married them, and that was all free, all paid for through that, so Dad always used to pull Mum's leg he said "I didn't buy you!"

Oh, that's a lovely story. And so you went to school here, up on the hill?

Up on the hill. And Sunday School.

Who was the head of the school? The Primary School?

When I first went there? Oh, the Popes, of course. There was Mr Thomas Pope and his wife. He took the top classes, and she took class 5.

And then you stayed there until you were how old?

Sixteen.

And then you went to the Post Office?

I had four and a half years there. I wanted to go into the Exchange at Canterbury, to the telephone, but at that time – I had an interview and everything, but they didn't take girls from the rural areas, only the town girls.

Oh, what a shame!

But when they wanted somebody, when they had an exchange here, the master, the head postmaster – Smith's it was then, the postmaster – he gave them my name, and they took me, and I went up there to work.

And you stayed there four years?

Four and a half years, and then I went to Beasley's [the Canterbury Cleaning Firm then in Stour Street] in the office, and I was there – I went there in '21 and I left in – I went in March '21 and I left in November 64.

That's amazing!

And I'm still friendly with the family, they'd got his son's wife and their children by then.

Did you know Mr. and Mrs. Baines in the Post Office?

Oh, yes, because when I was in the Post Office it was Tooks was the postmaster then, and when he went away for the weekend the Baines' used to come and stay there, because they didn't know the running of the place, and I used to have to get up at four or half-past in the morning to do the mail, because they had six postmen in those days. I used to have to get up and let one in to get his bike and go to Canterbury, and they just fed me. I had to stay up there, you see, because nobody else knew anything, and they didn't know the post office or the telephone, you see, so I knew them before they came.

And you went to Sunday School?

I went to Sunday School

Where was Sunday School?

Up at the school. First of all they had it in the mornings, at 10 o'clock I think it was, and then the older ones used to come down to the 11 o'clock service, but they came out before the sermon. But the younger ones, up to a certain age, we stayed behind, and then when we got older we came as well.

Did you have any Sunday School outings?

Oh, yes. One particular one – we used to go everywhere with lorries, most times; but the very first one I remember was in the Reverend Brewer's time. And like they do now, the children go away for an outing, don't they, and the mums go with them and take the younger ones. Well, that's what my mother did, she took me. And Stanley was in the Sunday School, but I wasn't old enough then. And I can always remember going to Whitstable – we played on the beach, 'cos in those days it was all going round Tankerton we went, there was all sideshows and things. You remember these things – perhaps you can't remember them – you stood in a basket and the balls used to come up and you caught them, and the swings, all sorts of things. In fact, we all thought that was Whitstable, because we arrived there on the train, which is where the reservoir was. I expect you know Whitstable market is on it now, right opposite the harbour; well, that's where the station was. We used to go on the Crab and Winkle Line [The Canterbury and Whitstable Railway]. Not many people can say that, can they?

So what about Sturry in the war? Pretty awful, wasn't it?

Oh, yes. I was in ARP, first aid. When we first started we used to go on duty every night, and then we decided that was far too much. We used to go on at 10, until 6 in the morning, and then we split up, we had so many every other night, which made a break, because you couldn't go to bed early, you had to wait. We used to just lay down, just as we were, and get what sleep we could, come home at 6 o'clock, get ready for work and go off. That's all we did.

Can you remember some of the people you were with?

Oh yes. Noah was a warden, my brother was a warden. George French, he was a warden, and Bob Johncock, he was a warden: he went in the army, you know, the one that lost his parents and brother and sister in the blitz. Mr. Prior, I think he was a warden, there were several of those because he was grade one, you know. And the Home Guard used to be in what is the butchers' shop now; that was two cottages, and they had one as their post. And Mr. Charles Impett, the warden, used to go and sit in there in his house that was in Church Lane, and we had the Parish Hall; and of course the soldiers were billeted at the Junior King's School. They took over the King's School, the King's School went to St. Austell's in Cornwall.[1]

What about the doctor? Who was the doctor then?

Doctor Ince [Dr A.Godfey Ince, F.R.C.S.] in those days. And when we were blitzed, and the Hall went, that was the first-aid post really, he opened his place. I remember when I went into the village, someone gave me a message to take up Mrs Capper there, and she had left her children in a cupboard, and I had an awful job with her, she kept saying, "Oh, you're taking me the wrong way," and she was worried about her children.

Sturry High Street after the bombing in November, 1941

She said "I hope my children are all right, they're in a cupboard." I said "All right, I'm going back to look for them." And I come back and do you know, that I got back and went in, and the warden said, "What are you looking for?" and I said "I'm looking for two children, a little boy and girl, because I've had to take their mother up to the doctor's - she's worried about them." "Oh." He said "Was they in a cupboard?" and I said, "Yes," and he said "They've been blasted in there." It was just blast; all the children it was just blast, they weren't hit.

They were killed by the blast?

Well, you know, it was just the same with the Johncocks and little June Peel, and Roy and his sister Audrey, she was younger than him, and John Collins, all those – it was just blast. [2]

And, of course, the bodies had to be indentified?

Well, yes. You know that big place up Staines Hill belonging to the Convent – not Brooklyn House there, the other place. I don't know whether one of the Fathers used to live there – St. Anne's Villa. [It was the Revd Father Joseph B. McCarthy]

Oh, I know, right on the top.

Yes, two cottages, yes, well, they classed that as a mortuary. They had to get someone to attend to them and lay them out, and then the relatives had to go up there and identify them. But the nuns were wonderful. They used to go up there to help you, and go down and make you a meal. They were wonderful.

Was Miss Cruttenden the headmistress then?

Yes, she was the headmistress then.

Because that must have upset her when all those children...

Yes, she was the head – because she thought a lot of the children. I think this one does, too, doesn't she?

Yes, I think she does.

Out of all those people, my brother had to make nine coffins, mostly children. Some of the others out there had other people, but out of the sixteen that were killed – there was Mr and Mrs Hampshire lived over the butcher's shop, that was Hedger's then and they were just blasted, they were more of less blown up into a tree almost. But they lived over the shop.

And then the Vicar was Mr...?

Mr. Samuel Risdon-Brown [Vicar of Sturry 1938 - 1949]

So he had to take the funeral services. Was it one mass funeral?

No, they had separate times. The Johncocks, you see, were buried at Thanington, that's where their grandparents lived, 'cos with father and mother and two children, that was the family more or less wiped out. There was only the son, Bob, left; he was in the army.

Were there many survivors? Were many of them buried and then dug out?

Oh yes. I was up there, I should have been round the hall. I got stuck right in the village and I was standing by my brother with blankets and stretchers as they dragged them out. And when they got the Johncocks out, they were saying that John Collins and June Peel had gone over there to play with the other two Johncocks, you see, and they were down the shelter, but she was over them, trying to shield them. I only know that by what Stanley said. But at Chislet Colliery, the miners they were very good, they came down and propped places up so that they could get them out.

Sturry stayed desolate for a long time, didn't it?

Oh yes. We had had it, we were blasted, hadn't got a window or a door. I stayed at home and saw it go up in a ball of fire. But Stanley, my brother, he was standing at the bottom of the stairs, he'd just got my mum and dad down the shelter – at least, he'd got Mum down, Dad got himself down – and he came back for something and it was getting rough and he stood at the bottom of the stairs, and as he stood there the front door came in and something on the back door whizzed by him and just missed him.

So the village was really bad.

Oh, it was terrible.

All the shops went, didn't they?

The next morning it had all been roped off, because you got no end of people coming looking, you know, like they do – I mean, I've never seen so many people down here this way as we did the next morning.

And all the little shops had gone?

Oh yes, and Brockman's that was a shop then that had all the batteries, all the stuff that they had for the cars and that.

Who was the little old man that had the sweet shop?

Cork? Yes. Well, she was – they couldn't find her. They asked me, "Do you know Mr and Mrs Cork?" I said,

"Yes, he's probably gone to find her." So we were going over the rubble and I said, *"Well, perhaps they've gone home,"* you see, because they used to live in the lane where the Evans live now. Because it was built for her sister and they had to go back and they'd taken her down to the King's School, because that's where the worst cases was, but she did land up in hospital because she was shook up rather.

Mr. Parker, he had the butcher's, he kept going, didn't he, although the shop was gone?

The shop was gone; well, he went down to Friendly Hall, some outhouses down there. And Dorothy Spiller's, that went.

The Post Office was all right?

The Post Office, that part was all right, it was right through here, you see.

So, most of the people in the village, they used the shops, didn't they, they didn't go into Canterbury for shopping?

Oh, no. Mrs. Holmes, they'd had a grocery. He'd died, but she ran a grocer's shop. She went to live at number 4 Church Lane, the cottage this end, and she had a little shop in the front room. Oh no, they were very busy. We had a nice draper's shop, too, before the war. Skyrmes had it, the parents of Joy Skyrme. They left here and they went to Canterbury to Castle Street. When they gave up, Joy had it. She still called it 'Joy Skyrme's'. But I don't know whether she's still about, I can't find out. Somebody said – I used to hear information from – I don't buy the paper now – the Lyons girl –

Vera?

Vera Lyons, yes, because she used to work for her; I used to get information from her.

Did you have any other friends that you used to run around with?

Yes, there was Doris Salmon. They lived in the village in a little low oak wood cottage. I had to go in and persuade them – the warden came along and he said, "Do you think you could go in and get them out? They won't come out and it's not safe for them to stay there.

Do you think you could go in and get them out?" So I went in, and made myself known, and I got them out, and someone else came along and took them down to the school. I seem to have been sent running round everywhere, pushing people out!*

Have you got anything else you can recall? What shout this house? Did you have an outside toilet?

Yes, still got it. We had an outside toilet.

So it hasn't really changed a lot?

Oh no, this house is pretty nearly the same. We never did pull it to bits, but all the other houses, they've been pulled about – we've got so many new people. I don't think there's very much left of the original, they've taken out walls and made an open staircase, but when this is sold it'll be just the same, but I'm not spending any money on it to alter it.

Because it suits you?

It suits me all right.

So the years have gone by. Are you still happy here in Sturry?

Oh yes. That's why I want to stay here as long as I can. I've got a stair-lift because I couldn't get up the stairs otherwise.

It would be awful to have to move now, wouldn't it?

I don't want to. Well, I'm as well off here as if I was to go anywhere else, because I'm on the ground floor now, and I've got the stair-lift. . .

[1] Robin Edmonds THE HISTORY OF THE JUNIOR KING'S SCHOOL FROM 1879 TO 1956 (Parker Print, 2008)
[2] It has been recorded in GROWING INTO WAR by Michael Gill (Sutton, 2005) that after the parachute mines fell the body of a child was found clutching a bag of buns. This legend arose because Thelma Bubb, (the late Mrs Stanley Bush), who had been rescued alive and taken to hospital, returned unharmed to the village that night still firmly clutching the bag of sweets that her Mother has given her when she first took shelter.

A Child's View of the Bombing of Sturry

Margaret Johnston (née Bull)

Interviewed by Heather Stennett, 3rd April, 2000

My earliest memories are of 18th November, 1941, when I was 5½ when Sturry was bombed (but I do remember the old house that we lived in that my sister, Betty Marsh, has talked about)

The evening of the bombing I can remember, I was there playing with my toys in front of the fire. My mother had gone out, so had my brother, Douglas, because he had gone to the Youth Club. I listened to Children's Hour on the wireless and my father was shaving, he always had his shave in the evening. He was standing in front of the mirror shaving and I can't remember at that time whether there were sirens or not [there weren't] or whether it was just the sound of the aircraft that alerted him. He gathered me up and we had an indoor shelter then that was built with sandbags in an inglenook. He gathered me up and suddenly it was as though the world had ended for me, for being that age, you know, an enormous explosion. The air was full of noise and dust that seemed to get thicker and thicker. While we crouched there the cat raced past us at about 90 mph because the back door and the front door had been blown in and it disappeared outside and I wanted to go after it. My father - I know he grabbed me and threw me back. Anyway, it was pitch dark as well as all this dust and noise and things falling. You could hear all the house above you falling. When it went quiet we crept out and immediately my father hit his head on a beam which shot him forward and he put his foot into the wireless which had fallen on the cabinet. So it was very noisy – he said a few words, too!

We groped our way to the front door, and it was very dark, although there were fires burning and people running about. I saw soldiers, who at the time were billeted at Milner Court. The school had been evacuated, my sister with it, to Cornwall.

While we stood there I imagine that my father didn't know what to do next. He didn't know whether to look for my brother, who would have had to come past where the bomb had been dropped, or my mother who had gone to the Island Road and there were people who had been injured or dying in that direction. We stood there, undecided; we could hear Mr. Cork screaming in the shop opposite. He was shouting "Help, murder, police!" At that moment the two Misses Tharps, who had the haberdashery shop opposite, came running across in a terrible state and Dad said to me "You stay with Miss

Tharp and I will go and see to Mr. Cork". I wouldn't let him go. I just put my arms around his legs and was so petrified. It was a terrible time. Luckily at that point my brother came running up. He was just a teenager at that time, he had seen all these dead bodies and he was in an awful state. Because he had tried to get past this bomb crater and they said "Sorry, son, you can't go up there." He said "I must, I must, I live at the end of the High Street".

So with him in tow, the three of us started walking towards the Island Road, luckily to meet up with my mother who was coming to find us. So we stood in the dark, hugging each other. It was a most awful experience. We went back to friends in the Island Road and stayed the night there. We then went to stay with relatives of my mother's in Canterbury until after Christmas, then we moved back into Sturry. Although the war was still on and this house we moved into had a great hole in the roof and it was bitterly cold, Mum and Dad were pleased to be back in Sturry. Back home.

Back into Mill Road, not into our house because by then the whole of the High Street had been pulled down.

Life for me carried on much as before, for me being that age. Because we carried on going to school although there were numerous air raids, we were taken to the shelters and back into the school, in and out, time and again. I do remember the air raids at night. We were constantly woken up and taken down to sit in this perishing cold shelter. We shared it with neighbours - an elderly lady and her daughter. It was an Anderson shelter.

I remember the war ending and then we had the street parties. We had VE Day party and the VJ Day parties. Where Sturry had been bombed was a lovely playground for us when the war ended because it wasn't rebuilt for a long time and having an enormous bomb crater in the

The bases of the concrete road blocks in Sturry High Street.

A cheval-de-frise or tank trap outside the Swan Inn, Sturry High Street.

High Street then, we used to go and fish newts out of that and pick wild flowers on the bomb site.

The only thing I can remember being left still standing in the High Street was the back of the chapel that had been there. [1] I used to go to the chapel in the afternoons and the church Sunday School in the mornings. We went on two outings and we had two Christmas parties!

The Sunday School outings we usually went on a coach, occasionally on a train, usually to Minnis Bay or St. Margaret's Bay. That was great fun. We all trooped off to a hall to have the sandwiches, not very exciting but great fun when you were taken there.

Going back to the Air Raid, what happened to Mr. Cork?

He wasn't actually injured, he was a large man, a bit like Mr. Bumble! He had fallen down behind the counter apparently, and couldn't get up. He wasn't injured but he was given to shouting. . .

After the war there were lots of children in the village, so there was constantly someone to play with. Most evenings in summer you either played rounders in the park or on the cricket field, and there was always lots of you to play with. Or swimming in the Mill Pond, or playing underneath the arches. The bigger boys would jump off and swim in the Mill Pond.

We went to Brownies and Guides with Miss Cox. That was at the School. When I became Patrol leader, my friend and I, Ellen Whittaker, [now Mrs Coombes] went to help take the Brownies with Miss Raven who lived at Milner Court where she was assistant matron. She was Brown Owl.

The Corks were sweetshop owners. On Sundays when other shops were closed my friends and I used to walk to Fordwich because the sweetshop there was run by Mr Arthur Boys. He must have dreaded seeing us because there were about 6 of us and we would all take ages to choose the sweets and he wrapped them all in little pokes of twisted paper. 2oz. of this and that. That was, of course, when rationing was over. Before then sweets

Mr Arthur Boys' sweet shop at Bridge View, King Street, Fordwich

were very scarce. You couldn't buy them. And I remember going into the chemist on the way to school to buy liquorice because we could buy as much of that as we liked.

Do you have memories of any particular weather conditions?

I remember the winter of 1943/44. The snow was very, very deep. It went on for weeks. How I remember it, my father got pneumonia and he was quite ill. My brother got mumps and I got measles. All at the same time. To save fuel both our beds were put in one room, my brother's and mine. It was a chance if I got mumps and he got measles but we didn't. We kept to our own diseases. The snow went on for a long time. The doctor was Dr. Ince. For a short while after Dr Ince died there was a Dr. Green, who came as a locum tenens.

I got scarlet fever. My mother guessed it was something like that and I was very ill indeed and he came and said he didn't know what it was although a lot of children at that time had scarlet fever and he might send an ambulance for me or he might not. Well, luckily I survived it.

I remember the plague of rats in the village. There were a lot of rats. The houses were really old but when you got into the attics there were ways right through them, for rats anyway. The cat we had then was really wild. No one except Mum could touch it or could even get near it. It was a really fierce animal. One day there was this noise and we all ran out. The cat had got into the roof space and driven out what seemed hundreds of these rats. The whole yard was black. They all came out, one after another from this hole in the building next to us. This congregation of rats then just went off. Where to nobody knew. They just disappeared beyond the allotments. The cat just stood there looking very pleased. If the rats had turned they could have attacked and killed him but he cleared Sturry High Street on the left hand side of rats. The cat vanished later, and was never seen again.

Sometimes in the war lorries used to go through [the High Street] packed with prisoners. Lots of soldiers and airmen, too, who had come down in their planes and had survived. We would all cheer them and call out. When it was the prisoners there would just be silence and everyone would just look at them as they were driven through the village. Nothing was ever said. It was quite eerie really. . .

There would always be a rush if a parachute came down, had been sighted anywhere. The boys with bikes would get there first and get the parachute silk and cut lumps off it and take it home for their mothers to make things with . . . underwear, underclothes.

[1] "Dissenters" by Ian B. Moat in CHISLET AND WESTBERE (1979) p 109

Selwyn Gauden and Megan Richardson

Interviewed by John Line in May 2000

Where did you live before you came to Sturry?

Selwyn: *I was born in 39 High Street, Abertridwr, near Caerphilly in South Wales, and moved to Sturry when I was three. My dad was a miner. He was born in Stourbridge, in the Midlands and he came down to Wales with the coal mining industry. Then when Chislet Colliery opened, he came up to Kent and he lived for a while with my Auntie Lil in The Poplars, Hersden, until finally he managed to find rooms for us at Ulster House Sturry, on the corner of Chapel Lane and Mill Road.*

The same roughly applies to you, Megan?

Megan: *I was born in 82 High Street, Abertridwr, and we came to Kent when I was seven.*

So you were born in 1929. You said that your dad lived with his sister. A lot of miners that I have spoken to so far said that they got lodgings in Ramsgate and have horrific stories of how they had to travel from Ramsgate, walk a long way and go home all dirty. So your dad managed to miss all that, because he had a sister already living here?

Selwyn: *That's right.*

What about schooldays? Did you start school here?

Megan: *No, I started school in Wales when I was 5. Our school was in Abertridwr. We started at 5 and left at 14. But I hadn't all that long started school and I had diphtheria and I was in the isolation hospital for 10 weeks.*

Selwyn: Don't know why they let you out, Megan!

Megan: *I had my 6th birthday in there.*

And you recovered fully?

Megan: *Yes, fine. We used to have good times in that school.*

How many brothers and sisters did you have?

Selwyn: *Just the one brother and the one sister.*

Megan: *That's me.*

Selwyn: *Tommy was Dad's son by his first marriage. We two are both from the same second marriage.*

And you (Selwyn) didn't go to school until you lot came here?

Selwyn: *No and then I went to Sturry Primary, Church of England.*

Did you enjoy school?

Selwyn: *Eventually, but originally I was a little swine. I would get up to all manner of tricks to avoid going to school. I would get as far as crossing the road then would run away. Then the only way they could keep me there in the first year of my schooling was to let me play on the toy cars that we had. Pedal cars. They used to bolt the door because I used to kick hell out of it.*

Megan: *They used to bring me out of Assembly to go and sit with him.*

To quieten him down? To make him sit still, I suppose. Do you think it was because you just didn't like school or was it something about a teacher?

Selwyn: *No, the teachers were all right. They were nice teachers. Miss Mason used to teach the Infants. Miss Anstey used to teach the next class.*

Megan: *They were sort of in between because Miss Ravine used to teach another class. She used to have those beautiful blouses and had her hair in a bun. . .*

Selwyn: *The most beautiful handwriting from a person that I have ever seen. She used to write with the old school nib pens, and the pointed nibs. She used to have an inkwell with red and black and she just dipped the pen in and it was beautiful.*

Megan: *She was Miss Ravine. The one with the bun and the pretty blouses. . .*

Selwyn: *They used to give us a treat on Fridays by opening a tin of sweets and you had one sweet.*

So you had happy days once you got going in school? I went to the Convent first. And so did a guy named Ray Gardener who you probably know. We used to spend a good deal of time up a conker tree just by

the back gate into the Convent because we knew that the old 'penguins' couldn't catch us up here or couldn't get us down either. So, if we wanted to get out of a lesson we would go up this tree. That was mainly because we had piano lessons and the Nuns had 18 inch rulers which they brought down on your fingers, quite rapidly, if you did anything wrong on the piano. And I didn't like that very much, nor did Ray. So we used to go up the conker tree. Enough of me….. Where did you go after Sturry School?

Megan: *I went to Sturry Central when I left the Primary. Mr Draper-Hunt was headmaster. Selwyn went to the Langton.*

Enjoy it?

Selwyn: *Ahem! It was tough to start with. But, yes, I enjoyed it. I think it was a fine school. Really is.*

You never actually lived in Hersden did you?

Megan: *No, we lived in Sturry High street. We moved from Ulster house to 17 High Street. Then we moved to 19. Albert Price had the one with the bay windows. Next door to Mr Southon. Betty Marsh was a neighbour. We had lots of shops in the High street. We had the draper's shops and everything. That was the Misses Tharp. We had three bakeries, Neames, Thompsons and Westons. Old man Weston on his bike. Then there was Mr White, the baker along Island Road. Lovely homemade bread. Mr Parker, the butcher was down there, just down the Fordwich road. They lived right opposite the Red Lion that was bombed. We used to go across to the Jug and Bottle at the Red Lion and get an arrowroot biscuit for 1d. A great big thing. We also used to search around for the empty bottles to take them back to get the money buy the biscuits. We had two newsagents, Mrs Morris and Mr and Mrs Cork. We had a bank, too. Lloyds Bank where the carpet shop is now and the Mailes lived there then.*
Then they moved over the road. A big concrete house called Fairview.

That house was actually knocked down for the new road. It was still standing after the war and they knocked it down for the road.

Megan: *That's where Reg Maile and his wife lived with their children because after Dunkirk they used to bring the ambulances through from Ramsgate through the High Street. And everybody in our street used to make tea because they were on standstill. If the back of the ambulance was closed you knew there were serious injuries; but if they were open and they were sitting up you could go give then a drink. We use to take them out trays of tea and a drink and all sorts.*

Selwyn: *It was the same as when the Queen Mary's, (the RAF recovery vehicles), used to come through with planes on. When they stopped we used to be there nicking the glass so we could make rings and crosses.*

Megan: *Oh, we had some lovely Perspex rings. And then parachutes - we had things made out of parachutes. Oh, I'd a lovely parachute dress, I did.*

Yes. It is remarkable when you think of what has gone through that little tiny High Street in Sturry. Two way traffic with plane carriers – unbelievable now.

Selwyn: *When you think double-decker buses passing in the High Street.*

And the old Charabancs. They used to come through the village.

Selwyn: *I used to stand on the door step in my gingham check suit and they used to throw pennies to me. I used to make a fortune on a Sunday when the traffic stopped.*

We used to sit on the bridge, Black Mill bridge, and watch them all go past. It was like a train, wasn't it, when the coaches went through?

Megan: *Do you remember the excitement there was the night that the Neaves' paint shop and everything went up? Monty Neaves. . .*

Selwyn: *He was a fireman, and the Sturry Brigade had gone out to deal with another fire, I think it was at Wingham ... or somewhere like that. And they were called back 'because there was a fire in Sturry'. And as he drove round the corner, which is now the carpet shop, he could see that it was his own building in flames.*

Megan: *Where the Library is now. Just round there. That's where his big place was. Oh God! Paint tins exploding!*

Selwyn: *All the village was up in its nightwear.*

Megan: *There was old Percy Tuff, the barber, at Laurel House, where the dentists are now. . .*

Selwyn: *Percy with his cucumber sandwiches. . .*

I remember he cut my hair many times

Megan: *Yeah, well, my husband never went anywhere else. Only to Percy.*

Selwyn: *He was the News of Surry, wasn't he? Any snippets, he knew it. And him and his wife used to cycle to and from work on a tandem.*

I remember that. They used to come down to the school. Cut my hair down there.

Megan: *Every Friday Night. Remember Dolly Amos? She had a bicycle. And we used to buy fish and chips - Friday night was fish and chip night. And Megan used to have Dolly's bike and a bag on each handle. And I used to cycle along Sturry Road. I used to go to Adley's, the fish shop, and I used to get fish and chips for everybody.*

Selwyn: *It had a little restaurant with all sawdust on the floor.*

Megan: *Well, I used to cycle in there, but on the way back, if I saw a car coming, I'd stop. You didn't see many cars then but I'd stop because I'd got these two damn great bags of fish and chips on the handlebars.*

Do you remember the War?

Selwyn: *Vividly. We were here in the Battle of Britain. We watched it take place over us and above us.*

Megan: *Do you remember Mr Bull? We'd been to Canterbury. Mum had taken us to Canterbury. And we came home and then there were all these aeroplanes [Focke-Wulf 190 Fighter-bombers] and Mr Bull was out in the garden like this and shouting 'GET INDOORS. . .GET INDOORS'. You could see all these tracer bullets coming. Well, we didn't think, did we? We just thought it was fun just watching it. Oh dear.*

Selwyn: *We were also on the East Kent bus along the Sturry Road that was machine gunned and bouncing bombs and everything else. [October 31st, 1942]*

You were actually on that bus?

Selwyn: *Oh, yeah, there was about twelve killed on that.*

Megan: *Mrs Dodson from Oxley House, Popes Lane, she was killed outright. [Mrs Florrie Mona Dodson, aged 25]*

Selwyn: *You had to clamber over her feet to get off the bus. Her little daughter was standing there crying.*

Megan: *She was screaming. She wasn't two, poor little thing.*

Selwyn: *I had shrapnel in my fingers. They took me down the doctor's. Well, in fact, when we got off the bus, we were walking towards Sturry, and an ARP warden came across with his son, who had also got an ARP helmet on. He was eating one of those big bars of Palm Toffee. And he offered me a bite and it looked disgusting.*

And they said 'Well, with your injury, you had better go back into hospital,' and that's when I started crying. I wasn't going back in there, because there was still smoke rising over Canterbury.

Megan: *We went to Dr Ince's, didn't we?*

Selwyn: *We went to Dr Ince's, but there was a queue waiting for help at the doctor's. It was amazing how many people had been hit with bits and pieces.*

Whereabouts was the bus when it actually got hit?

Selwyn: *It was by South Street*

Megan: *On the Sturry Road*

Selwyn: *Yes. We had been to see 'The Defeat of the Germans Near Moscow' in the Regal cinema and the film 'Gone with the Wind'. One of the bombs blew the screen into the auditorium. I was sitting up front, upstairs on the bus with Johnny Kirkham. His father [Alfred Kirkham] used to take us to the pictures every Saturday because you had to be accompanied by an adult if it was an 'A' picture. And we saw these planes come skipping over low across the Vauxhall Lakes and the next minute, I was at the back of the bus. Somebody said 'It's all right. They're ours.' And, all of a sudden, all hell was let loose. I could see sparks dancing round my fingers as they were on the rail, and I didn't know I'd been hit until about five minutes after we got off the bus. Megan was down below me, downstairs.*

Megan: *I'd just sat down like that, and a cannon shell flew over the top of my head. . .*

Selwyn: *It went straight through the back of the bus.*

Megan: *If I had been standing up, I would have had my head blown off as well.*

Selwyn: *Mum and Dad had asked a couple of kids to go up the shop for them and they had just come back with whatever they had got for them and they could see these planes coming across from Pleydells in Popes Lane, and their wings were twinkling. And Mum and Dad had to fight like hell to grab the kids to pull them in, pull then under the stairs. When they came out after the raid as over, there were all these cannon shells right through the front of the house, as if the Jerry pilot had seen them and was having a go at them. So, yes I remember the War all right.*

Selwyn, having finished school at the Langton, where did you go to work then?

Selwyn: *I went to Seeboard as a clerk/typist. I went into the Fleet Air Arm in 1951 and when I came out from* the Fleet Air Arm I went to the Bridge-Blean R.D.C. Then from Bridge-Blean to Clark and Eaton's. And from Clark and Eaton's into the pit. I spent five years down the pit.

As a face worker?

Selwyn: *As a collier, yes.*

Was the track you were on full height or were you bent over?

Selwyn: *It was the main road. Full height.*

If you were to say the shift came from another 'district' that was another face?

Selwyn: *Another set of faces because there used to be the Southeast, the Main East and the Drift. That was the three districts, and if you had not got enough to work one face then you would take those men and put them on another face that needed a couple of men. But I never regretted going on the coal face because it taught me a lot about life.*

Did you work with pick and shovel or did you have pneumatic drills, etcetera?

Selwyn: *We worked with pick and shovel. You would have drills if the coal was tough. The cutter would have come in and cut what they call a 'jib'. That would cut four foot six underneath the coal seam. Generally speaking you could fill the coal onto the conveyor and you would be all right. But if it was tough and hard then you would call in a pneumatic drill. They would put explosives in and blow it and you learned the angles to get the best results. We all took up safety positions and then once it was blown, away you go.*

Was it hot or cold down there?

Selwyn: *Depended which district you were in because, with mining, you've always got two shafts. The fan used to pull in the cold air, circulate it through the pit and up. So if you were in the Southeast, like I was, you had the hot air. If you were in the Main East, you had the cold air and if you were in the drift, it was medium.*

Megan: *My father, when he worked down the mine, they used to have to crawl and all he ever wore was a pair of bloomers, women's bloomers, nothing else.*

Did he work here?

Megan: *Yes, my Dad did. But he had a hundred percent silicosis. He died at fifty four, my father. He was in the mine from when he was fourteen. He never knew anything else. He had pleurisy and pneumonia. On November 18th, 1941, when he had been very ill*

in bed, he had just started getting up again as my Auntie had come from Hersden to see him. In the black-outs then you had to be ever so careful. She was catching this five to seven bus to Hersden. We walked down to the bus with her by the Belisha beacons they were then. We put her on the bus and we just walked back up the High Street, we could hear this plane. Couldn't we, Selwyn? We just got indoors and my dad was sitting reading a book called "The Vanishing Corpse" [by Anthony Gilbert, pub Collins, 1941] when the land mines fell. That was found on the roof, that book.

Selwyn: *Mother sat on the fender box*

Megan: *Yeah. We just sat there and the first one — it's a good job it did — the first one dropped over in the allotments. And then the house went and she grabbed Dad and us onto the stairs, and as she went to pull the door to, it went out of her hand. The lights went out, too. We was in pitch darkness and we was so lucky, it was only a bit of plaster fell down, wasn't it, Selwyn? On to us, from the staircase. But we sat there for ages and the smell was horrible. Then you got all the wardens coming round shouting 'How many is in there? Is everybody all right?' Well, luckily, we were. They eventually managed to get us out and they took us to Milner Court, down to the soldiers there. (Laughing) My! We looked like a load of ragamuffins. We were filthy!*

Where was number 19?

Megan: *It was a wooden house right opposite where Tharp's - do you remember Tharp's, the draper's shop?*

Selwyn: *You've got a couple of houses in between Franklin House and Alldays now. Opposite there. That was the Tharp's and Mrs Nellie Holmes had the grocer's shop.*

Megan: *About where the Fire station is. Roughly there, we were.*

Selwyn: *Dad always used to say that if he stood under this beam that used to run through the living room, oak beam, that he'd be safe. And if he had stood under that beam he'd have been cut pieces because for some reason or other. . .*

Megan: *Blast*

Selwyn: *The entire fireplace, stove and oven came out from where it was situated, went through one door and another door and ended up in the garden. It would have taken him with it. But my mother grabbed him and put him on the stairs. Another abiding memory of that night was being taken down to Milner Court and being given a big hot steaming mug of tea with evaporated milk in it.*

Megan: *Oh, beautiful it was! Gorgeous! They did us proud, didn't they? They made sandwiches, we had cakes, everything that night.*

Selwyn: *After the bombing we went up to Hersden and stayed with Dad's sister, my Auntie Lil.*

Going back to that incident with the bus on Sturry Road, were there any other Sturry people on the bus? [Lilian Mabel Setterfield of Providence Place, Sturry, age 37, died later from her injuries]

Megan: *Mrs Porter from Herne Bay Road, she was on the following bus. I'd lost my hand bag with our bus fares and everything in it. And I started to walk home, and when the next bus stopped along by Vauxhall, she came to me and she could see the mess I was in and she said 'Get on the Bus'. I said 'I can't I haven't got any money' I think it was a penny she paid for us.'*

Selwyn: *No. The conductor said 'Have you got off that bus back there?' and you said 'Yes' and he didn't charge us.*

Megan: *No, because she was going to pay. And when I got to Sturry I took Selwyn into Dr Ince, then I had to leave him and go up and tell my dad. When I got home my mum took one look at me and said 'Where's Selwyn?' I told her what had happened. Dad was helping to dig out the . . .*

Selwyn: *Fred Allfree's house in the Herne Bay Road.*

Megan: *Not Fred Allfree's. The one at the bottom.*

Selwyn: *Fred Allfree was trapped. There was four houses, two semi-detached pairs. Just as if you had lifted them out from Herne Bay Road and that they had never existed.*

So there were bombs up there, too ?

Selwyn: *Yes. On the daylight raid.*

Megan: *Marriots. My dad was helping to dig them out. We had to go tell him about Selwyn and he went straight down to the doctors to get him.*

So, they got the bus and they bombed two pair of houses on the Herne Bay Road?

Megan: *They was just dropping everything. They must have been in trouble and they were dropping everything everywhere, weren't they, Selwyn? And they were machine gunning. . .*

Selwyn: *They reckoned they were only lads.*

Whereabouts on Herne Bay Road?

Selwyn: *Herne Bay Road. Numbers from about eleven down. Completely destroyed. As you come right into Herne Bay Road into Deansway Avenue turn immediately left. Just over the slope, that's where it got hit. On the same day there was Ned Thompson and a few others in Deansway Avenue when they came over and they dived flat on the floor and the bomb landed, it would be, in Jimmy Reid's garden, went under the fence, came up in Cullen's. It was what they called the bouncing bomb and it flew over the Broad Oak Farm and killed a cow in the field.*

Megan: *I was thinking about when we got home. My mum was trying to wash my hair to get everything out.*

Selwyn: *Oh, there was a stench!*

Megan: *Terrible! She washed it about a dozen times. And I could still keep smelling it, you know. And I had got this towel wrapped around my head when they came and said that everyone had to get out. There was an unexploded bomb in the Cullen's garden. And they took us down to Mr Prior's on Sturry Hill.*

Selwyn: *Yes, because he'd got a safety wall built underneath his stairs and we all had to stay behind there, but the unexploded bomb was the one that had bounced and left its mark and bounced into the field at Broad Oak Farm.*

Megan: *But it had left the fin in the garden. They thought it was the bomb. But it wasn't. It was the fin of the bomb. So then we were back home again.*

Selwyn: *The back of our house and the roof were all shattered with cannon shell.*

I need to sort out where you were then.

Megan: *Deansway, 50 Deansway Avenue.*

Selwyn: *The council had requisitioned an empty house. A family from London had decided that despite the bombings in London they wanted to go back.*

There was certainly more damage than I ever imagined there.

Selwyn: *It was a frightening time. It seemed like hours, but it wasn't, because what Jerry did, he came over in the day and did all the damage he did and then when we transferred down to Mr Prior's, they came over on a night raid. So we had another bash.*

It may seem a funny question but where there any funny things which happened in the war?

Selwyn: *Well, there was the incident when Mum used to allow the soldiers from Pleydells to come and have a bath, because the officers had commandeered the baths there. And one evening we were standing by the door, watching things go by and the next door neighbour, you may remember him. He was a Sergeant Major in the Home Guard, Fred Edwards, Just then this Mosquito plane, they had not long been flying about, came roaring over and Fred Edwards looked up and said, 'Ah yes. I know that one well'. So the soldier said 'That's a Mosquito.' Fred Edwards said 'No, it's not. It's a twin-engined Spitfire'. So the soldier said 'I'm sorry but that's a Mosquito, a new fighter bomber we've got.' Fred Edwards said 'THAT is a twin-engined Spitfire' so the soldier said 'I'm telling you that's a Mosquito' So Fred Edwards said 'Look here, son, we in the Home Guard know things that the Army doesn't even know'. Everyone dissolved into laughter.*

Megan: *He was funny. He really was. Then when Canterbury was bombed I used to go up the school and help with the food for all of them. Get on my old bike. The Central School. [Now the Spires Academy] This was before I left school. I used to cycle there along Popes Lane.*

What? Were people living in the school?

Megan: *Yeah, they had them billeted in the hall. The school was closed for a few weeks after the bombing. I used to go up and give them a hand. When I left school at fourteen, I went to work in the kitchen. I used to get fifteen shillings a week, four pence for a stamp - national insurance stamp - fourteen and eight pence then.*

I certainly didn't realise there were so many bombs in Sturry. I knew about the bus. And the village itself and the bomb craters down Popes Lane there.

Megan: *There were two buses bombed, you know.*

Selwyn: *There was one bus went off the road at Calcott. The driver had bullet through his cap and he hunched up, an automatic reaction to put your arm up to defend yourself, and the bus toppled over. I don't think anybody was hurt in there.*

Megan: *The worst one was Sturry Road. We just had to climb over the dead bodies to get out, didn't we? [1]*

Selwyn: *Terrible! That's something that will never leave us*

Megan: *It sticks in your mind.*

Selwyn: *I can still see that woman.*

Megan: *Oh, so can I. Lying on the pavement.*

Selwyn: *I had a fellow behind me with a bullet right through him. I turned round to look and he was just awful.*

You never forget horrendous incidents like that. So… what were conditions generally like then?

Selwyn: *Oh, atmosphere-wise, everybody pulled together. It was great years for that, all camaraderie and help thy neighbour.*

It's about the only time we English did pull together.

Selwyn: *You - English. We - Welsh!*

[1] There is another account in HOW THE GIRL GUIDES WON THE WAR by Janie Hampton (Harper Collins, 2010) pps 162-4 written by June MacKenzie now Mrs Jack Wood

A War-Time Childhood in Sturry

Derek R. Butler

My father obtained a driving job in Canterbury in 1938 and we moved from Lenham to Sturry, renting a house in Popes Lane, one of Major C.H.H.Kenworthy's properties in the then new development which also covered Deansway Avenue and the Herne Bay road. An early memory was seeing the village fire engine parked outside Percy Brooker's house, "Gillyflowers" in Popes Lane. He was the First Officer of the Sturry Fire Brigade, whose engine had been converted from a Hotchkiss taxi by Bligh Bros, the Canterbury coachbuilders.

There was a little stream that ran under the road and alongside Charles Cruttenden's bungalow, "White Lodge". It was of particular interest to the children who lived in the area, including the Davies and Southon families. As a family we used to enjoy walks along Popes Lane, leading into Hawe Lane, passing Mr G.H.Denne's house "Pleydells", since demolished, and also Hawcroft Farm owned by Paul I'Anson Headley.

I clearly remember the outbreak of the Second World War on Sunday, 3rd September, 1939. When the air raid siren sounded my father started to fit protective boards in the windows and to prepare blackout material. To a five year old it seemed fairly exciting and throughout the war years we lived with a mixture of excitement and fear. There was no doubt though that the children of our time didn't really appreciate how perilous the times were – our parents, of course, had no such illusions.

After the bitter winter of 1939/40 we moved down to Island Road, the south side of which was actually then in Westbere parish. Our new home was opposite Homewood Hall, the family home of the Woods, which had been built by Alderman Thomas Wood in 1889. He was the founder of a pork butcher's business in Sun Street, Canterbury.

On the day we moved in to Stortford Villa, (now numbered 100 Island Road), we met Roger Goodman, whose parents ran Fairview Nursery at the bottom of the lane which ran beside our house. "Fairview" still remains today but is surrounded by the 1960's development named Fairview Gardens, which followed the death of Harry V. Young of "Elim". I learned to ride Roger's bike in that lane, which also served as a cricket pitch and for other games. Just after the war Mr Goodman planted the conifers for Robert Brett Ltd which border the railway line.[1]

Stortford Villa was a semi-detached 3 bed-roomed house, with a sitting-room (always referred to as "the front room"), a living/dining-room and a kitchen/scullery that housed a sink, an old range and a built-in copper. The fire in the front room was only lit at Christmas, unlike the

one in the living-room which was lit most days. It did not adequately heat the whole room and those who sat furthest away suffered somewhat as my sister Pam can testify.

Our wireless was very important to us and this was worked by a wet battery or accumulator that had to be topped up periodically with distilled water either at Arthur May's shop in the High Street or at Brockman's Garage in Mill Road. We also had an old wind-up gramophone which took the old-fashioned steel needles supplied by H.M.V.

By 1940 the war was beginning to make an impression on our lives and we were drawn into the adventure of it all. We quickly became accustomed to over-flying aircraft and we would wave to convoys of soldiers that trundled past on the road. The Wood family vacated Homewood Hall which was requisitioned by the Army. A detachment of the Royal Fusiliers moved in, as they also did to Milner Court, and some of them became regular visitors to the extent that we are still in touch with their relatives today. They were succeeded by some Lancashire Fusiliers, among them Eric Westwood who played for Manchester City Football Club for many years.

At the outbreak of war an Emergency Measure known as the National Service (Armed Forces) Act introduced compulsory military service for males between 18 and 41 years old. On 14th May, 1940, a new force for home defence was formed known as "Local Defence Volunteers", soon changed to the Home Guard, and fondly remembered as "Dad's Army". My father joined this and his free time was spent with the local platoon under the command of William Gee, of "Alderley", Island Road, who owned a tobacconist's shop in Canterbury.

Their headquarters were conveniently in the property next to The Swan Inn. Mrs Louisa Lucas was the licensee at the time, to be succeeded by her daughter, Mrs Muriel Roy. It was also the meeting place of the local Buffaloes, or more formally, the Royal Antediluvian Order of Buffaloes, a Friendly and Benefit Society.

The evacuation of the British Expeditionary Force from Dunkirk in June, 1940, resulted in a large number of troops arriving at Ramsgate who were then transported by road and rail through Sturry. When the trains slowed down Roger and I threw apples to them from his father's nursery.

By then there was plenty of military activity around. An Ack-Ack battery with Bofors guns was located at the top of Staines Hill. We saw plenty of aircraft as RAF Manston was only a few miles away and there

Very rare film of people running towards the crashed Dornier aeroplane at Fox Hill, Calcott, Sturry

were occasions when very large formations of German bombers passed overhead en route to London. The Battle of Britain officially ran from 10th July to 31st October 1940 and is particularly etched on my memory. As a family we witnessed the aerial dog-fights on Detling airfield on Sunday, 18th August, referred to as "the hardest day". [2]

That day a British pilot, Pilot Officer John W. Bland, the son of a clergyman in Bristol, crashed in the field in front of the Convent in Westbere. His Hawker Hurricane was one of four shot down in a matter of minutes by a German ace, Oblt. Gerhard Schopfel. John Bland was stationed at Gravesend and is buried in the town's cemetery: his name is remembered on a memorial at the airfield site.

At much the same time another R.A.F. pilot, Flying Officer Franciszek Gruska, a Polish national, was shot down on the Westbere marshes near Stodmarsh. The site of this crash was not properly excavated until 1975 when the remains of the pilot were recovered and buried with full military honours at Northwood cemetery. [3], [4]

A few days earlier, Tuesday, 13th August, we had heard a German bomber in trouble after being attacked by fighters. The Dornier Do17 plane was forced down with the help of local anti-aircraft guns at Puxton Farm near Stodmarsh. A group of soldiers from Homewood Hall, who claimed to have shot it down with their Bren gun set off to find the plane but were beaten to it by the anti-aircraft gunners, who captured the crew of four. The plane was one of 74 that had set out to bomb Eastchurch

Aerodrome and Sheerness Docks on the Isle of Sheppey. It came down at 6.45 a.m. and the crew must have been surprised to be detained by a bunch of gunners clad only in tin hats, Army boots and underpants!

On August 28th, 1940, a Mark I Spitfire piloted by Squadron Leader Donald Finlay (a Great Britain Olympic Hurdler) was attacked over Ramsgate and although wounded, he managed to bale out and land near Staines Hill, his plane, too, crashing in the Westbere marshes. And at 12.40pm. on Sunday, 15th September, a Dornier Do17Z-3 crashed in flames near Fox Hill, three of the crew being killed. The Revd. Samuel Risdon-Brown, Vicar of Sturry, conducted a burial service before their interment in Sturry Cemetery (together with another German airman shot down at Reculver). For many years their graves were tended by someone unknown. In the nineteen-sixties they were re-interred at the German War Cemetery at Cannock Chase.

Our cellar was used as our first air raid shelter and I remember one occasion when father literally jumped from the top of the wooden steps when the hissing of a high explosive bomb was heard. This dropped, I believe, near the gasholder beyond Providence Place on the way to Canterbury. In due course our Anderson shelter was delivered and my father set about excavating a site for it some 7 or 8 yards from our back door and not too far away from our cesspool!

My first personal experience of a German air attack was when in Canterbury on the morning of 11 October,

1940. I was with my mother and quite near Lefevre's Department store, (now Debenham's) when the air raid siren sounded and we rushed into the Precincts to take shelter in the Cathedral crypt. Nine people were killed at the top of Burgate in that raid.[4]

The war really came to Sturry with a vengeance on Tuesday evening, 18 November, 1941, when 2 parachute mines were dropped on the village. I can still hear my father saying that the droning aircraft overhead was "One of ours": The Home Guard were trained in aircraft recognition but perhaps were not so hot when it came to recognising engine sounds! The whole family knew it wasn't one of ours when the mines exploded, one in the High Street by the Red Lion Public House and the other forty yards away, mercifully on waste ground. (The crater of the latter was to remain a source of great interest – and danger – to local children for years to come.)

The mine which landed in the High Street devastated the heart of the village and caused 15 deaths, seven of them children. As a family we knew some of the victims personally and one in particular, Audrey Johncock, was a special friend of my sister, Jean [Mrs William Catterick]. Audrey's brother Roy and their parents were also killed and are all buried at Thanington. (Ironically, the family had returned to England from New Zealand in 1931 after experiencing an earthquake in Napier.) John Collins, the only child of Mrs Rose E. Collins of Church Lane, was also killed whilst visiting the Bubb family at 13 High Street as was 10 year old June Peel. Both sides of the High Street were completely wrecked and the late Thelma Bubb [Mrs Stanley Bush], who was trapped for four hours, was fortunate to escape serious injury.

The Parish Hall at the far end of Church Lane collapsed although strangely enough the wooden post on which the Red Lion pub sign hung survived the impact and remained in place until the redevelopment of the village in the Sixties. It was in the Parish Hall that we had been fitted for our gasmasks, Allan, my brother, being young enough to get one of the "Mickey Mouse" variety.

The "Baedeker" raid on Canterbury on the night of May 31st/June 1st 1942 is still vivid in my mind and on Saturday, June 6th, a number of bombs fell quite close to our house. One fell in the rear garden of 1 The Springs, badly damaging No 2, and tearing out the side of 4 Maida Vale Cottages, the home of Mrs S. Seath. There were casualties among the soldiers in Homewood Hall opposite from the bomb which fell in the orchard there. The damage to our house meant that we were temporarily evacuated to Sturry Secondary School (now The Spires Academy) which had been designated a Rest Centre and where the caretaker, Fred Clayson, had his work cut out in a difficult situation.

I shall never forget Saturday, 31st October, 1942, my eighth birthday, when 20 or so Focke-Wulfe 190 fighter-bombers, part of a force of some 50 enemy planes, attacked Canterbury and the surrounding area, including the Regal Cinema (now called the Odeon) where the film "Gone With the Wind" was showing. The raid only last a few minutes but considerable damage was caused and there were many casualties.

The planes came in very low late in the afternoon and my modest tea party was ruined as the living-room window blew in and the table was covered in glass. One bomb dropped on the property just up the road called The Bungalow, a wooden structure, where fortunately the Dobbin family escaped unhurt. There were considerable fatalities, though, when buses on the Sturry Road and at Calcott were shot up that day.

By the end of 1941 Morrison shelters were distributed and we had one in our front room. They were shaped like a large table with a steel top and wire mesh sides and could accommodate 2 or 3 people sleeping in them. We often slept in ours at the time of the V.I. doodlebug or buzz-bomb offensive, although luckily for us most found their way up the Thames Estuary on their way to London. "V" stood for the German word "vergeltung" meaning vengeance or retaliation. I saw one of our fighters attacking one over the woods towards Stodmarsh and will always remember the first one I saw close-up when in the garden of "Claremont" with the Pickford family. It was obviously off course and heading in the direction of Herne Bay and hopefully the open sea.

When victory over Germany was finally secured we duly celebrated VE (Victory in Europe) Day on May 8th 1945 with a large bonfire on the field opposite the Humps. This was after a lively sing-song and drinks at the Swan Inn, with Mr William Cole of Chapel Cottage, Mill Road, on the piano. We burnt an effigy of Hitler on the bonfire and had a Victory Tea held for the children in the Milner Court Barn, where we enjoyed a good spread after the deprivations of the war years.

[1] Gill, Michael GROWING INTO WAR [Sutton, 2005]

[2] Brooks, Robin J. KENT AND THE BATTLE OF BRITAIN (Newbury, Countryside Books, 1999)

[3] A memorial to both pilots was unveiled on 18th August, 2010, at Westbere.

[4] A booklet relating to these pilots entitled "Five Minutes Apart – A Story of Two of 'The Few'," is available from Derek R. Butler, the proceeds going towards the cost of the erection of the memorial stone at Westbere.

An Old Sturry Family

John Moat, (1927-2008) (O.J.) interviewed by Heather Stennett on 4th January, 2001, then aged 74, with young John Moat (Y.J.) in attendance

Y.J. *This house (Vale View, Fordwich Road) was two farm workers' cottages at one time. I don't know if you saw at the back of our house there is an old granary that's been there converted to a house.*

O.J. *Old granary and there's cellars underneath. There's pantries underneath one part of it and cellars under the other, too.*

H.S. That's unusual because in this area with the very high water table you don't often get a cellar, do you?

O.J. *You don't, no. When you have got one if the water table gets high you put your gum boots on to go down there or make sure that you have everything down here you want is above level.*

H.S. How long have you lived in this house?

O.J. *Soon after the war – yes, it was in the 50's because I was in the army in the war, no after the war actually by the time I was conscripted. I had two years in the army which was quite enjoyable.*

Y.J. *I think, granddad, you told me that you were in the A.R.P. in the war.*

O.J. *I was a motorcycle messenger in the ARP. Night fire-watching, too, but it all goes back too far now.*

H.S. Were you born in the village?

O.J. *I was born in the house next door, Ferndale. That's where my son and wife live now and their 3 children.*

H.S. How many were in your family?

O.J. *Mum and Dad and four children. I was the 3rd. My older sister is now in a nursing home, my brother lives at Ripple Court down Dover way and I live here. My younger sister lives in Sussex.*

H.S. Did you go to school in the village?

O.J. *Yes, Sturry C of E School halfway up the hill with Captain Riley. Then I went to Sturry County Secondary Modern School. [now Spires Academy.] A row of air raid shelters was built in the land adjoining the school. In the war when the sirens used to go off we all had to go and sit in the air raid shelters. It was cold and damp but they had oil lamps or something for lighting.*

The Moat family home on Fordwich Road taken before the First World War. The sheep belonged to the drovers staying at The Welsh Harp

Y.J. *I think, Granddad, you said when the bomb fell on the street you were in the shelter there.*

O.J. *I was up at the school and I used to go to day school and go back for the evenings. For evening school, I always rode a bike and there was one evening that we were there and we heard a few bumps but we didn't take much notice. Then we found the lights all going down and down and down. It was gas lit, so we thought that we had better get out of here before they go out all together. So we all got out. I got on my bike and cycled down into Sturry but the crossing gates for the railway crossing were closed. I couldn't really understand why but anyway I got through the little wicket gate at the side and I started to go down the street. I had to get off and walk, I was going over all sorts of rubble. I didn't know what I was going to see so eventually I did go down through the High Street and then I went through the churchyard out onto the Canterbury Road and then I came here. My family were all standing outside, wondering where I was and whether they would ever see me again.*

H.S. Of course, to most people it's just a story about the bombing of Sturry, but for somebody who has lived through that period of time it's very different.

O.J. *Quite a lot of my school friends - I think 6 or 7 of my school friends – were killed. I had to go to the funerals being Head Boy then. But they were exciting times.*

H.J. Could you describe to me a little bit what Sturry was like under siege – during the war. Was it much different to normal life?

O.J. *I don't think so. I don't know how to compare it with anywhere else, because I was born & bred here so I can't really compare it with anything else.*

Y.J. *You told me about the Prisoner-of-War Camp in Trenley Park Woods.*

O.J. *Oh yes, you couldn't go through the woods from Fordwich to Stodmarsh then. Some of my relations lived in Stodmarsh, you had to go out through Littlebourne and round because they had closed the roads. It was full of troops, I don't think it matters that I am telling you this now. It was very secret at the time. It was cut off from the general public, no transport, only army transport went through as far as I can remember.*

H.S. I believe that a lot of soldiers were billeted in what is now the (Junior) King's School. What was your role in the ARP?

O.J. *I was a messenger. I had a bike and I had special lights for bikes in those days and I used to run messages occasionally but not very often.*

H.S. What about after the war?

O.J. *I was eventually called up. I went to Canterbury Barracks to join up, everyone else seemed to come from miles away and I turned up on my bike. I was at Canterbury for 6 weeks, when I was being interviewed for all sorts of things. They said it was time for me to go abroad. I went the old-fashioned way. An old Dover passenger boat to Calais and a troop-train down to Toulouse and caught a troop-ship across the Mediterranean to North Africa and Egypt.*

H.S. You certainly did get to see the world!

O.J. *After that I was sent to Benghazi to a small workshop there. All the local people who had any dignity wanted to drive a motor, you see, and that meant that I spent a lot of time on just ordinary repairs in an advisory role. I came back and went back to my old job. Then my brother and I opened up an engine machinery workshop in Canterbury and I used to rebuild engines. In those days new engines were very scarce. You could buy new ones, but you had to re-condition the old ones so we had the necessary equipment to rebore cylinders and regrind crankshafts and all the little machinery jobs that you need to do to put engines together that will go, and will go properly.*

H.S. Was your Father involved in that trade?

O.J. *No, he was the local carrier. He took the business over from my grandfather who used to run a horse bus from Canterbury to Herne Bay every day. Then when my father took it over the Horse Bus was rather old fashioned so in 1929 he bought a Trojan van, solid tyres and all. Then in 1934 he got an Austin Light 12cwt van. I thought that was really reaching the heights then and he drove that all through the war but eventually it had to go. Then he got one of the first A40 vans.*

H.S. What would have been opposite here, because that is recent development?

O.J. *Originally it was a field, with a fence around the outside and the farmer used to graze cows and sheep there. I can remember that.*

H.S. In this house, do you feel that you are a Sturryite or a Fordwichite?

O.J. *Oh, definitely a Sturryite, I'm this side of the bridge.*

[In 1987 the ancient Parish Boundaries between Sturry, Westbere and Fordwich on the Fordwich Road were changed and since then Fordwich extends to the north of the bridge.]

H. MOAT,
CARRIER

DAILY SERVICE BETWEEN
CANTERBURY &
HERNE BAY

Including :-

Sturry	Hersden	Maypole
Fordwich	Upstreet	Herne
Broad Oak	Hoath	Beltinge
Westbere	Chislet	Broomfield

MAIN DEPOTS:-

CANTERBURY :—Bacon & Son, 1 Palace Street.
Bligh Bros. Ltd. Garage, St. Radigund's St.

HERNE BAY.—T. Cade, Florist, Canterbury Road

POSTAL ADDRESS:-
FERNDALE, STURRY.

Stevens & Son, Printers, Northgate Street, Canterbury.

Poster of Moat's carriers

Trenley Park Camp

K.H. McIntosh

Trenley Park in the Stodmarsh Road in Fordwich was once the ancient hunting ground of the Abbots of St Augustine's Monastery in Canterbury. Recorded in the Domesday Book as belonging then to Odo, Bishop of Bayeux, it has remained substantially the same in area and outline for the last thousand years. However, the wood took on several new roles during and just after the last war, all clearly remembered by Penny Lewis who lived nearby. The first was early in 1943 when ammunition began to be stored there in preparation for D-Day on June 6th, 1944. A Howitzer gun had earlier been sited in the garden of "Merryfield" in the Stodmarsh Road. A balloon without ears, possibly a radio one, and rather smaller than a barrage balloon, was moored behind Mote Cottages, near the fourth tee of the golf course.

Fordwich, Sturry and Hoath supplied some of the platoons of the Home Guard which had the care by night of the road to the coast there. Thomas Haimes, one of their number, recorded that "there were shells as big as a dining-room table and enormous high explosive bombs, some stored underground. The Military Police were always there, too, with tracker dogs".

John Marsh from Puxton Farm was a member of the Wickhambreaux Home Guard and had orders to shoot any unauthorised person who attempted to go beyond the camp and one night did take a shot at a motorist who failed to stop. Fortunately he missed because the next morning a very irate American Air Force officer, who had been on his way back to Manston Aerodrome, turned up to complain!

After the ammunition had gone, the site was used as camp for Germans taken prisoner after the invasion of Normandy. They were housed in the Nissen huts erected all down the track beside the house called Trenley Lodge, opposite the entrance to Christ Church University playing fields. There is no record of prisoners-of-war having been there during the First World War. [1]

The prisoners themselves did not know their exact location save that they were near Canterbury. Many years after the war I was asked by the Canterbury Library if I could direct a German visitor to the local prisoner-of-war camp where he had been encamped as they couldn't and he himself didn't know. He wanted to pay a sentimental visit there – and did. One man, Hugo Reidinger, lived on in Sturry after the war.

The prisoners worked on local farms, notably at Tile Lodge Farm in Hoath Road. They helped with the threshing at Hawcroft Farm, confirmed by Monica Headley who well remembers them being there. They

Entrance gates

wore brown overalls with great coloured patches on them designed to stand out should they try to escape. They also were taken on Banks' buses to Stodmarsh for hop-picking.

The prisoners-of-war were repatriated immediately after peace was declared in 1945 when they were succeeded by some the 70,000 most unfortunate casualties of conflict called Displaced Persons who were given refuge in the United Kingdom.[2] These were men mainly from Latvia, Lithuania, Estonia and the Ukraine. In the case of the Ukraine it was said that some of the men had been blamed by the Russians for not resisting the German invasion strongly enough and later by the Germans for not resisting the Russian one and thus they had no place to go. Their spokesman here was called Michael Stepoliak.

Those from the Baltic were in an even worse plight because their countries had been over-run by the Russians during the war. They were not able to return to their homes there for resettlement and indeed the Allies would not sanction their forcible repatriation. [3] They were a pathetic group and I found it heart-breaking to be shown cherished photographs of wives and children whom they didn't know were alive or dead and were unlikely ever to see again.

Remains of an underground entrance

Difficulties were compounded by the variety of languages spoken in the camp and by the unreliability of those purporting to be translators. This was particularly so for my father when it came to diagnosis and medical treatment. Life in the Trenley Park Camp cannot have been ideal for any of them but at least it was safe and they were as well looked after as possible first by Mr Eley who was in charge, then Mr C. Morgan and finally by Mrs Simmonds and Mrs Mavin, who lived in what used to be called Fern Villa in Sturry High Street and is now Georgina House.

There were other sources of comfort. Mrs Pamela Willson (nee Butler) was then a member of The International Friendship League that met at the home of Miss Margaret Parry at North Holmes Road, Canterbury, at which the men were made welcome. Other diversions included Cossack dancing and singing songs from their various homelands. A favourite rendez-vous was the back room of the Fordwich Arms Public House and the

riverside there, Saturday evenings often being spent at the Wingham Casino. There was even an entry by the League in the Canterbury Carnival.

I remember that several of them used to come to Evensong in St Nicholas Church at Sturry, perhaps being reminded of home by the service, and patently enjoy the singing there.

Not all local relationships were so friendly. An elderly cat owner in Fordwich was very disturbed when, in the very harsh winter of 1947, she saw one of the men wearing a fur hat that she was convinced had been made from the skin of one of her cherished – and missing - pets. The internal relationships did not always go smoothly either. In June 1948 there was a hunger strike by the Ukrainians there who had been told that they were being moved by the K.W.A.E.C. (the Kent War Agricultural Executive Committee) to a camp at St Mary's near Lydd where there was a shortage of workers. Eventually they did go to St Mary's, where they reported they liked the new camp there very much better!

The use of the camp came to an end with the revocation of the Direction of Labour Act when demand for agricultural labour eased and many of the Ukrainians found employment in the textile industry in the North of England.

[1] List of Places of Internment (published by the Prisoner of War Information Bureau, 1919)
[2] Bygone Kent Vol 30, No 1 Jan/Feb 2009
[3] Ben Shephard THE LONG ROAD HOME: The Aftermath of the Second World War (The Bodley Head, 2010)

Carnival entry including Pam Butler and Selwyn and Betty Lewis

Little Doors of Escape
Sturry Sunday School Remembered
By Derek Butler

We joined the St Nicholas Church Senior Sunday School soon after moving to Sturry and there came under the influence of Mrs Elizabeth Risdon-Brown, the wife of the Vicar, to whom I personally owe a great deal. I have fond memories, too, of the Infants Department led by Miss Margaret Newman, (later Mrs Clark), whose mother was the verger. Miss Louise Simpson was the school cleaner – it was her sister, Jessie, who pumped the bellows for the church organ for over forty years, keeping a keen eye on the lead wind gauge the while.

Miss Bertha Elliott played the piano as we lustily sang "Hear the Pennies Dropping" when the offertory was taken. For most children it was probably half-pennies or even farthings that went into the plate. The Vicar and Mrs Risdon-Brown organised the Senior Sunday School, assisted by their daughter, Monica and her friend, Pat Askew. [1] Each Sunday we were given a copy of "The Classmate", issued by the National Sunday School Union. An undoubted highlight was the story that Mrs Risdon-Brown told about Stephen, a fictitious character based on fact. Those attending hung on every word and could hardly wait for the next instalment the following week.

Following the bombing of the village in November, 1941, Mrs Risdon-Brown wrote to two famous Children's Hour broadcasters – "Uncle Mac" (Derek McCulloch) and "Romany" (the Revd G. Bramwell Evans, 1884-1943) and had two warmly sympathetic replies, Romany describing our Sunday School meetings as "little doors of escape from mental strain".

It was particularly kind of "Romany" to write a personal reply since he was ill – even so he hoped "that when the last siren had sounded it might be possible to pay Sturry a visit" but he died the following year.

Uncle Mac wrote: I know you have suffered and endured as have many of us. My own little girls went through innumerable bombings in Bristol but, like you, came up smiling. Like you they go to Sunday School. . . . If I may send you a message it is this – 'be brave'.

In 1991 on the 50th anniversary of the bombing we organised a reunion of the Sunday School which had helped us so much in our formative years, many members coming from long distances to join us.

[1] LETTERS TO STURRY From Patricia Askew to Monica Risdon-Brown - June 1940 to November 1940 (edited and pub K.H.McIntosh, 2003)

The Reunion of Sturry Sunday School, 1991
Back row: L to R, Len Smith, Derek Butler, Brian Southon, Roy Edwards, Selwyn Gauden and Allan Butler
Front row: Michael Yeomans, Monica Headley (née Risdon-Brown) and David Davies

Sturry Primary School (1943-1949)
A Boy's View
By Allan Butler

I started at the Sturry Church of England Primary School in the spring of 1943. I therefore joined the gang from the Island Road who met up with Jean Larkins and walked to school via the Council Road (now Sleigh Road, where the council kept their road mending equipment), the "Humps" (the rough land of former gravel pits now Delaware Close) and to a path that led to a stile at the top of the school playground.

Our Headmistress was Miss Edith Cruttenden, who lived in a bungalow in Fordwich Road and had joined the school in 1935. Once a week the Vicar, Rev. Samuel Risdon-Brown, would attend, give a short talk and lead the prayers.

Serious misdemeanours were duly entered by Miss Cruttenden in her famous "Black Book" and the most serious would result in a caning. This took place in the porch adjacent to her classroom where she would mark a chalk cross on the floor and order the miscreant to bend over it. Very serious offences included leaving the school premises without permission, entering the next door Vicarage garden to collect conkers, fighting, disobeying teachers and racing from the road up the sloping concrete retaining wall to grab the railings at the top.

My first teacher (Infant 1 class) was Miss Mason who later became Mrs. Skinner. In this class we concentrated on learning the alphabet and sounds and numbers and practised our writing. We were also able to play with plasticine and do colouring.

In Infant 2 class I had Miss Anstey (later Mrs Howells) for a term and for the remainder of the year Miss G.H.Smith (the deputy head from 1945 to 1957) was our teacher. She was quite strict and under her we worked hard at our "tables" so that by the time I was eight, unlike most children today, I knew by heart (and still do!) up to times twelve. In this class I was placed second behind Brian Smith of Woodbine Cottage, Island Road, who was a friend who walked to school with us. I recall at this time sitting first next to Ivy Birch and later next to Shirley Arnold which resulted in some teasing by the other boys.

In these years up to the end of the war in Europe in May 1945, I recall only once or twice having to go into the school shelters because of air raids. The shelters had brick-built benches with wooden slats for sitting on. There were occasions, however, when we would be late going to school because the "all clear" had not sounded following a night raid.

The year 1946 found me in Junior 1, the class of Miss Hichens who had joined the school in 1924 and left in 1952. I sat next to Michael Twyman and behind Reggie Whittaker and Ronnie Murray. In Junior 2 we had the young and attractive Jean Dreaver as teacher. Miss Dreaver never lacked volunteers to stay behind to help tidy up and I was usually the first to put up my hand! It was in this class that Peter Price, who had just moved to Sturry, joined us and there began a close friendship which has continued to this day. In Junior 3 we used to play charades and indulged in a limited amount of drama and played cricket against Eddington House School at Herne Bay.

My brother, Derek, and I devoured the weekly comics which came into the house - "The Wizard", "Rover", "Hotspur" "Adventure" and "Champion". Once when we boys were doing gardening with teacher, Mr. Parker, I was sent to Miss Cruttenden for misbehaving. I feared the cane but my punishment was to sit with the girls who were doing needlework and complete two pages of mathematical problems. I remember that my partner in Maypole dancing was Mary Batt. The most exciting happening was the class outing to London where we visited the Houses of Parliament and were given a talk by the Canterbury M. P., Mr John Baker White.

Entrance to the school

Dinner Ladies, Sturry Church of England Primary School - L to R Mrs Nancy Gay, Mrs Peggy Rowland, Mrs Rose Collins (Head Cook) Mrs Mary Davison and Mrs Kathleen Holness.

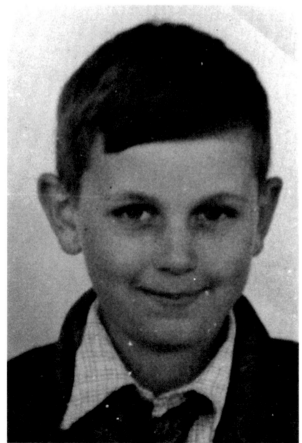

A young Allan Butler

92

I think ten of the class later sat the 11 plus examination and six passed.

Mrs. Rose Collins, the head cook, and her staff daily cooked more than 200 meals which were served from a long trestle table at the end of the room. I was not very partial to school dinners which were often rissoles or salads with scotch eggs and chopped up beetroot followed by semolina pudding.

The school grounds or 'playground' had five distinct parts to it. The lower part nearest to the road was mainly used by the infants. Next there was a concreted area where we often had our P. E. lessons for which we were provided with a straw mat to sit on. Beyond the concrete and the shelters, adjacent to the Vicarage tennis court and the top of the drive, was an area of gravelly, sandy soil with a base of grass where the older boys played football and other games. Popular among these were Chase, British Bulldog, Feet-Off-Ground and Creeping In. We also played marbles, conkers and various ball games. Sometimes we were enticed to join the girls in hopscotch and skipping.

The next section fenced off from the football pitch was a scrub area containing gorse bushes and a sufficiently large enough grassy space to enable us to play hardball cricket there. The final part of the grounds before you came to the 'humps' was where the boys had their small gardening plots where we attempted to grow vegetables. This must have been the school's response to the exhortation to "Dig for Victory".

Other memories which come back to me from 60 years on are of how cold the classrooms could be in winter, seeing children from Broad Oak farms being conveyed to school by horse and cart, and a member of our class about to be caned in the porch. Whilst Miss Cruttenden closed one door he ran out of the other and made his way home. Punishment deferred to another day! And then there were those awful visits by the health inspector when you put your head on her lap and it was inspected for nits!

My main friends in the junior classes were Peter Price, David Bubb and John Bubb and we four used to sit together for our dinners. Other friends were Reggie Whittaker, Michael Twyman, Brian Smith and Ken Rogers who was a year ahead of us. Shirley Munton, Rowena Davison and Margaret Race were among the most popular girls in the class. Apart from those already mentioned other contemporaries included Christine Harris, Irene Benchley, Stella Petts, Violet Chittenden, Agnes Roy, Heather Baker, Bill Jordan, Gerald Keem, Roy Kemp, Keith Baker and Brian Yeomans.

We were all sad at leaving the school in 1949 and I remember Miss Cruttenden shaking us all by the hand and asking us what our aspirations were for the future. This fine lady retired through ill health in 1955. She was denied the retirement she deserved when she died the following year.

Sturry Primary School
A Girl's View

By Doris Thompson (née Mayo)

The class of 1948
Back row: William Palmer, Terence Keem, Peter Gay, Peter Banks, Peter Dodge, David Todd, Christine Ades, Rose Lamb, Sarah Webb, Marion Jones, Patricia Jakeman, Terence Pickford
Middle Row: Brenda Ruck, Geoffrey Barton, Ken Peel, Paul Jarnell, Eric Gisby, Joan Mayo, Doris Mayo, Janet Whittaker, Jennifer Dale, James Mayo, Ronald Wanstall,
Front Row: Valerie Ward, unknown, Jean Rogers, unknown, Susan Bennett, unknown, Molly Croxton, Helen Edwards, Michael Wheeler, Dennis Holland, Brian Baker, Stuart Allfree

I began my time at Sturry Primary School shortly before the end of the Second World War – roughly 60 years ago.

I remember having to take a gas mask to school, and also being in the school air raid shelters, although whether this was for real, or a practice drill, I'm not sure. Miss Hall was the teacher in the first primary class throughout my time at the school. Memories of her class include writing on slates, being allowed to choose a toy from "the chest" to play with and having a large rocking horse at the side of the room - a lovely wooden one. When the pupils were restless or noisy Miss Hall would have us rest our heads on our hands on the desk and close our eyes for a little while to calm us down.

Miss G.H. Smith taught the next class, a very severe looking lady with very short bobbed hair, virtually shaved at the back. Although appearing severe she was a strict but fair teacher – well, that is, apart from the time

she mistakenly thought I, (along with several boys) was amused that another boy was being punished by her. The guilty boys had to go to the front of the class, lie across the teacher's chair and have the seat of their pants dusted with the cane. I was saved this indignity and received my punishment on the back of my hand and arm. Nowadays, of course, this isn't supposed to be allowed but I can honestly say looking back that physical punishment left far less unhappy memories than the unfair treatment of sarcastic hurtful remarks from a teacher and you can't legislate against that.

In Miss Smith's class we learnt our times tables up to 12 by chanting them from charts on the wall as Miss Smith pointed to them with her stick and we were tested on them and our spellings every week.

There were large open fireplaces in the classrooms and the teachers had to keep the fires fed coal from the scuttle.

The staff of Sturry Primary School about 1950
Back row, L to R: Miss Jessie Powell, Mr Robert Scott, the Revd T.G.Williams, Mr Clark, Miss M. Hichens
Front row: Miss Evans, Miss Edith Cruttenden (Headmistress) and Miss G.H.Smith

Miss Hichens taught the next class and there we progressed to £.s.d. Miss Hichens had a tiny bucket and about 2 inches high. If a child began to cry Miss Hichens would take the bucket from the cupboard and pretend to catch the child's tears. As I remember the bucket was needed rather frequently in Miss Hichens' Class.

The next to the top class was taught by Miss Jean Dreaver. She was a very attractive 21 year-old. I thought 21 was so old! We progressed to "pen & ink" in this class and I remember our weekly oral spelling tests.

We had a male teacher in our final class and his name escapes me. This was the class where we took our 11+ exam for possible grammar school place and I remember the bitter disappointment of one or two boys who got through to an interview stage but weren't successful. Miss Edith Cruttenden was our headmistress and a lovely caring, if eccentric, lady who knew her pupils well and showed she cared by her unbiased attitude and interest in us. She could rivet a classroom with her famous screeching, foot-stamping routine.

We had bucket lavatories in an outside toilet block. There was one toilet for teachers only which was a bit nicer than ours! The line of washhand basins in one of the cloakrooms seemed a luxury. The teachers had a large jug and bowl situated in the seniors' cloakroom & it was a pupil's job to make sure there was a jug of warm water for the teachers at lunch time. If they forgot,

Miss Cruttenden would appear in the "dining room" brandishing the jug, and you were glad if you weren't the culprit. Miss Smith's classroom was re-arranged daily to become our dining room.

Mrs Rose Collins was the school cook & very good meals she and her team provided, too. School dinner money was half a crown (12½p) by the time I left the school. We had 1/3 pint milk each, every school day, provided from Mr. Peel's farm just down the hill from the school. Sometimes in cold weather Miss Smith would warm the bottles of milk somehow near the fire. The cardboard milk tops, which were removed by pushing a small, serrated circle out of the middle, made an ideal basis for making pom-poms with scraps of wool.

Another off-shoot from the war was that every so often batches of cod liver oil and malt were supplied from 'somewhere' and Miss Cruttenden would distribute the lot of it amongst the pupils. I loved it!

School medicals and immunisation sessions took place in the top classroom; what happened to the pupils of that class that day I don't know. The "Nit Nurse" was also a regular visitor when each pupil would have their hair examined by the nurse using one of a number of combs standing in a beaker of disinfectant. I also have a horrendous memory of having a tooth pulled out, whilst in the first infant class, by a very unsympathetic dentist - no such thing as an injection or gas in those early days.

More pleasant memories are of the Christmas party when the partition walls between Miss Hichens', Miss Dreaver's and Miss Hall's classrooms were removed creating one long room for the festivities. This was decorated with paper chains we had previously made.

Near the end of my time at school some recorders were obtained and an after-school recorder club started which I enjoyed & continued right through secondary school. For a short time I was in an after school Brownie group run by Miss Sylvia Cox. My most vivid memory of this is being taught to darn only to find I had stitched my sample to the skirt of my dress. Another after-school activity was the Kings Messengers which Miss Cruttenden held in her own home at Sturry. [The junior branch of the S.P.G – the Society for the Propagation of the Gospel]. We played numerous games in the playground. Games such as Skipping, hand-stands, marbles, cigarette cards, 5 stones or Joeys, Catch, 2 balls (juggling 2 balls against a wall), "What's the time Mr. Wolf", etc. Along the border of the school with the Vicarage was a line of Horse Chestnuts (Conker) trees; as well as providing conkers for our games the heaps of autumn leaves gave us a lot of fun and often formed the walls of our make-believe houses.

For some reason there was a rule that pupils must not catch the service bus up the hill from Dr. Mac's Surgery to Sweechgate Post Office, Broad Oak (The bus then continued on to Herne Bay). It cost one old penny to do this journey and (with at least another mile to walk through Broad Oak village from Sweechgate). If you happened to have a penny and the weather was bad, temptation occasionally got the better of us. If you were caught standing at the bus stop you had to give in gracefully and get walking!

I was sad to see on one of my return visits to Kent that the old school buildings had gone but life moves on and anyway we still have our memories.

The Countess of Huntingdon Connexion Chapel in Broad Oak. One of only 23 in the country, it was built in 1867.
The author was the first person to have her marriage solemnized there.

The School on the Hill
A Teacher's View

By Jane Freeman

My links with Sturry Church of England Primary School began on one Monday morning with a knock at the door. It was a gentleman who introduced himself as Headmaster of the local primary school – yes, Mr Royce Payne. He had heard that an infant teacher had moved into the area and he was desperate for a supply teacher. That was in 1972 and for the next two years I was a supply teacher. My appointment as a permanent teacher was in 1974.

I retired in 2004 and became a supply teacher once again! Full circle!

Much changed in those thirty-two years but some things remained the same.

The Infant syllabus took up less than a side of A4 paper. During my career I dread to think how many A4 files I was given as new initiatives were introduced (e.g. The National Curriculum, The Numeracy and Literacy Strategies, etc.,etc.) and these changes made life as a teacher increasingly time-consuming and challenging. What remained the same was the huge privilege and great pleasure of working with young children.

So some memories of teaching in the 'Old School':

Staying with the curriculum – the daily timetable for Infants was

---

1 hour - Creative activities. Painting, Modelling, Needlework, Woodwork, Houseplay etc.

2 ½ hours - Directed activities Number, Reading, Writing, Story, Poetry, Drama, Nature, Singing.

20 mins – P.E. or Music and Movement

25 mins – Assembly

30 mins – Breaks

The Revd Peter Gausden (Rector of Sturry 1968-1997) viewing the vandalised old school building in April 1988

How interesting to compare today's Teacher Directed and Child Initiated time in Reception classes and the emphasis on more time for Physical Education. From the Infant Syllabus it can be seen that record keeping was compulsory then as now! When inspectors visited they observed lessons and wrote a report. Although that experience was always daunting it was not as threatening as to-day's OFSTED inspections.

So it was a very structured day, but with a great emphasis on learning through play. Amazingly, some of the play equipment from the 'Old School' is still in use today – large plastic bricks and some wooden toys. It was expected that every child read to the class teacher every day [no extra adults in class in those days]. This was difficult and although I did see teachers skilled enough to hear up to six children at once I could not listen to more than two at a time. The reading schemes used were Happy Venture featuring Dick and Dora and Janet and John. Thankfully the modern reading books are so much more interesting and attractive.

Assemblies were daily and usually consisted of a hymn, a sung prayer and occasionally a story and often a chastisement for some misdemeanour. On Thursdays Mr Payne, or "Sir", as he was known, led the assembly and those assemblies included the Lord's Prayer and often the following prayer that I often thought must have sounded

quite frightening to infant children, but perhaps they did not listen too carefully!

Reach downward from Thy hidden throne
And take my hands in prayer,
And hold them, hold them in Thine own,
In school and everywhere;
And I will lift them up to Thee
Quite often in the day;
Do Thou each time take hold of me,
That I may never stray. Amen

Discipline has changed greatly. Children could then be punished with a smack. In my experience this did not often happen but the 'golden slippers' were notorious and many were threatened with that punishment! Although I did not see these infamous slippers I understand that they were a pair of ballet slippers – one was kept in Mrs Hadlow's room at the top of the dark staircase and the other in Miss Carpenter's cupboard.

Miss Carpenter taught one of the two junior classes that were still housed in mobile classrooms as there was then no room on the Park View site. There were seven infant classes – two in the original school building and the rest in mobile classrooms. All the infant classes were 'family' or 'vertically' grouped and this meant that in the same class there would be five, six and seven year olds. There were many advantages to this system and one was that the teacher really got to know families; often teaching two, three or more of their children. Those starting school entered a secure environment where older pupils were able to help the younger ones and routines and rules were very quickly learned.

Links with the local church were always important and the Rector attended school each week, not only to take assemblies but also to teach one class each week in turn. We attended a Harvest Festival service in church and the Church Fete was an important event. Every year children would perform traditional country-dances and often Maypole dancing took place too. The school grocery stall always made plenty of money and staff all attended. Absence from this event was not an option. My class was often instructed to create the banner that decorated the stall.

Two odd memories remain with me – one was during a very cold spell of wintry weather. The playground was so treacherous that the only way children could be allowed to visit the outside toilets was if the whole class went together, so we did. How time-consuming but the children thought it was fun.

Sports' Days took place on the grassed area and one year there was a 'fathers' race' – the ground shook as the dads ran and many of the children were terrified and started to cry!

A Post-War Childhood in Sturry

Peter Gay

Perhaps it was growing up during the war that removed any fear of danger. Rushing for the shelter when the siren sounded or falling flat on our faces when low-flying fighters flew overhead were safety-first routines drilled into us. At home we lived behind a blast wall, built after our windows were shattered when a bomb fell on Herne Bay Road.

The poignant remains of Sturry High Street and the centre of Canterbury were constant reminders of the perils of war but in the Anderson and Morrison shelters we felt safe even if they offered little protection in the event of a direct hit.

By the time the war was over we were prepared for any adventure. In the late-1940s prowling the old Home Guard shooting ranges we found .303 ammunition. Removing the bullets from the cartridges with a pair of pliers, we laid fiery cordite trails. Percussion caps gave a very satisfactory bang when hammered with a nail but our attempts to make our own bombs in old tin cans stuffed with cordite and buried in the sand never produced more than a puff of smoke.

In our play we were as territorial as the Lavender Hill Mob. I was a Sturryite, our manor was Den Grove Woods, the sandpit, the Humps and the White Mill Pool and the river. Our nearest neighbours were the Broady Oakers, who would occasionally venture onto our patch and were tolerated even though they had a mysterious territory of their own - the brook, or Sarre Penn, [1] the finest great-crested newt pond in the district and even a haunted house, or so we called it. [This would have been the then derelict Broad Oak Lodge.]

To the south of the village was the land of the Fordwichites. There weren't so many of them but they had a wonderful area to explore – the river, the lakes, the remains of an old abandoned cottage below Trenley Park, and even their own old Home Guard range which we would raid when we ran out of ammunition for our own experiments. We knew, too, that there was a fourth tribe to the east of us, the Hersdenites beyond Staines Hill who we would occasionally encounter skirting the sandpit in Hoades Wood when we were looking for sand martins or catching newts in the ponds.

A watercolour painting of the Mill Pool at Sturry between the wars by E.W.Hazelhurst (1866-1948)

The Mill Pool in August, 1952: rear David Longley, Roger Pay in front of him. Tony Pay to the left and Reg Whittaker with the dog.

Our weapons were bows and arrows, our aim to see who could fire furthest, never at each other. We did occasionally think of arming them with darts in the forlorn hope of hitting a rabbit or squirrel but our light hazel bows lacked power. The woods and sandpit offered year round pleasure and exercise. We hung ropes from trees and swung from branch to branch, sometimes clambering from one tree into another. We practised mountaineering on the then steep slopes of the sandpit, letting down a rope and hauling each other up.

In the long snowy winter of 1947 when there was no salt for the roads and they were too steep and slippery for a van we earned a few pennies helping to deliver groceries on Sturry Hill.

In late spring we went fishing for trout in the Black and White Mill pools or for roach and dace along the river banks, always with an eye open for the bailiff. I only caught one trout and it bit my finger but it tasted good.

In the hot summer of 1949 dozens of us swam in the White Mill pool, never the fearsome Black Mill which, we were told, had a dangerous undercurrent. We jumped or dived into the deep water by the mill race and sun-bathed on the bridge wall as the traffic roared by. The water was none too clean in those days and I caught jaundice which delighted the Foreign Office doctors years later who thought it might confer immunity to more unpleasant varieties in Africa and South America.

I like to think that the Sturry villages bred a tough breed of children. We were protective of each other, were aware of dangers but had the freedom and confidence to roam far and wide from dawn to dusk at weekends and in the holidays. And we were supported by strong community ties : regular summer outings to Minnis Bay in Mr Banks' coaches, Fire Brigade parties, summer fetes and family walks to the lily banks at Trenley Park in the spring or for chestnutting in the autumn.

[1] THE SARRE PENN – The Story of a Stream by Jean Anthony, Allan Butler, Monica Headley and Veronica Litten (1995)

A Post-War Childhood in Broad Oak

by Irene Newing (née Dunn)

I was born in 1941 at a house called Rosendale in Broad Oak. My father had come there from Durham before the war to work at Chislet Colliery. Over the years he had had a number of accidents there. On one occasion there was a big cable problem while he was in the shaft which was very worrying for Mum. Dad was laid up again after a cable snapped down the pit and badly injured his knee. He was very unlucky and had various injuries over the years. After one of these he learned to play the piano and the violin. There was never much money but we were always well-fed – sometimes Dad would buy winkles from a man who came round with them in a basket on the front of his bicycle. He was in the Home Guard in the war.

I have a sister, Lovona, who is four years older than me and a brother, Malcolm, two and a half years younger. My Mum was a very regular attender at the Countess of Huntingdon Chapel in Chapel Lane at Broad Oak. Many a time we would fall asleep there cuddled up with Mum. As we got older we went to Sunday School regularly there – and had some good parties there, too. Doris Mayo (now Thompson) and I used to have piano lessons from Mrs Taplin in Babs Oak Hill and after one of these parties I fell into the ditch opposite the Chapel and cracked a bone in my arm. This was the day before my piano examination and Mum was not best pleased.

We also each Christmas all enjoyed really good parties in the Broad Oak Hall. They were organised by Mr Albert Hadlow from Sweechgate Stores.[1] They were a great treat. A game that we played at home was with a stick in a bucket. It was spun round and you had to catch it before it stopped spinning.

I am not sure what age I was when Mum asked me to go to the other shop in Broad Oak. This was situated on the edge of the road between The Golden Lion and The Royal Oak and run by Mr Ronnie Birch. I suppose I would have been about four years old and I saw real bananas there for the first time. I must have known from pictures what they were because I rushed home and told my Mum who sent me back to buy some. What a treat!

The Mayo family lived nearby opposite Goose Farm and Doris Mayo and I became (and have stayed) great friends – more like sisters. My brother, Malcolm, played with Jimmy, Doris's brother, and my sister, Lovona, was a friend of Doris's sister, Ellen and of Betty Fabb. They used to go roller-skating on the rink in Herne Bay.[2] On Guy Fawkes' Night Doris's family and ours would each have a bonfire and fireworks and we all enjoyed both. At about the time of the Mary Poppins film, Doris and I were up in her bedroom seriously considering doing a Mary Poppins with an umbrella out of her window.

Sturry home-guard. c1941

Sturry Home Guard photographed outside the requisitioned house "The Poplars", Field Way, in 1941. Among those thought to be present are Fred Edwards, Jim Daniels, Chas Croxton, Ron Larkins, Sid Butler, Vic Cockle, George Tugwell, George Dodge, Jack Saffrey, Ernest Jones, Stan Fullager, Bob Lawrence, Bill Thompson, Bill Hammond, Bill Harvey, Percy Newman, Ted Dunn, and Fred Whittaker.

There was a lovely tree in the field by the Chapel and Mum caught me up the tree with my arm in plaster. Another time I sort of fell out of the tree and slit the seams each side of my dress and the one down the front. Doris and I laughed and giggled all the way home. Mum wasn't best pleased about that either. She never knew, though, that, although we had apples in our own garden we would scrump from next door and also climbed over the barbed wire fence at the bottom of the garden and scrump from the orchard there. Much more fun!

We walked to Sturry Primary School on our own – Mum was working at Milner Court (Junior King's School) by then. I was very young and a bit late once and dashed across the road to the school on the hill and a car coming down just missed me. I rushed into school really scared the driver would come in and complain – but he didn't.

As we got older we played a lot in the woods behind Goose Farm and made a camp from branches. Doris and I would take matches, a bean can, some sugar and pinch a bit of rhubarb which we cooked over a camp fire. We liked to play in a ditch nearby and we had a rope to help us cross the stream.

We also used to play in Dengrove Woods leading down to Sturry but we were never able to make friends with the children living in the row of just pre-war houses, known as Baldwin's houses, between us and the caravan site. In fact we very often had stinging nettle – our only weapon - fights with them. Mrs Twyman, who lived there, was a great friend of Mum's, and we always visited her on Christmas Day, taking our presents with us to show her. And I was a bridesmaid at her neighbour, Ruth Bailey's, wedding.

In the summer at jam-making time, we would go to the sandpit in the woods opposite Babs Oak Hill. We had a jam jar each and once we had filled these with blackberries we would have fun playing in the sandpit. I was also a Brownie in the 1st Sturry Pack and we would sometimes go to the Junior King's School, where Brown Owl, Miss Jessie Raven, taught us to work for our badges. We also had exercise classes in the Chapel. Doris and I stood out, both standing taller than the other children.

We joined the St John Ambulance Brigade, too, and cycled into Stour Street in Canterbury every week. Mrs A. Ford was one of our leaders there. We learnt a lot about bandaging, etc., and would practise our drill outside in front of the building. [The Poor Priest's Hospital.] On a few occasions we were able to attend the morning picture showing at the Odeon without having to pay.

We went to St Leonard's-on-Sea camping with the St John's and had a great time. Had a ride on the speed boat off the pier, too. We learnt knots and many other things and, of course, bandaging, too.

Doris and I stayed very close friends but as time passed we obviously brought other aspects into our lives. Roy Newing and I married in Sturry Church in 1963 and moved into what was originally the shepherd's cottage in Sweechgate – now number 62.

[1] H.Stennett & K.H.McIntosh BROAD OAK – A Kentish Village Reconsidered (2006) p 39
[2] Roger Pout THE EARLY YEARS OF ENGLISH ROLLER-HOCKEY (Herne Bay, 1993)

Married Life in Westbere

Recollections of Westbere by Mrs. Jean Ralphs

Recorded by Norman Smith on 5th January, 1991, and undertaken on behalf of the WVPS (Westbere Village Preservation Society) as part of an oral history archive of Westbere, and reproduced with their permission.

When did you first come to Westbere?

In 1948

What brought you here?

We were looking round for a house and we wanted to live out of the town and this was a village.

Were you local people?

I came from Cliftonville in Thanet

101

Did you actually know Westbere before you came house hunting here?

My husband had done some business here

So you had some idea of the sort of community you were likely to come into?

Only up to a point. We were just looking for a house and that's all there was to it. It was a pretty village.

That was your first impression, was it? It was a pretty village and a nice house?

Yes. We had a large garden and I had two kiddies and it was heaven to me after the war after having to put up with a flat. A school was close, the Convent at the top of the road and from then on, I was just an inhabitant. There were some very nice local people whom I soon got to know for the very reason that we all walked and you met these people when you went to meet your children from school and it was very nice.

You mentioned the Convent School, was there a village primary school as well?

Yes, there was a tiny village school up Church Lane. There was a headmistress and an assistant headmistress. The assistant was a Miss Powell who lived in the village and I used to see her going to work every morning up the hill. She was a wonderful teacher of the old-fashioned kind and most of the local village children went there.

There were a lot of children in the village in those days?

Yes, I suppose there were. There were three at the Yew Tree and several along at the cottages here and we all knew one another.

From what I've been told, it was a working village in those days in the sense that most people worked locally.

I suppose so. The mines were the main centre for people to go to work. It wasn't the same as it is now with people going up to town every day, commuting. That has changed dramatically.

So there were a fair number of people from Chislet Colliery living locally?

Yes, there were five cottages that were owned by the Coal Board and people rented those cottages from the Coal Board, not from outside, people that worked at Chislet Mine, electrical engineers and so on. They were a varied bunch.

What five cottages were they?

Cecil Cottages.

Were there other people associated with the mine as well, other than in the cottages?

The landlord of the Yew Tree worked at the mines and in his spare time, he worked in the Yew Tree, probably at night when he was not on shift. His wife ran it up to a point. His name was George Harvey. Later the landlord was Joseph Taylor.

Was there any shop in the village in those days?

Not as such. There was a wee shop right at the top on Bushy Hill run by somebody who lived up there who used their front room. It was very handy. You could get butter and sweets and chocolates, but it soon closed down and we haven't had one since.

So you used to walk to Sturry to do your shopping?

Yes. I walked in the first few years. It was very nice going down the main road, not a lot of traffic. Then I used to cycle and that came to a stage where it was not very pleasurable.

I suppose Sturry itself was pretty small at that time?

Yes. There wasn't the bypass there then. All the traffic went through the village. It wasn't very nice for the pedestrians. I can't remember the year the bypass was built but I suppose it must have been an advantage.

So in the late forties, Westbere had a pub and a school and of course it had a church and I presume this was very much more important at that time?

Yes. The bells rang every Sunday morning and there was a very old vicar when we first came. I can't remember when he died. His name was Father Reeves [the Reverend Charles Varnam Reeves, Rector of Westbere 1931–1952] and he would walk about the village in his bedroom slippers and a biretta, hailing people to go to church. He was a great man. Then we had one or two rectors after that. [The Rev R.W.Lee and the Reverend E. Charles Craft, Rector 1952-1963].

I have heard people speak of Father Reeves and there is a little memorial plaque to him in the church.

He got all the boys going to church. It was very active. They'd have a Sunday School and a party at Christmas. The teacher who worked at the school was in the Sunday School and so it was a very close-knit place.

I suppose it was a church school?

It was.

Now obviously there are a lot of houses in the village now which weren't there then. Can you remember if

CONSTITUTION OF
THE WESTBERE VILLAGE
PRESERVATION SOCIETY

(adopted 14th October, 1969)

Cottage orné by B.J.Green

there were a lot there then that aren't there now that have been demolished?

No. I was thinking about that. There was one up Church Lane, next to the church where Joseph Taylor lived called Quinta. It was made of wood and that was demolished and in its place is the retirement home now. There's plenty been built because there was a lot of land. The most famous is the Walnut Tree Lane beyond Walnut Tree Farm.

I would guess that was built in the Sixties. Just thinking back to those early days, presumably as well as people working in the mines, the farms were pretty active.

You mean in the village itself? There was Kemp Hall Farm. It was the Seaths. When we first came here there was a Grandfather Seath and his wife, they lived in the first house. Then there was a Bill Seath who was the father of Rosemary Butler. Then there was Sidney Seath who had the farmhouse at the bottom of Bushy Hill, at the top of Walnut Tree Lane. He had cows. They didn't seem to do a lot of farming, but mostly had cattle. Right opposite Kemp Hall Farm where there are now three big houses, there were sheds and places for the cattle and that went straight through down into the marshes where he used to take his cows. The grass was so lush there that people came from all round when there was a drought. Brett's works weren't at the bottom of the village, they were further to the right. They moved along there and dredged and dredged and

that's how the water came about. [2] Before that it was lovely; beautiful for anybody who was interested in wildlife.

There were a lot of piggery buildings too, behind Westbere Lodge.

Yes, the piggeries were adjacent to the Kemp Hall Farm buildings on Westbere House land. It was some people who lived in Westbere House who had the pigs, a man called Bilby Robinson and he had these beautiful Saddlebag pigs which were prize pigs and he used to take them to shows. He had a converted bus in which he slept at show time and the pigs slept up the other end. He was very proud of them.

Was he the occupant of Westbere House when you arrived?

No. He was the second one. He came out of the RAF as a navigator and the previous owner was Anthony Hue-Williams. They weren't there very long and then Bilby Robinson came after them. When they sold up, this is when it was sold piecemeal, the house, the grounds opposite Westbere House, right the way round the back, the field opposite here. All the way up here was meadow that belonged to Westbere House.

Can you remember roughly when that was?

'52 or '53 – something like that.

Carey Bros, Andover Villa, Westbere, sausage-makers.

St Anne's Convent Schoolboys, 1952. L to R back row Conrad Edal, Michael Clark, David Longley, Colin Elks, Michael Waite
Front row: Michael Stringer, Tony Pay, Michael Brooks, Ivan Chapman

You mentioned Bretts.[1] I seem to recall that there's a little rail trackway that runs behind Kemp Hall Farm which I was told was something to do with bringing gravel from up above the main road. [2]

That is out of my ken. There was gravel up there but I thought that was Ovenden's.

You don't remember gravel coming down to the village from up there?

No. I wouldn't have seen it, it would have been up the back. It's quite possible.

Were there any orchards around?

Yes, there was one very big one at The Oaks. It grew Cox's Orange Pippins mainly, beautiful apples. The land was owned by a Mr David Patterson, a Scotsman and retired tea-planter, and he owned all that land round there. He must have owned an awful lot of land, the ground going up to the main road where the bungalows are now. That was trees and conifers.

Did he have any buildings?

There were two buildings there but I think a lot of the apples did go up to London to the hotels, although that is hearsay. The buildings were just where there are now two large houses, to the right of The Oaks. There was also a house called Russet Orchard up near the main road where Mr Taylor grew apples.

Was there ever a bus service in the village?

There was the main bus service running along the main road from Thanet through to Canterbury which we all used but nothing ever came down into the village itself.

In the immediate post-war period, was the village all wired up and on gas mains, with mains drainage?

Yes, there was gas there already and electricity but no mains drainage when we first came. We had cess pools. It was only a year or two afterwards that we had the main drainage through the village. But there were a number of houses, my own included, that were not linked. We were too low down but after a few years a pump was put down there in one of the cottage gardens and all the sewage was pumped up to the road which runs through the village and it joined the pipe that was there.

Can you remember who bought Westbere House from Mr. Bilby Robinson?

Mr Hilary and the Hon Jennie Bray, I think. They built the swimming pool, I think. They were there for several years. Then after that, the Parkers lived there for a while. Then the Stevens.

Can you remember when the village school closed?

Yes, but I don't know the year. I think it was when the education system changed in Canterbury and they were cutting out village schools.

That was in the Sixties. We haven't talked about Westbere Lodge. Did that change hands a lot?

Not a lot. I can only remember one big family – the Harris's. There were nine children, but it's a very big house. I think they left their mark, a lovely family. Then I think the Sharratts came there. It's a very well-built house and it's not all that old.

No. Edwardian, I think. Built by the Wotton family of Tomson and Wotton Brewery. [According to Miss Jessie Powell it cost £1,000 to build]. I suppose the gravel workings must have gradually become more apparent?

They went right up to the Drove, near the gatehouse and the path that leads down to the river. They came up to there then I think the seam of gravel wasn't good enough. They had barges going up and down, taking the gravel down to Fordwich to be processed.

Did that create a lot of noise?

Yes, but it was nothing to what we have to put up with now. There was one time when one crane turned over. They had cranes taking the gravel out and they were working all day. It was a great fishing spot then; everybody went.

Then the Seaths decided to pull out of farming and the land was sold for building. Do you have recollections of this time? Did it cause a lot of anguish locally?

At first I think they got turned down from the local council and possibly the county but they got their permission in the end.

I imagine that development must have changed the village totally.

Absolutely, because it started traffic going through. There was a lot of works traffic, great big lorries, one killed our cat.

So the late Sixties was the time when the really big changes took place in Westbere with the closure of the colliery and the new development. Can you remember any real village characters?

There used to be three that went to the Yew Tree regularly and played dominoes etc. and there was another game there where they used to swing a ring, a sort of traditional thing. These characters, one was Tom Greenwood, who lived at the Gatehouse. He had been in the mines.

There was another one – I don't think I'm speaking out of order but he was very often 'under the weather'. He told me he was the Mayor of Westbere once. Then there was an Italian man – Carlo – who used to be the

All Saint's Church, Westbere

chauffeur of Mr. and Mrs. Bray at the big house. The Yew Tree was a small place then and they used to go there pretty well every night. They were characters that people knew. There was Miss Kathleen Harding at "Luckwell" in Church Lane. [3] We had a lady who lived in Ashby Cottage, a Miss Gwen Clarke-Hughes, a lovely person and a very good neighbour of mine. She kept a pedigree herd of goats and chickens and rabbits I think she became quite a character in the village but she wasn't eccentric at all. She was a friend of Miss Flo Green and her family.

The Greens were quite prominent in the village, weren't they?

Yes. That land on which the house called Utterhay is built belonged to Miss Clarke-Hughes. She had three and a half acres of ground around that cottage. I think Miss Green was a girlhood friend and when she retired she came down here and had Utterhay built, I think there were two or three Greens, Flo, Madeleine and eventually there was Basil. They were a great asset to the village and the church.

The Misses Tates are still with us in the village. Were there more Tates around?

They came later. That house Paigles was built for them. I remember when it wasn't there. The Misses Powells (the schoolteachers) were very active in the village, too. I remember going to a party there and we had a whale of a time. But they were all friends and did a lot of good work in the village.

Westbere still is a fairly close community and people seem to get on well so it seems it's always been like that.

In a different way perhaps, but I think it's very good. The place has been cleaned up too. The rats were dreadful.

They went with the barns and the cattle, I suppose.

Yes, because of the animals, but I thought that was what living in the country was. And flies! You hardly see a fly now.

Were there any chicken farmers around?

Well, Miss Clarke-Hughes had poultry. They were all free range. They wandered over three and a half acres of ground.

Was she a very elderly lady when she died?

Late sixties, that's all. Then things changed from then on. The land was divided up into pieces as it is now. The extension was built at the back.

So you've lived in your house for nearly fifty years.

Well, for over forty. It's a long time but it's surprising how it goes when you're bringing up a family.

Thank you very much, Jean. Do you have any final thoughts? Judging by what you have said, you seem to think that most of the changes have been for the better.

Definitely. People take a pride in their homes now. Westbere Cottage (Shaws), that was two cottages once and they belonged to the big house. Two gardeners lived in them, a Mr. Petts and a Mr. Aldridge. I remember them very well.

Did that all change when Bilby Robinson sold up?

A German lady called Lansdoff bought those two

cottages. She eventually left and the Munro's bought them as one. That must have been at the time when the land was sold. Of course they're beautiful now but they were thick with damp at one time, green up the side of the walls and so on.

Did Westbere House have elaborate gardens in that period?

Yes, they had all the land in the front, all the land behind my house. That was a kitchen garden, peaches on the wall and so on.

It was a walled garden, was it?

Yes, it still is. I have a wonderful wall, must be worth a lot of money. It runs right down to the railway line almost. I keep it quiet.

Did you acquire more land when they sold up?

Yes. Rowe bought a lot of the land, then he had a heart attack and just gave it all up. He sold a lot to my husband.

Thank you very much, Jean, and I hope that this will be the first of a number of tapes.

[1] Paul Tritton ONE FAMILY, ONE FIRM, ONE HUNDRED YEARS (Bosun Press, 2009)
[2] WESTBERE HERITAGE TRAIL a community project pub Westbere Preservation Society (2006) p 4
[3] Ann Pope TELL US ABOUT WHEN YOU WERE YOUNG (Canterbury Environment Centre, 1977)

Miss Cecelia Mack (1912-1991) and Miss Gertrude Mack (1912-2010) of St Anne's Villa, and known to generations of pupils at the St Anne's School

We Moved to Friendly Hall I

by Lizzie Shirref (née Gross)

We moved to Friendly Hall in the Fordwich Road, Sturry, from Canterbury in 1952. We had been living in a school, with shared premises and garden, and now a whole new world opened up for my brother and sister, aged 10 and 4, and me, aged 8. Not only did we have what seemed like a huge garden, complete with its resident toad, all to ourselves to play in; it also had what every garden owner in the late 40s and early 50s aspired to, a chicken run. Over the years we had some hair-raisingly aggressive cockerels, particularly Black Michael and later Ivan the Terrible. With neither of these were we allowed in the chicken run, and our intrepid mother would collect the eggs armed with a broomstick and tea cloth to ward off the cockerels' desperate efforts to peck her ankles. Sometimes there was definitely blood. In contrast, one of our hens, Buttercup, laid and laid, and was allowed out to wander with us round the garden clucking chattily all the while. She was dearly loved, grew very old and we buried her eventually, none of us having the stomach to eat such an old friend.

We also for the first time had access to village shops. Mrs East at the bakery had to put up with our noses pressed against the window as we drooled over the sights within, desperate for sweet things in that rationed and sugar-free age.

But best of all was the river. It became our playground. We swam, fished (roach mostly, which we ate only once, disgusting and gritty), rowed and canoed. Above all we explored. In our summer holidays, we were always on or in the river, both in Fordwich and in Sturry. I remember hours spent playing on the small weir above the Sturry bridge, sliding down it, shooting its rapids in a flat-bottomed rowing boat packed with children, clambering back up, swimming in the pool below. My brother Charlie was quick-witted and agile, his friend James Hamilton a year younger but about a foot taller and very strong, Sally Paine from Fordwich slightly older and marginally more sensible but full of wonderfully adventurous plans; where these three led, the smaller ones followed. In my recall, we played entirely unsupervised by adults, though often they arrived with picnics. If not, we all trailed home for meals and went straight back out afterwards...

Friendly Hall viewed in the distance on Fordwich Road in the flood of 1909

We Moved to Friendly Hall II

by Philippa Nice (née Gross)

We moved to Friendly Hall, Fordwich, (then actually in Westbere parish) in 1952 when I was four years old. My parents remained in Fordwich for the rest of their lives. They later moved out of Friendly Hall into Friendly Lodge which my father had built (with help) in part of the kitchen garden.

We inherited Mr Howard Parker, the butcher, who rented part of the stable end of the house. [Howard Parker's shop in the High Street had been destroyed in the bombing.] The rent was the Sunday joint. We kept chickens (a luxury food then) and I picture, even now, with a shudder, Mr Parker – a rotund, red-faced man with a bloodied apron – coming out of the run with a dead chicken. This was always preceded by my mother instructing him which chicken we were going to have for lunch this week.

Mrs. Parker, a smiley lady, was always plucking chickens and surrounded by feathers. The butcher's boy used to give me rides in the basket of his delivery bicycle – thrilling!

By the time I was six, I was allowed to walk up the road to the baker's.

Mr and Mrs East's shop smelled of warmth. Mr East sometimes appeared – a tall man, very pale and totally covered in white flour. Mrs East would send me home with a warm, white (and enormous) sandwich loaf which I hugged all the way home.

Over the main road, Mrs Nellie Morris ran the newsagent and sweetie shop. If I was being exceptionally irritating to my parents, I was allowed to go and get an ice-cream from the rather frightening Mrs.Morris. She seemed disapproving when handing me my purchase and, as I recall, was always in conversation with someone else at the time.

In Fordwich I experienced a "Swallows and Amazons" childhood, always messing about in boats with my two older siblings and Jamie Hamilton and Sally Paine. Fordwich village shop was run by Sam Gilling who supplied my brother, Charlie, and sister, Lizzie, with bottles of "Dandelion and Burdock", a foul-looking black drink which seemed to bring Jamie and Charlie much excitement.

We didn't worship at Sturry Church because my father was a King's School master and had to attend their services in the Cathedral. My only experience of Sturry Church was at my sister's wedding in 1964 and I don't remember much about that – I was a bridesmaid and too busy.

Friendly Hall in the Nineteen Thirties.

Sturry Nomads Sports Club
A Year to Remember (1952-1953)
by Allan Butler

For a boy growing up in Sturry in the late 1940's there was no organised cricket or football for youngsters outside school. The few matches we had were arranged by ourselves against teams from Littlebourne, Hoath, Beltinge and Bekesbourne. More parochially we had my Island Road team competing against the Sturry Hill side of Ken Rogers. We then combined to take on the boys from Fordwich and Broad Oak. Home fixtures were played on the Sturry Cricket Field or Peel's Field in Island Road (west of Sleigh Road).

In December 1951 (when I was 13) our cricket and football became properly organised when my brother Derek Butler formed the Sturry Boys Club and arranged football matches against teams from Boughton, Herne Bay and Littlebourne. These were played on a field at Mr Dick Line's Whatmer Farm adjoining the Cemetery.

In February 1952 the club accepted the invitation of the Nomad Sports Clubs based in Canterbury to become an affiliated member. The Nomad Sports Club was the brainchild of the twenty-one year old Gerald Baker from Canterbury who was later to become the City Architect. The Clubs would adopt a Christian ethic and foster good sportsmanship and loyalty. It was instilled in the boys that it was more important to take part than to win. Inspired by Gerald Baker's enthusiasm a central committee of Norman Butterworth (chairman), John Line (Vice-Chairman), Derek Butler (Secretary) and Gerald Baker (Fixture Secretary) began planning for the year ahead with cricket matches, a football league and inter-section competitions in athletics, cycling, swimming, rowing and cross country running.

Before the start of the 1952/53 Football Season the Sturry section had to find a ground and with nowhere available in Sturry, Derek went to see Mr Daniel Brice, the Fordwich farmer and landowner, who readily made available part of East Field by Spring Lane. Long poles were obtained from Homersham's wood yard and put together as goal posts. The white-lining machine was borrowed from the vicar and a pitch duly marked out. It was a rough and bumpy field which earned the sobriquet "Molehill Stadium". Permission was obtained to use the Old School Room for changing.

The football league for under fifteens would comprise five teams – Canterbury A and B, Sturry A and B and Littlebourne. The regular squad members were as follows:-

Sturry 'A'	Sturry 'B'
Ken Rogers (Captain)	John Line (Captain)
Mick Homersham	John Bubb
Ken Peel	Keith Baker
Bob Murray	Willie Palmer
Allan Butler	Roger Pay
David Larkins	Brian Wells
Brian Adams	David Longley
Reggie Whittaker	Peter Price
Tony Whittaker	Roy Davies
David Bubb	Ron Wanstall
Michael Holness	David Martin
Alan Peel	Larry McNulty
George Robey	Jimmy Lipyeat
Brian Hall	Chris Jarvis
	Mick Marsh

Other occasional players were Colin Elks, Stan Wright, John Harvey, Roger Amos, Bill Line and John Ladley.

The knock-out cup competition was won by Sturry 'B' who prevailed over Littlebourne in a thrilling final by 5 goals to 4 at Victoria Recreation Ground. Goal scorers were Peter Price 2, John Line 2 and Brian Wells.

John Line's goal scoring record of 26 goals in 15 matches was very impressive.

In addition to the league and cup matches for the under 15's there were friendly combined fixtures and first eleven matches which enabled the senior members such as Derek Butler and Arthur Bubb to have a game. These two did sterling work as referees during the season. Opponents in these matches included St. Mildred's Boys Club, Spring Lane, Sturry Road Social Club, Herne Bay and Hersden. In addition on 1st March, 1953, a fixture mix-up led to an adult side from North Deal turning up at Fordwich instead of the expected boys' team. The match went ahead and we managed to keep our losing score down to 6–0!

During the season match reports appeared in the regular newsletters which Gerald Baker edited: "The Nomad – The official newsweekly of the Nomads Sports Clubs Association in Kent". Mid season the circulation had reached 90. The editorial in edition 8 on 13th November, 1952 was designed to shake us all up:-

Sturry Nomads "A" team 1952/53
Back row L to R: Brian Adams, Allan Butler, Mick Homersham, David Bubb, Reggie Whittaker and Bobby Murray.
Front row: David Larkins, Michael Holness, Ken Rogers, Tony Whittaker and Ken Peel

Sturry Nomads "B" team
Back row L to R: Roy Davies, Dave Martin, John Bubb, Roger Pay, David Longley, Ronnie Wanstall.
Front row: Willie Palmer, Keith Baker, John Line, Brian Wells, Peter Price.

The statistics for the season were as follows:-

Sturry 'A'

	Played	Won	Lost	Drew	Goals For	Goals Against
League	12	7	4	1	36	20
All Matches	16	11	4	1	76	34

Leading goal scorers:

	League	All Matches
Brian Adams	14	23
David Bubb	12	19
Ken Rogers	--	6
Tony Whittaker	4	4
Mick Homersham	4	4

Sturry 'B'

	Played	Won	Lost	Drew	Goals For	Goals Against
League	12	5	5	2	54	44
All Matches	15	8	5	2	63	49

Leading goal scorers:

	League	All Matches
John Line	26	26
Peter Price	15	15
Keith Baker	3	4
Willie Palmer	3	3

"For goodness sake let's Toughen up the Game. It's all the same – with all our football – the curse of timidity. Read below of the latest league match: turn over and hear about Canterbury's 1st team's waiting game: take any of our matches. Take them and look at them: tear them to pieces: analyse them as you may: turn the teams inside out: spend a whole season experimenting: then sum up. There's only one thing wrong with our present standard of football. It's more suited on the whole to girls' netball matches, where you must not hurt Priscilla or she'll tell teacher. Oh! For goodness sake, let's have a bit more tough stuff. Keep it clean – let's not lose our good name – but do, oh do, get stuck in!!"

The issue of January, 1953, announced that Lt. Comm. E.C. Talbot Booth, RD., RNR, had been elected president of the association for 1953. The Sturry section Annual General Meeting and Prizegiving was held at the Social Centre on 25th November 1952 with John Line in the chair, when Lieutenant Baker presented the prizes as follows:

Cricket

Batting Ken Rogers
Bowling John Ladley

Outstanding Performance Mick Homersham

Football

Most Improved   Peter Price
Most Promising   Willie Palmer

Clubmanship   John Line
Sportsmanship   Reginald Whittaker

The Athletics Tournament was held at the Victoria Recreation Ground on 6th April, 1953. Sturry were the winners with notable performances by Brian Adams, Reggie Whittaker, Mick Marsh and David Longley. The end of the cricket season though brought the closure of the Sturry Nomads Sports Club. No football was organised for the 1953/54 season and most of the keen lads were playing for their school teams. Ken Rogers and myself had already made our debuts for the Sturry Cricket Club. In the early 1950's a number of us sang in the church choir and attended the Sturry Youth Club and Westbere Boy's Club.

The Nomads gave us organised and competitive sport when we would otherwise have been just kicking a ball about or hitting one with a piece of wood. It had all been very enjoyable, great fun and well worthwhile.

A Fordwich Childhood

by Sally Kington

We came to Fordwich in 1948, my parents Robert and Phyllis Paine, my brother Nick aged fourteen, me aged seven and my sister Sandra who was three. Give Ale Cottage was our new home, converted by my architect father from three dwellings under one roof into one. Two of the three staircases were removed, making way for the coat cupboard at the bottom of one of them, the bathroom at the top. The ceilings were low and the beams even lower so my tall father and brother were forever banging their heads. The house flanked the churchyard and was rather sunk into it, so that a gravestone stood tall outside the kitchen window, and the legs of the people going down the church path were at eye level when you were doing the washing up. It was named with another house in mind, another medieval building, long vanished from the village, from which the church dispensed ale at festivals.

Sandra was still too young, Nick was pre-occupied with school, but I immediately fell in with the other children in the village. They were among others the Murrays, the Robeys, the Collins, the Pickfords, the Todds, and Eileen Smith. We played in the street, in the wide part by the village sign - largely cricket of sorts, with the wicket on the gate in the wall to Mr Villiers-Stuart's house, Yew Tree House. The ice cream cart came along sometimes. We played in the meadows, but only in the first field. An energetic aunt did once walk Sandra and me all the way along to the woods at the end. And even though she'd bought a large bottle of cherryade from Mr Boys at the sweet shop, it seemed too far. Also we saw a snake on the way.

We did sometimes venture up from the end of Spring Lane towards the pine trees. This was past Miss Edgell's. She rode a very tall bicycle down the back path from the top end of Spring Lane where her house was down to School Lane and on out to the church. Up at the pines, there were also some good trees for climbing.

We were drummed up into the choir. Colin Brown was a boy of about eighteen who came on his bicycle from Canterbury to play the organ. On Friday nights for choir practice, we had to light the gas mantles and pump the organ ourselves. Father Williams was the vicar when we first came. Then there was Canon Clayson, whose daughter Mary, not much older than me, had us all in the old schoolroom on Saturday mornings making things and singing songs. Later Mary had a pony, and she and I with bike and pony went over to the blacksmith at Wickhambreaux.

With his architect's sense of place and his sense of civic duty, my father involved himself in the conservation and governance of the village. And the village, being actually a town, had a mayor, a position he took his turn at filling. Each year the mayor and council, the mace-bearer and the town crier processed from town hall to church, and they were memorable years when my father led the way, the mayoral chain looking heavy on his shoulders. We sang 'All People that on Earth do Dwell' at those particular services.

My mother trained at the Royal College of Art. Her contribution was to the arts and crafts of stalls at the village fetes (held at By The Way House where Mr Daniel Brice, the farmer, lived). She would make blotters or whatever it was that were bought and sold, and one year she painted the board with the open-mouthed face on it for the Aunt Sally. She did a bird's eye view of the village.[1] She painted the Fordwich coat of arms on a series of wooden plates to sell to commemorate the coronation in 1953. And I think she made the shields of arms for the coronation procession.

June 2nd 1953 Coronation Day Procession, Fordwich High Street led by Colin Brown with George Robey and James Hamilton as banner bearers. The Queen was Sally Paine with attendants Daphne Collins, Freda Robinson and Mary Clayson. Others in the picture include Pam Murray, Ruth Clayson, Janice Robey, Jennifer Collins and John Boxall

I led that procession, for I had been made village queen. This was much to my astonishment, because Eileen Smith was the oldest of the girls in the village and to my mind she should have been chosen. But I had recently been on crutches after 18 months' hospitalisation for what turned out not to be TB, and people thought I was courageous.

My brother went to King's and was an oarsman, [he was to row for Oxford in 1956] so he would appear on the other side of the river where the school had boatsheds and landing stages. Sandra and I had a little boat ourselves and Nick was embarrassed by the presence of his younger sisters paddling about among the skiffs and fours. It was better when he became a superior oarsman and went down to row in the eights at Plucks Gutter. Better for us too, because then we could spend more time on the King's side with the school boatman, who let us help by rowing out to rescue boys who'd capsized.

In our boat we could reach the river wall of the little garden at the back of the Town Hall. It was fenced off otherwise. We would sit there out of sight, under a large Laburnum tree, dangling our legs. The Town Hall was a sanctuary in another way when we would dash up from the boat when the rain came on and shelter under the deep overhang of the upper floor.

Another place where we would go ashore was at the bottom of the garden of Watergate House, where there were steps up from the arched gate in the stone wall of the old quayside and where James Hamilton lived, a slightly later addition to the troop of children. We took heed of my father's tales of stone from Caen being unloaded here in the 11th century and carted over to Canterbury for building the cathedral.[2] Some of it came back to Fordwich, discarded during restoration in the 1940s and acquired by my father for a rockery at Give Ale Cottage.

Veronica Hawkins standing between two topiary crowns created by her Mother, Mrs Dolly Hawkins, at 2 The Springs, Island Road, Sturry, for the Coronation.

Once a year the weed-cutter came, and the weed-cutter was the name both for the strange raft of a boat that had the knives under it and the man who manoeuvred it. Then we were out in our boat dragging the newly severed, heavily floating water weed away from the overhanging tree branches it got caught in, and sending it on its way downstream.

We tied our boat up at the Fordwich Arms, in the corner where the path led from the road along to the landing stage. The publican's grown-up sons let Sandra and me help with the boats they had for hire, baling them, manoeuvring them. One wet August we all set off in one of their bigger boats to row up to Canterbury, lugging the boat over the weir at Sturry, getting into shallower and shallower waters until grounding well short of our objective and turning for home.

Coach parties came on their way home from Margate, to end the day with a sing-song round the piano at the Fordwich Arms. They were loud, and went on until closing time, and the noise through my bedroom window kept me reluctantly awake but fitted me up with a fund of music hall tunes.

Mrs Whittaker was our cleaning lady. She lived in Monks Hall, in the row of houses opposite and at right angles to our house. Sandra and I found every excuse to visit her, in by the side gate in the Drove that led across the bottom of the other houses in the row, down the path to her back door. Never through the front door into the room with heavily beamed and bossed ceiling which had the piano in it. Nor did we go into that room when we went in by the back, but into a little room alongside, much too small for the gathered family - plump Mrs Whittaker, large Mr Whittaker who drove the County Council steamroller, and their four grown-up children. There was Elvina who played the piano, Olwen who worked on a switchboard I think, pleasing everyone with her Welsh voice, Cyril who was very smart, and Sid who worked on the farm. They were our entree not only to an entrancing patch of land down the Drove where they kept a pig and chickens and rabbits but also, thanks to Sid, to the even more fascinating farm.

We hung around the milking shed, going into the farmyard by the top gate. We gazed at the huge horses and the very small horseman (he had a cleft palate and communed with the horses better then he did with us). They were at the stables in by the bottom gate, by the oast house. We choked on the dust in the noise of the threshing outside the big barn, which was past the stables. We rode on Sid's tractor. We followed our noses up across the fields beyond Fordwich House to the edge of the woods in the gloaming where the men who had been hedging and ditching all day had a fire of the brushwood.

Mr Sam Gilling eventually moved into Monks Hall, setting up his shop in Mrs Whittaker's former room with the special ceiling. But in our young days he was at the corner of Spring Lane, in a nice square shop with a deep counter round three sides and a nice looking, comfortable living room you could see through to at the back. We took the shopping list along each week - written out by hand by my mother or by me at her dictation, always in the same order, always starting butter, sugar, lard.

As the Fifties moved on, my horizons widened. I remember the oddity of being among new friends who said, 'Let's go to the George and Dragon!' It seemed so daring and grown-up. But Fordwich in the smaller compass had already provided me with an engrossing childhood, and I still dream about it.

[1] K.H.McIntosh FORDWICH – THE LOST PORT [1979] page 114
[2] Veronica Bowyer-Smythe – FROM CAEN TO CANTERBURY (n.d)

The Sturry Good Fellowship

by Allan Butler

The Sturry Good Fellowship was formed in 13th September, 1943, at the instigation of the Vicar, the Revd. Samuel Risdon Brown, and Sir Arthur Pugh, its aim "to preserve and foster among the male population of the village the spirit of good fellowship and mutual understanding prevalent in these dark days of war."

Meetings were held fortnightly from May to September first in the Primary School and from 1949 in the Social Centre. There was an annual Ladies' Night and in the Spring an outing. The Fellowship maintained its aims for the following 25 years, being wound up in 1968.

Gerald Button was the first secretary and was succeeded in 1952 by Len Morgan. I joined in 1961 and still have my rule book. I was elected to the Committee in 1964 and as it transpired was the chairman when it was wound up in 1968. H.Clyde Lovely was a prominent member and frequent speaker, while former police sergeant, Wm Fuller, who was also chairman for a term, regularly presented talks on "Famous Crime Cases".

Other members who spoke included Sir Michael Nethersole; P.T.S.Brook (Fruit Farming); the Revd Father Joseph B. McCarthy (The British Legion); Frank Jenkins (Religion in Roman Times); Dr R.A.C.McIntosh (The Mixture as Before); A.J.Brooks (Fifty Years of Coal Mining); R.C.Sage (Impressionist Art); Sergeant R.C.Grayling (Policeman's Choice);and Major E.Elliot (Military Experiences). Dr M.S.Harvey, after delivering his talk on "A Matter of Health", was subjected to a grilling on the addition of fluoride to the public water supply.

Coming into their own later, newer younger members also gave talks such as Alf Matthews on Cross-Channel swimming, David Dungey on Captain John Smith and the Jamestown Settlement; Derek Butler on Sturry in the Early 1900's and Jack Cooper on House Purchase. Other memorable talks were given by our postmaster, E. Newson, on the Battle of Jutland and H. Clyde Lovely who delivered "Dishonest to God", a forceful rebuttal of Bishop John Robinson's 1963 book "Honest to God".

Special guest at the 1964 Ladies Night was Mrs Olive Stephens, wife of the Vicar of Chislet, who had been a participant in the radio quiz "What do you Know?" and its T.V. successor "Ask me Another" and who was to become "Brain of Britain".

Other members whose names I can recall were Messrs R.G.Collingwood, C.Haggis, Major Paget, Trevor Jones, Arthur Bournes, G. Williams, Ivor Gay, J. Reid, Maurice Spillett, W.Joiner, H.Pitcher and J.B.Wild. They were a cross section of the male population of the village with a respect for one another and all would contribute to the lively and stimulating discussions.

Looking back from the prospect of 2010 our programme might not seem very exciting but as Jack Cooper, a former Secretary, said "I miss the Good fellowship for what it offered and wish we had something like it today. . . how much more enjoyable to have an evening out in good company at the Social Centre. . . than in today's world to be sitting at home in front of a computer screen".

Grandfather's Garden

by Diana Brown

My grandparents moved to their house, which had been built in 1913, when Sir William Rice and his family, who had lost two sons in the First World War, left the village. They created a four-acre garden there and my sister, Margy, and I would like to take you on a tour of it as we remember it in the 1950's when we were young.

So come with us, starting on the wide terrace in front of the house with its magnificent views across the marshes to Stodmarsh. There was a telescope mounted there through which you could watch the great crested grebes nesting in the lakes below.

Beyond the gravel drive is a flight of brick steps taking us down to the terrace below. If you look back now you can see the magnificent wisteria sinensis that covers the veranda. The steps have Mexican daisies growing in the cracks while the banks at the sides are covered with Rose of Sharon (Hypericum). There used to be a tennis court here but this was dug up in the Second World War and then became our Aunt Mary's rose garden. However, roses proved hard to grow and she later had vines here with the intention of making wine. This was not successful either - our father describing one hilarious evening in which a series of bottles exploded one after the other during supper just like a 12 gun salute.

The herbaceous border at the side of this with its lavender hedge beyond is full of lupins and phlox and other flowers grown for picking. This way takes us to the first pond where we'll pass the dahlias - I like the spiky ones best. The pond is a rather unusual shape and used to have a rustic bridge over it but now it has a very fine stone one. One of the capstones is a reused part of a memorial stone to Great Uncle William Gilbert Pidduck, who built "Oaklands" on Staines Hill. It is surrounded with alpine plants to remind grandmother of her time in the Swiss Alps.

From here you can see the shrubbery, the azalea beds and the greenhouses – one of these seemed to be always full of flowers. I particularly remember schizanthus, gloxinias, hyacinths and agapanthus. Grandfather grew wonderful honeydew melons, tomatoes and grapes, too.

Sturry Women's Institute Choir circa 1950
Back row: includes Mrs Gymneth Williams, Mrs Irene Kennett, Mrs Ida Spillett and Mrs Ada Bubb.
Front row: includes Mrs Vera Pay, Mrs E Newing, Mrs Alice Fabb, Mrs Vera Cullen, Mrs Mary Reid and Mrs M Button.

There is a cypress hedge through an arch of which we can now get to the Round Pond. It is built in the Italian style and we can stop here to turn on the fountain. The water makes a lovely sound splashing over the water lilies. The goldfish like it, too.

I think all four of we children fell in the pond in turn – our elder sister, Ruth, when trying to catch a frog, Margy while attempting to walk on the lily pads, our brother William when racing round it and me while I was trying to wash the back of the statue of Pan – my grandmother's water guardian. This pond was surrounded with herbaceous perennials – the delphiniums are my favourites here.

There is a little ornamental folly by the pond, covered in variegated ivy, consisting of the pillars from the entrance of grandfather's pre-war office rescued after it was bombed in 1942. And a sunrise step with a mosaic made of pebbles leading to a camellia path. The paths were a great delight – we liked exploring and running along these, especially the one which ran round the outside of the hedge sheltering the greenhouses. There was a pergola near here covered in clematis, when we would run on past the new azalea mollis bed into the round garden and out to the top of the old quarry in the wood up

through the root vegetable garden and eventually past the blue spruce and cedar trees. The steps to the cowshed and stables led down through the quarry.

There is another vegetable garden, too, growing such delights as rhubarb, celery and – joy of joys - flowering artichokes. Pears were grown along the paths here and we helped carry the ones that grandfather considered ready for eating up to the house. (Grandmother used to say that there was just one hour in the life of a pear when it was fit to eat.) Oh, and then there was a cherry-plum orchard (watch out for wasps) and quince trees. You could see Canterbury Cathedral from here (if you weren't afraid of geese). If we found hen's eggs anywhere we had to hand them to grandmother, telling her whether or not they were still warm. Giant puff balls (calvatia gigantea) grew here. Grandfather enjoyed eating slices of these fried.

Then there was the wood of coppiced hazel with bluebells growing beneath them. Granny would show us the purple and white violets near the apple and pear store which had come from a special bank in a wood near where she had lived at the now-demolished Milton Manor on the road to Chartham. We realised even then that it was a garden of memories for her as well as it has been for us ever since.

Guiding in Sturry

by Jean Anthony (née Larkins)

We seemed to spend a lot of time in the Vicarage garden on Sturry Hill in 1945 when I was a Brownie. One of my first memories is of sitting on a raffia mat when Miss Jessie Raven was our Brown Owl. We still used the garden when I went up to Guides in 1948. Miss Sylvia Cox was our Captain but sitting on raffia mats was not encouraged then! We had to be active – games, tracking and cooking dampers (flour mixed with water, the resulting dough stuck on the end of a stick and cooked over an open fire).

We had weekend camps in the Vicarage garden, too, before going away to camp each year. It was hard work collecting wood for the fire, carrying buckets of water (usually uphill) and erecting Hessian screens round a hole for the lats (latrines) - which I hated. We were taken to different locations every summer, my first being at Barham – on the top of a hill, of course. I think it was at Mr A.J.Ross's Out Elmstead Farm.

In 1954 I became a warranted Scouter and helped Kathleen Taylor of Dengrove who was Akela of the Sturry Cubs. Back to sitting on raffia mats under the

Vicarage trees, although the Cubs enjoyed games and generally running around. The trees proved good hiding places in the games.

Years later – in 1983 - I became a Guider. No more raffia mats then. We had "sitter" tins that held our Guide bits and pieces and were individually decorated. We still used the Vicarage garden for enrolment ceremonies and camp-fire singing.

Over time Guide camps improved in comfort (for example, no more Hessian lats). Janet Paul was our Captain and Daphne Bullock was Quarter Master and I was assistant Q.M.

The Guides still had to collect wood and carry water, though. They still tended to undercook bacon, too, and to complain about smoke getting in their eyes. We saved large catering-size tins and cooked chocolate pudding in them. We all loved chocolate pudding but our favourites were "blackbirds" – fried jam sandwiches coated with sugar.

Happy memories, indeed.

Ist Sturry Guide Company.
Top row L to R: Mary Truscott and Sylvia Cox
Middle row: Jill Metherell, Ellen Whittaker, Jean Larkins
Front row: Rosemary Barrance, Molly Croxton and Ann Metherell.

Name	Role	Start date	End date
Miss Newman	Leader	June.1940	Not known
Mrs Couchman	Asst Leader	Dates not known	
Miss J E Raven	Leader	Aug.1950	Nov.1955
Mrs M Burton	Leader	Dec. 1963	Sept. 1968
Miss M Mearns	Asst Leader	Aug.1957	Nov.1958
Mrs R.G.Purkiss	Leader	Oct.1969	May.1970
Mrs L Dance	Asst Leader	Dec. 1963	May.1968
Miss A M Blythe Smith	Asst Leader	Dec. 1968	Sept. 1969
Miss M Brown	Asst Leader	Dec. 1969	May.1970
No details known			
No details known			
Miss Sylvia Cox	Leader	Nov. 1950	July. 1956
Mrs B L Stanwix	Leader	July. 1957	Not known
Mrs G M Lindsell	Asst Leader	Nov. 1950	April.1951
Miss Truscott	Asst Leader	Oct. 1951	Nov. 1953
Miss M Race	Asst Leader	July. 1957	Sept. 1958
Miss S.Munton	Asst Leader	July. 1957	Sept. 1958
Mrs M Harris	Asst Leader	Nov. 1961	Octo. 1962
Miss J Donohue	Asst Leader	Mch. 1968	May. 1971
Mrs B Eddington Edmonds	Leader	Dates not known	
Miss A E Bing	Asst Leader	Dates not known	

An incomplete list of Guide and Brownie Leaders in the 1960's to which should be added Mrs Monica Headley and Mrs Margaret Grayling and certainly others.

Sturry Guides at camp in 1982 including
Wendy Anthony, Kate O'Flyn, Alison Stockbridge, Marion Louch, Erica Dungey, Emma File, Elizabeth Foad, Sharon Kirk,
Elizabeth Todd, Angela Newbury, Julianna Beard and Joanne and Jacki Tompsett.

A Crowd, a Host of Golden Daffodils

The Reverend George Philip Haydon, 1846 - 1913

The full history of Mr. Haydon appears in the account of his home, The Oaks, in Church Lane, Westbere, published in WESTBERE HERITAGE TRAIL [1]. He lived there from his retirement in 1898 until his death, when he was succeeded there by his brother-in-law, Sir Charles Warren. He had been Vicar of Hatfield [2] for some twenty years before coming to Westbere and continuing devoting his time to the breeding of daffodils. By happy accident a later resident is able to write about them below.

From Sally Kington, former International Daffodil Registrar

My parents moved to Westbere in 1960. Theirs was a house they designed for themselves on a steep field above Westbere Lane, opposite Dr Moloney's house, called Summerhill. I came home from university in the holidays, and then when I was living in London, I came down at weekends for walks across the marshes and jaunts to the Yew Tree Inn, and French cricket on the wide level lawn my mother had carved out of the slope for just such purposes.

Much later, after my parents had moved back to Fordwich, Kinn McIntosh drew my professional attention to Westbere. I was working at the Royal Horticultural Society (RHS) by then, serving as Daffodil Registrar, tending the International Daffodil Register, a descriptive list that the Society had been keeping since 1907 of all known garden daffodils. These were not the wild daffodils, of which there are about 150 species and wild hybrids, mostly native to Spain, Portugal and North Africa, just two of them native to Britain. No, they were the man-made hybrids, the daffodils which in the 1840s were first discovered to be so easy to breed from the wild ones. The Dean of Manchester was the pioneer. A businessman from Lancashire called Edward Leeds came not long after, and then a banker from Yorkshire called William Backhouse.

Enthusiasm for daffodils has not abated since, either for breeding them (the UK leads the field), propagating them (the Dutch do this on a large scale) or planting them (the world over). The Register now comprises upwards of 27,000 different varieties.

What Kinn told me was that a multitude of daffodils still came up each year on land formerly attached to The Oaks where the Rev. G.P.Haydon had grown them in his retirement. I knew about Haydon. I knew about him from daffodils of his listed in the Register, from articles about him in the Daffodil and Tulip Yearbook and from his own writing in the RHS journal.

In 1884, when Haydon was still Vicar of Hatfield, the Royal Horticultural Society held a conference, at which the newly created daffodils were named and put on the market. Haydon was among a string of skilful growers who, taking up the threads from the pioneer hybridizers, bred from the conference daffodils. Renowned contemporaries of his were the Irishman Guy Wilson and yet another churchman, the Rev. G.H.Engleheart.

Looking at the daffodils at Westbere, I could see that few were the wild ones, few were even the old varieties that had been growing in English gardens over the centuries, naturally occurring sports and hybrids of the wild ones. On the contrary, most of them had the air of being the man-made hybrids - some tentatively ascribable to the varieties Haydon was using as parents, others probably his own seedlings.

If the success of his seedlings is anything to go by, proficiency and creativity lay behind Haydon's hybridizing. Not only did they command high prices, but they were also winners on the show bench. Seven were given the RHS Award of Merit, many more won prizes at the Midland Daffodil Society at Birmingham or at the Kent, Surrey and Sussex Show nearer home.

His advice on the cultivation of daffodils was apparently respected, for while he was still at Hatfield he was invited by the RHS to give a lecture on the subject in London. His ideas on conservation seem to have been progressive, as he closed that lecture with remarks on "the destructive animal, the tourist" and the need for laws against unregulated collection of wild plants.

The daffodils at Westbere are the remarkable legacy of a notable man. They are the survival, in quantity, without admixture of more recent varieties, of some of the finest daffodils of late Victorian times and choice offspring from them.

[1] WESTBERE HERITAGE TRAIL - a community project pub The Westbere Village preservation Society (2006) p 48
[2] Crockford's Clerical Directory (1912)

Boxing Day in Sturry - 1965 and After

by Derek Butler

When I was Secretary of the Sturry Cricket Club I read about the Yorkshire Cricket Society's annual Boxing Day match and suggested we had a similar game. This idea was taken up with enthusiasm and the first match was held on Boxing Day 1965 when the Sturry team took the field against the Canterbury Choughs Cricket Club in aid of the Friends of the Canterbury Hospital.

It was reported in the Kent Herald by Alan Bensted that "the frost was swept off the pitch" before the Matron, Miss D.M.Leachman, "no mean cricketer herself" (in fact, a former England player, who always kept an eye on the Kent Cricket Club scores from the hospital) bowled the first ball for Sturry and "in red sweaters, crouching menacingly at mid-on and cover point, Sturry bowled out – or slid out – the Choughs for 30". Sturry passed this total for the loss of 6 wickets. The umpire, Sid Burton, doubled as Father Christmas! Donations from a procession of cars through the village helped swell the funds for this worthy cause, raising £21 – the equivalent to £270 today.

The next year, again in frost, the two teams played for the benefit of the St John's Ambulance Brigade's Building Fund. The Mayor of Canterbury, Councillor Bernard Porter, one of the sponsors of its Appeal, thrashed the first ball to the boundary watched approvingly by Dr R.A.C.McIntosh, another sponsor. This time the reporter, Alan Bensted, had to concede that he didn't know who won on account of feeling a little frail after Christmas

Day and leaving early! The sum of £35 (£463 in today's terms) was raised.

Boxing Day, 1967, was rainy but this did not deter the Sturry and Choughs teams who played their charity match in aid of the Dr Barnardo's Home in Canterbury. Mr Frank Butler, the Superintendent of the Home, bowled the first ball under the watchful eye of the umpire/Father Christmas, Ken Rogers. The Choughs won and £25 (£322) was raised.

In 1968 the first ball was bowled by the Chairman of the Parish Council, Miss Kinn McIntosh, and the proceeds of over £30 (£385) donated to the Sturry Over 60's Club. There is no record of who won...

Over these years the participants included Jack Cooper, Les Dinnage, Bert Ogden, Dave Stanley, Dave Jenkins, Allan Butler, Peter Price, John Worrell, Geoff Archer, Martin Cannon, Billy Alder, Maurice Collingwood, John Line, Derek Payne and Ken Rogers, the last three also doubling as Father Christmas in the fund-raising processions.

Boxing Day, 2009, saw the 60th anniversary match between the Northern Cricket Society and the North Leeds Cricket Club in aid of St Gemma's Hospice at Moortown in Leeds but I'm afraid we didn't keep it up at Sturry.

Boxing Day Cricket: Bowler – John Worrell; Batsman: Malcolm Longley Umpire: Sid Burton

Sturry Bellringers

Standing L to R: H.R.French, Bert Luck, Stanley Bates, Harry Rogers.
Sitting clockwise: unknown, Mrs Rogers, Mabel French, George French, Mrs Elizabeth Thompson, Valerie Bradshaw, Mrs Violet Bradshaw, Mr Wm Thompson and Mrs Clara French.

Patrick Harrisson (on the stairs) Barbara Durkan, Roger Button, Geoffrey Thompson, Mary McKenzie, Martin Harrisson, Keith Davies, Christina Bouldin and Derek Standing.

Pen to Paper*

by K.H. McIntosh

The first and most important book ever written in Sturry was DE REBUS ALBIONICUS by John Tywnne (1507-1581). It was set in the grounds of Sturry Court and was published by the Elizabethan printer Edmund Bollifant in 1590. Written in 1549, it comprised an imaginary philosophical dialogue between Man and the Devil as they walked to and fro. Twynne Close is named after him.

In 1562 ("Times when the ministry was full of danger",) the Revd Thomas Becon (1512-1567) became Vicar of Sturry in plurality and a Six Preacher.[1] He was one of the most prolific theological authors of his time, although some of his scurrilous limericks are too vulgar, not to say obscene, to reproduce today.

Later authors to have lived in the earliest Vicarage at Sturry have been Robin Collins, who wrote romantic fiction such as GO WITH A SPLENDID HEART and MY CITY FEARS TOMORROW in the nineteen-sixties under the pseudonym of Robin Cranford; and Emeritus Professor of Law, Peter Fitzpatrick, whose most recent book (with Ben Golder) is FOUCAULT'S LAW (2009).

In 1935 H.Clyde Lovely, who lived at Cranford in the Island Road, (now the doctor's surgery), wrote a book about his early life at sea under the pseudonym of Clew Garnet. Called HAMMERED SHIP-SHAPE it was described as "A Saga of the Sailing Ship Apprentice" and still makes good reading.

Writing at much the same time was J.V.P.D. Balsdon, of St Aubin's, Sturry Hill, sometime Rector of Exeter College, Oxford. CHARITY BIZARRE, published in 1935, is only one of Dacre Balsdon's engaging, light-hearted books far removed from the world of scholarship. His brother, Wing Commander Denys Finlay Balsdon, is commemorated on the Sturry War Memorial - the incident in which he died is described in ENEMY CPAST AHEAD by Guy Gibson.

A post war writer, who set one of his many detective stories in Sturry, was Harry Carmichael (pseudonym of Leopold Horace Ognall, 1908-1979). His book THE DEAD OF THE NIGHT was published in 1956.

The famous Ian Fleming chose the name of his friend, Hilary Bray, who lived at Westbere House, for a character in his James Bond novel ON HER MAJESTY'S SECRET SERVICE (1963) giving him a fictional knighthood. Another connection with Westbere House appears in TEN MINUTES TO BUFFALO - The Story of Germany's Great Escaper by Ulrich Steinhilper and Peter Osborne (1991). This German pilot, whose plane had come down

in the Chislet marshes in October, 1940, was held here for interrogation.

At Hollydene on Staines Hill there lived for a time a distinguished writer of children's books, Richard Parker (1915-1990). Whilst his BOY ON A CHAIN (1964) is perhaps his best known book, SECONDHAND FAMILY (1965) was ahead of its time in having as its subject a boy from a Children's Home who was fostered in a mining village.

The Revd. J.Neville Ward, Methodist Minister here from 1974 to 1977, was the author of a series of theological books in the 1970's, including FIVE FOR SORROW, TEN FOR JOY and FRIDAY AFTERNOON.

THE TOWNSEND JOURNALS – An Artist's Record of his Times, 1928-51, was published by the Tate Gallery in 1976 following the death in 1973 of William Townsend, son of Mr and Mrs L. Townsend of Devonshire Villas, Broad Oak.

Eugene Vinaver, a Russian by birth, who lived at Greenacres in Fordwich Road, and died there in 1979,

Hammered Shipshape

was the author in 1947 of a magisterial three volume work on the writings of Sir Thomas Malory of MORTE D'ARTHUR fame. It is said that the famous American novelist, John Steinbeck, had a great desire to write his own version and came to England in 1957 in search of Arthurian sites and visited Winchester to see the Vinaver manuscript there. He came to England in 1958 to spend more time with Eugene Vinaver.

Roger Higham, who also illustrated STURRY – The Changing Scene and FORDWICH – The Lost Port, lived at 39, High Street. He is a travel writer and author of books on Kent, Scotland and France where he now lives and writes.

In 1983 Michael Occleshaw of Hersden published a book called THE ROMANOV CONSPIRACY about the assassination of the last Tsar of Russia and his family.

Gerald Van Loo, who lived in Yew Tree Gardens in Fordwich, wrote a biography in 1989 called A VICTORIAN PARSON – The Life and Times of Thomas Prankerd Phelps, Rector of Ridley in Kent 1840-1893.

Benita Brown, who lived for a time at Blackthorn Gardens, Hersden, is the author of many family sagas set in Tyneside.

Robin Q. Edmonds of Wolverley Cottage, Church Lane, has written THE HISTORY OF THE JUNIOR KING'S SCHOOL FROM 1879 to 1956, published in 2008. Alfred, Lord Milner, whose home it was, was the author of ENGLAND IN EGYPT (1892), ARNOLD TOYNBEE: A Reminiscence (1902) and numerous articles. Rudyard Kipling, a frequent visitor there, used names from the graves in Sturry Churchyard for characters in at least one of his short stories.

Whilst it would have been pleasing to record that that most illustrious author Joseph Conrad had also lived in Westbere House, alas he died on the very day in August, 1924, that he was due to move in there from his home at Bishopsbourne.

*a comprehensive article on the many works of fiction associated with Fordwich appears in FORDWICH – THE LOST PORT, (1975, p 208).

[1] Derek Ingram Hill THE SIX PREACHERS OF CANTERBURY CATHEDRAL. (pub K.H.McIntosh 1982)

Sturry Silver Jubilee 1977

by John Line

In 1977 Parish Councils and groups all over the country were making plans to celebrate the Queen's Silver Jubilee. Sturry Parish Council was no exception and was determined to make sure that the event was enjoyable and memorable for all the residents of the Parish.

A new association was formed with members of the parish council and other "willing" volunteers. I, as already a long-serving Parish Councillor, agreed to chair the newly formed Sturry Community 77 Association. I was quickly joined by Maurice Collingwood, Colin Danton, Pat and Richard Fagg, Mike Stilwell, Brian Johnson and others.

The committee was agreed that the celebrations should be traditional in style but also accessible to all. They quickly settled on there being a Carnival Parade followed by a Fun-Day on the Primary School playing field. To this end it was also decided to hold a "Jubilee Queen" competition so that the lucky winner could lead the procession on the special day - Sunday 2 June 1977.

Posters were distributed to all local businesses and the committee were thrilled to have so much interest. The main competition was held at the Ship Inn, Upstreet, which comprised a disco during which the candidates were interviewed by a panel of local business people. The first Sturry Jubilee Queen crowned was Gill Stilwell with Vera Webb as her Princess.

The Committee was simultaneously putting into place all the arrangements to ensure that the Carnival parade and Fun day were successful. Obviously this meant liaising with local bodies - Police, St John Ambulance etc, all of whom were enthusiastic and helpful. The Fun Day was planned as traditional fete with the usual fairground stalls, hot dogs and ice cream and an "It's a Knockout Competition" in which teams of local residents would compete for a trophy. There was also to be a Fancy Dress Parade and all the usual games required to give all-comers something to do and enjoy.

When the day dawned, it was one of those perfect June days - the weather had been kind – a real contrast to Coronation Day in 1953. The procession formed up along Brett's concrete road, off Fordwich Road. Local judges had been assembled to select the winners from a variety of floats that ranged from visiting carnival queens and miscellaneous other entries. All the local organisations had created the most marvellous floats full of playgroup

Fordwich Silver Jubilee Celebrations 1977

children, Brownies and Cubs, Guides and Scouts and many others. There were large lorries, small flat-backs, cars, bikes, horses, dogs and walking entries. Everyone involved was very excited as the parade left the marshalling area, led by the Jubilee Queen seated comfortably on a lovely pony and trap driven by Brian Peakall.

The route was lined with local residents and friends and the whole atmosphere was enthusiastic and joyous. The main event at the Sturry Primary School site went better than expected. There was a wonderful sense of community and everyone joined in the fun. The Fancy Dress Competition was very popular and produced some amazing costumes! The "Knockout" competition was very competitive - involving as it did a race around an obstacle course against the clock. There must have been two thousand people, old and young on that field that day. Everyone involved remembers the relaxed, happy atmosphere and the sense of achievement that a small village could put on a really good bash!

At the end of the day the tireless committee cleared up the field, took down the bunting and headed for a barbecue at a committee member's garden. During the evening, (after a few glasses!) it was decided to make the Carnival with a Miss Sturry an annual event.

Planning for the next year and another 20 years plus continued and as the years passed this Sturry village event remained popular with local organisations, residents and visitors from various parts of the county.

The late 1980's and the early 1990's were the peak years, with a carnival of up to 50 floats (including 18 visiting Carnival courts, 3 bands and 4 majorette troupes) and the Fun Day made up of stalls of skill and chance, laid out around an arena holding a programme of various activities:- Fancy Dress, Band displays, Majorette demonstrations, Gymnastics and Dog displays being a few. These were arranged firstly around a street "It's a knockout competition" and then an obstacle course competition between the visiting Carnival courts.

Once the year had died down Father Christmas visited the villages to say "thank you" and give sweets to the children. Whilst all the planning for these events was going on Miss Sturry and her Princesses were carrying the name of Sturry to all parts of Kent, always being well received and each year the reigning Court being proud ambassadors of the villages.

Other events were held on an annual basis, the Miss Sturry selection dance, a 5 mile fun run, which was one of the earliest of its type to be held in the area, attracting 750 entries at first, but down to around 100 at the end. A 10 kilometre road race was held in 1999. Other events held over the years were discos, Wine and Wisdom evenings and included active participation in other local events. On occasions the Miss Sturry Court also visited the village of Aire-sur-la-Lys in France with which Sturry is Twinned.

After many years of highs, lows, successes, disappointments and worries it became evident that the end had come. Our association had become yet another casualty of the high burden of insurances, Health and Safety legislation, Risk assessment, permissions and Policing requirements, including street barriers for road closures, made it impossible to continue. Having the Carnival is fun, but this sort of event is being taken away by bureaucracy, legislation and permissions. At the end of the 20th century there were 24 carnivals in Kent that Sturry would have been able to attend. Sadly this number is now down to 12.

Son et Lumiere in St. Nicholas Church
Sturry 1973

Son et Lumiere performed in St Nicholas Church, Sturry, November 1973 and November 1991

St. Nicholas, Sturry, Working Party

about 1981/2

St Nicholas, Sturry, Working Party about 1981/2
Back row L to R: Denise Float, Betty Marsh, Mrs Belsey, Molly Smith, Anne Holloway, Eve Bates, Stella Walter, ?Maureen Jannat.
Front row : L to R Anna Bound, Betty Marley, u/k, Margaret Harrisson, ?Mrs Blowes, Lou West, Mary Sutton, Mary Allsworth, Dorothy Weal.

Mrs Madge Needham

In conversation with Sybil Kent in 1987

Margaret Needham, always known as Madge, lived for the last thirty years of her life at 18 Mill Road, Sturry. She was born in July 1895 in Eccles and educated at Convents in Mill Hill and Lubeck. She studied music at the Louvain Conservatoire from which she had to beat a hasty retreat at the outbreak of the First World War. In line with her independent spirit and the opportunity to use her musical talents, she went on stage to perform in London theatres before marrying an ex-Army officer in 1920. He died when her only daughter was one year old.

It was the Second World that added a new dimension to her life. Having lived at home and nursed her parents until their deaths and with her daughter married, in 1940 she volunteered for war service. With fluent French she was directed to that part of the Civil Service that dealt with war transport and shipping and was very soon transferred to highly secret war work which she was still not allowed to discuss.

"It was the most exciting time of my life – lots of fun and lots of frights – but I wouldn't have missed it for the world. We ate on the job and slept on the job but it was vital work and so nobody minded. Altogether I stayed in the Civil Service for fifteen years and retired with a pension. I was 60 and bought this little cottage here. This was the first home of my own I'd had since I was widowed. I've been here for thirty years and – please God – I'm not leaving until they carry me out."

Mrs Needham lived into the autumn of 1994 just a few months short of her hundredth birthday, although in the words of a friend "she had quite escaped reality by then".

Mrs Madge Needham

Mayor's Tales

Fordwich 1994

The Mayor's Tales crew: Kinn McIntosh (author), Michael Beck (producer), Michael Kent (video and sound),
Joseph Epsom and Stanley Wilson (actors)

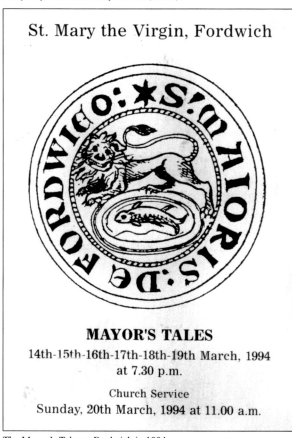

St. Mary the Virgin, Fordwich

MAYOR'S TALES
14th-15th-16th-17th-18th-19th March, 1994
at 7.30 p.m.

Church Service
Sunday, 20th March, 1994 at 11.00 a.m.

The Mayor's Tales at Fordwich in 1994

Taking a Butcher's

Douglas Garwood responding to a snapshot interview by Heather Stennett in April, 2000, for the Millennium Data Box.

The premises of Messrs Garwood & Nye, Family Butchers, of 10 High Street, Sturry, had then been a butcher's shop for 34 years, having opened in 1966. In the Second World War it was a Home Guard Station and then in 1948 a chemists' shop. Doug himself has been a butcher for 46 years to date and George Arthur Nye (6th March 1917-20th December 2009) even longer. The shop sells fresh meat and products, fish, delicatessen goods including sauces, cheese, cooked meats, pies and eggs and obtains almost all of its produce locally.

When it opened 34 years ago it employed two full-time staff – George Nye and Doug himself. It became more and more popular and after three years had two delivery vans and employed five or six men. There had been a significant change in trade over the years. Doug said "The 'Sunday Roast' people don't seem to have the same sort of roast as they used to – they're a different generation now. A real change is the Bar-B-Cue/Grill foods." Three quarters of the window display is now taken up with these types of food in the summer months. The more traditional fresh meats cuts sell better in the colder winter months.

The shop prides itself on its sage sausages. These won an award in a United Kingdom Champion of Champions Competition when it was a runner-up for the whole country in February, 1998.

"The supermarkets," said Doug, 'have affected trade but by diversification and listening to the customer, the shop continues." Doug has tried new lines, some being very successful and some – such as ostrich steak, kangaroo, crocodile tail steak and wild boar - didn't capture the imagination of the local shopper. These items are not stocked now but can be ordered.

Doug's day on a typical Saturday would start at 5am. By 5.45 am he and his assistants are at the shop – including Martin Keem - cut joints, arrange fresh meat on trays and dress the window. The other staff work on the cooked meat and internal cabinets. In all it takes two and a half hours to get fully ready for opening at 7am. During this preparation time pies, which have been made on the premises, are cooked.

Although the shop shuts at 5.30 p.m., cleaning up starts at about 4 p.m. The back of the shop is tidied first before moving onto the front. Over the Christmas period the day started at 3.30 a.m. and finished at about 10.30 p.m. Last year 236 Turkeys were sold, the pace of work best described as like being in a madhouse!

Post script: The shop was sold in April, 2005, and is now a Chinese Takeaway.

Living in Sturry - a Very Personal View
by Ken Adams

My life began when I moved to Sturry. No, I wasn't born here. As one of my former pupils remarked when we met some years back: "You were already an old bugger when you first came here." I didn't feel it at the time but with the benefit of hindsight, I realised that earlier places of residence seem to be the prequel to life where I felt I had settled. The word "settled" could suggest a period of no change. Far from it. The Sturry years, more than half my life, have known colossal change: three different homes; working at two different schools; a sabbatical year; promotion; bereavement; a second marriage; retirement and years that have seen me change from a father of two girls at primary school to a grandfather of adult grandchildren. Circumstances had dictated where I lived before; but Sturry was my choice.

People who moved to Sturry now or have arrived here in the last twenty or thirty years would be astonished if they could see the Sturry of 1962. Behind our first house in Deansway Avenue and where Heath Close is now were allotments. Beyond Woodside there were virtually no buildings. A few houses on Sturry Hill, the old primary school, the Vicarage and houses on the north side of Island Road were, apart from the cemetery, all

Hazel Castle, Joy Griffiths and Shirley File an the annual Strawberry Tea at 1 Sturry Hill.

that occupied the area south of Park View and west of Babs Oak Hill. I'm told there was a pig-farm somewhere on that land, but I don't remember it. [It was just below the cemetery.] I do remember the Humps, a wild area, now replaced by the playing field and much of the estate below it. How my nine-year-old self would have loved the Humps! Just the sort of terrain for our war-games or for acting out our Wild West fantasies derived from Saturday morning pictures. Just before we moved to Sturry someone told me quite seriously: "Oh, they'll never build on the Humps." How wrong he was!

Living and shopping in a village was a novelty for me. Above Deansway Avenue we could buy most things seven days a week at a little shop, now long gone. Or we could visit Mr Bill Pye's shop at the bottom of the hill. A bit further afield we could cram into the tiny shop of East's, the bakers, always well patronized. (Also tiny was the library housed in part of Grape House.) George Nye's butcher's shop survived until recent years. Until Vye's moved to the corner of Church Lane, it occupied the premises which later became Centrecraft and is now the restaurant, Kathton House. I remember the chemist and a greengrocer's shops, and it was always interesting to visit the Post Office and compare notes about Sunday's general knowledge crossword with Mr Newson. People were amused when I said that in Sturry we could shop at Nye's, Vye's or Pye's.

As today, the railway crossing played a significant part in Sturry life. Even when traffic was much lighter, the passing of a train caused noticeable delays to road users. On holiday once I mentioned that I lived in Sturry and received the reply: "Nice village, horrible railway crossing." Before the barriers were installed our first warning of the approach of a train was the sight of the signalman zooming down the signal box steps, a hand on each polished rail. In the face of the traffic he had to push the two heavy gates across the road.

The proximity of Chislet Colliery was significant. It was interesting to meet miners and retired miners who lived in Sturry. I was fortunate to realize a long-standing ambition by visiting the coal-face while the colliery was still operational.

Sturry was still showing its war-wounds in the early Sixties. A great gash in the centre of the village showed where the landmines fell in 1941. This incident, I was told, gave Sturry the unenviable honour of being the most blitzed village in the country. There are certainly more names of civilians than service personnel on the memorial to the dead of the Second World War in the church.

It was not long after we settled in Sturry that we became aware that big developments were on their way. A scar appeared on the ground making its twisting course from the Humps to Island Road. This scar became Sleigh Road and soon the first houses followed on the Homewood Hall estate. About the same time work started on the Silver Birch estate (Fairview Gardens). At first, all my Nimbyism came out. I feared that the planned huge development would spoil Sturry, but before long ("If you can't beat 'em, join 'em,") we had bought a house in Meadow Road. It's an exciting time watching one's new house grow where only a slab of concrete and a gas-pipe had been. It's quite an experience, too, moving in to a new development with houses being built all around, gardens full of rubble, no streetlights at first and a long wait for a telephone.

Now I live in Broad Oak, which is different again. Part of Sturry and yet not Sturry. Where Sturry has the advantage of south-facing slope and views of the lakes and Trenley Park opposite, Broad Oak largely backs on to orchards and farmland and beyond that woodland. In both Sturry and Broad Oak the main problem is traffic. Sturry's misfortune is that two road routes converge where both cross the railway: Broad Oak's is that it has become Sturry's relief road. Dorothy Gardiner in "Companion into Kent" wrote about Sturry: "What a blessed relief from noise and anxiety that long-promised bypass will bring." The book was published in 1934...

Continuing in Faith

by Ron Chadwick

What do I value in Sturry? Other contributors to this book will have told us what it is that they like - or possibly dislike - about the village and the district. I certainly value many things -among them easy access to city, coast and countryside, walking and cycling opportunities, friendly neighbours - and more.   But what I value most of all is the growth of Christian unity in this area.

Sturry has a particular distinction in this regard for it was here in 1970 that a Local Ecumenical Project between the Anglican and Methodist Churches was set up making it one of the earliest such projects in the country and certainly one of the most thoroughgoing. In 1995 on its 25th anniversary Kinn McIntosh edited and published 'In Good Faith' describing the development of the scheme and in which several contributors gave their honest opinions of it. I called it 'a pointer to the future'.

Now, as we celebrate the 40th anniversary, how is that future shaping up? My view is that during this period Christian unity has so grown and flourished within the parish that while valuing their respective traditions, Anglicans and Methodists now consider themselves primarily as Christians within a united church. Moreover, at the same time, despite obvious differences, we have enjoyed an increasing sense of shared Christian experience with our Roman Catholic friends. This has continued, over many years through 'Christians Together in Sturry and District'. This body arranges a local service in the 'Week of Prayer for Christian Unity', the delivery of Christmas and Easter greeting cards within the parish and the annual collection for the work of Christian Aid.

The churches of the Sturry district have not been immune, however, to the increasing secularisation of British society. Our local congregations are not as strong numerically as formerly and despite some encouraging work among young people at least two generations are largely absent from Christian worship. How far this is due to our failure to pass on the faith or to the pressure of the all pervading secular culture is a moot point.

It follows that there is now an increasing burden on mainstream churches in finding dedicated leaders and workers and in maintaining church buildings, especially medieval structures so expensive to repair. This last problem has led to the creation of 'The Friends of St.Nicholas Church Sturry' to raise funds for necessary building work; similar fundraising will be needed for All Saints, Westbere.

One church building which was closed in 2000, namely Hersden Methodist Church, has since been refurbished, with a modern extension added, to form the Hersden Community Centre. In view of the issues raised in the last paragraph it is clear that unity is not enough; what is required is a renewal of faith within our communities. A movement 'Fresh Expressions of the Church' is leading to many new initiatives nationwide. Such an initiative has, since 2006, been taking place, by the local 'Churches Together' through a monthly 'Cafe Church' in the Hersden Centre where faith matters can be explored in an informal way. Faith continues in Sturry and district; a stronger and more united faith in our Lord Jesus Christ.

Ron Chadwick, Les Neaves, Len Williams, Phil Craft

Transplantation

by Shelby Fitzpatrick

As we descended onto the runway and into the dark, dank, cold of an English winter thirty-five years ago, our colonial expectations were severely challenged.

So this was England, and this was Sturry, and here we would settle. Our journey from the other side of the world had emphasised the differences, with time lines blurred and uncertain directions ahead.

From our home in the earth's second largest island (Papua New Guinea) where one walked barefoot, knew no fences nor pollution nor television nor seasons, to a much smaller island of bleak winters melting into a Spring promise which, in turn, exploded into glorious Summer, we foreigners made a home here. It would take a few more seasons to appreciate the pleasures of Winter with its muffled snow, patterned frost and the many other reasons for seasons.

Once settled in Sturry, the myth of an English village became an exciting reality. There were paths to explore, routes to cycle, a river to hold our small canoe and drift us towards the Channel. There was history to learn through the land, the architecture, and the culture of the village. We followed the year with our routines and activities, some chosen, some prescribed. We began to understand the vortexes of village life and to play our small part in the composition of the mix. Friendships followed, along with participation in local events, many adventures and exciting discoveries. Daily we explored the interiors and exteriors of our place and were energized by new revelations.

A few simple principles were soon evident and eased us into the local scene. Walking our dog or our sock lambs (bottle-fed baby lambs that had been hand-reared) served as an excellent introduction to villagers, especially the children. The glories of the local horticultural society were essential for knowledge and support in gardening. Living near a church had huge benefits for understanding local dynamics. Once senses had acclimatized to our adopted place, the rewards steadily flowed. Over the years appreciation has grown exponentially - for the spirit and energy of this community to respect and preserve its past, for endless dimensions of the natural world accessible in the nearby lakes, woodlands, and river, limited only by curiosity, energy and time, for convenient transportation links to the rest of the UK and to the Continent through air, sea, road or rail, connecting us to lands beyond the UK.

We particularly appreciate what lies just outside our front door: the joy of being serenaded by nightingales,

The Old Vicarage at Sturry

the magic and beauty of emerging plants culminating in Spring, Summer, and Autumn spectacles, the surprise of first hearing - then coming upon - a rare bittern at the Fordwich lakes – events such as these combine with the hospitality, generosity, and diversity of the community to affirm that choice of a home so many years ago. Being surrounded by the natural beauty of this area has doubtlessly helped in times of loss or suffering by offering a retreat and solitude while quietly reminding us of hope and regeneration. But it is through the relationships cemented during our time here that we have had the most satisfaction and pleasure.

A consequence of not losing our own natural accents is that it is only our children who have broken the barrier of being "foreigners", yet our roots have gone deep into this community. The privileges that have developed from this connection have enriched us beyond any borders or expectations, and have provided a palate for our work and play both here and in the wider world. It is a great pleasure to be able to share this beautiful pocket of Kent with many visitors who invariably leave thinking it a little corner of Paradise.

We never disagree.

Fordwich Winter of 1963

Local Histories

Broad Oak – A Kentish Village Reconsidered
  ISBN – 978 0 9544789 3 3
Chislet and Westbere – Villages of the Stour Lathe
  ISBN – 0 9502423 4 9
Fifty Years Of Methodism in a Kentish Mining Village, 1979
Fordwich – The Lost Port
  ISBN - 0 9502423 2 2
Hersden – Chislet Colliery Village
  ISBN – 0 9544789 1 6
Hoath and Herne – The Last of the Forest
  ISBN – 0 9502423 7 3
In Good Faith – Twenty Five Years of an L.E.P.
  ISBN – 0 9502423 8 1
Letters to Sturry – A Wartime Correspondence
  ISBN – 0 9544789 0 8
Sturry – The Changing Scene
  ISBN – 0 9502423 0 6
The Sarre Penne – The Story of a Stream
  ISBN – 0 9526183 0 3
Village Views – Sturry, Broad Oak, Westbere and Hersden
  ISBN – 0 9513651 0 X
Westbere Heritage Trail 2006

K.H.McIntosh

Heather Stennett

Acknowledgements

We are very grateful for the support of many people including those listed below and would like to thank them all for their help and loan of photographs

Jack Brisley
Kate Darien-Smith
Margaret Sangster
Diana Poulter
Pam Willson
Molly Castle
Winifred Thomas
Terry and Julia Pickford
Marion Twyman
Geoffrey Neaves
Monica Headley
Veronica Ryn
Pam Carnell
Munro McIntosh
Jan Gaskell
Stella Walter
Margaret Gausden
Tony Pay

Joan Lock
Jean Anthony
Ruth Manley
Rosemary Mandeville
Hedley Basford
Maria O'Sullivan
Bruce Ward
Ian Kinnis
Don Bridger
Faith Chandler
Brian Thompson
Rita Conde
Anita Clarke
Pam Hart
Peter Gay
Tony Wenham
Derek Stingemore

Veronica Pilcher
Sarah Perry
Daphne Coombes
Gwen Petts
Marie Strong
James Styles
Tina Bouldin
Lynda Bakkaloglu
Freda Tassell
William Palmer
Jackie & Les Moran
Michael Homersham
Graham Kenmir
S. Wooldridge
The Kentish Gazette
Members of the Society of
    Sturry Villages

And especially Robin Edmonds, John Line and Allan and Derek Butler

Every effort has been made to trace copyright owners and corrections, if any, will be made in future editions.

Index

A

Adams, Brian 110, 111, 112
Adams, Ken 129
Ades, Christine 93
Alder, Billy 121
Aldridge, Mr. 107
Allfree, Fred 80
Allfree, Stuart 93
Allsworth, Mary 127
Ambrose and Foster 18
Amery, Julian 30
Amery, Leo 30, 39
Amos, Dolly 78
Amos, Mrs Percy 66
Amos, Roger 110
Annie, Nancy (nee Bellingham) 57
Anstey, Miss 76, 91
Anthony, Jean 99
Anthony, Jean (née Larkins) 117
Anthony, Wendy 119
Archer, Geoff 121
Arnold, Shirley 91
Arthur Taylor, Mr and Mrs 62
Ashley 17
Askew, Pat 90
Askew, Patricia 90
Asquith 27
Attenborough, Richard 62

B

Backhouse, William 120
Bacon, May 44
Bacon & Son 87
Bailey, Ruth 101
Baillie, Charlie 55
Baines, Mr. and Mrs. 70
Baines, Mrs. 51
Baker, Brian 93
Baker, Gerald 110
Baker, Heather 92
Baker, Keith 92, 110, 111, 112
Baker, Lieutenant 112
Baker White, Mr John 91
Balfour 27
Balsdon, D F 123
Balsdon, J V P D 123
Banks, Ernie 21, 48, 49, 50, 58, 88
Banks, Mr 99
Banks, Muriel 48, 49, 50
Banks, Peter 93
Barrance, Rosemary 118
Barton, Geoffrey 93
Basford, Hazel 24
Bates, Elsie 24, 25
Bates, Evelyn 69, 70, 127
Bates, Madeline 24
Bates, Stanley 122
Bates, William and Annie 25
Batt, Mary 91
Beard, Julianna 119
Beasley's 70
Beck, Michael 128
Becon, Thomas 123
Belsey, Mrs 127
Benchley, Irene 92
Bennett, Susan 93

Bensted, Alan 121
Bensteds, the 18
Beresford Jones, Mr. A.B. 34
Bill 44
Bill, Lavender 42
Bing, Miss A E 118
Birch, Ivy 91
Birch, Mr Ronnie 100
Bird, Mrs 50
Birds 50
Blake, Mr 66
Bland, Pilot Officer John W. 83
Bligh Bros. 87
Blowes, Mrs 127
Blythe Smith, Miss A M 118
Bobbington 67
Bodin, Mr W. 12
Bollifant, Edmund 123
Bond, James 12
Booth, E C T 112
Bouldin, Christina 122
Bound, Anna 127
Bourner, Mrs Maud 2
Bournes, Arthur 17, 44, 45, 50, 66, 115
Bowman, George 63
Bowyer-Smythe, Veronica 115
Boxall, John 113
Boys, Benjamin 11
Boys, Bevin 20
Boys, Harry 11, 12
Boys, Mr Arthur 62, 75, 113
Braddon, M.E. 24
Bradshaw, Mrs Violet 122
Bradshaw, Valerie 122
Brain, Mrs 64
Bramwell Evans, Revd G. 90
Bray, Hilary 105, 123
Bray, Mr. and Mrs. 105, 106
Bredin, Lt Colonel 54
Brenchley, Mrs. 52
Brett's 16, 54, 82, 104, 105
Brewer, Revd. H.P.B., Vicar of Sturry 1885-1914 70, 71
Brice, Mr Daniel 36, 62, 64, 110, 113
Brice, Mrs [Edith Maud] 64
Brickwood, Margaret 66
Brickwood, Mrs. 66
Brockman's 72, 82
Brooker, Percy 51, 82
Brook, Mr. P T S 18, 58, 60, 61
Brooks, A J 115
Brooks, Robin 84
Bros, Carey 104
Brown, Benita 124
Brown, Colin 113
Brown, Diana 116
Brown, Miss M 118
Bubb 84
Bubb, Arthur 110
Bubb, David 92, 110, 111, 112
Bubb, John 92, 110, 111
Bubb, Lily 45
Bubb, Mrs Ada 116
Bubb, Thelma 84
Bull, Douglas 57
Bull, Mr 78
Bullock, Daphne 117
Burton, J. 19
Burton, Mrs M 118
Burton, Sid 19, 121
Butler, Allan 19, 84, 91, 92, 99, 110, 111, 115, 121

Butler, Derek 19, 82, 90, 110, 115, 121
Butler, Frank 121
Butler, Rosemary 104
Butler, Sid 100
Butterworth, Mrs Molly 64
Butterworth, Norman 110
Button, Gerald 115
Button, Mrs M 116
Button, Roger 122

C

Cannon, Ernest 62
Cannon, Martin 121
Capper, Mrs 71
Carlo 106
Carmichael, Harry 123
Carpenter, Miss 97
Castle, Hazel 130
Castle, Luke 64
Castle, Pearl 61
Catterick, Jean 84
Cecil, Hugh and Mirabel 32
Cecil, Lord Edward 26, 27, 30, 31
Chadwick, Ron 131
Challen, George 11, 12
Chamberlain 27
Chaplin, Rose 61
Cheney, C.R. 3
Chittenden, Violet 92
Churchill, Mr Winston 18
Clark and Eaton's 79
Clarke-Hughes, Miss 107
Clarke-Hughes, Miss Gwen 106
Clark, Michael 105
Clark, Mr 94
Clark, Mrs 90
Clayson, Canon 113
Clayson, Fred 18, 84
Clayson, Mary 113
Clayson, Ruth 113
Clemenceau 28, 29
Cockle, Vic 100
Cole, Mr William 53, 84
Collard, Norah 45
Collier, Richard 7
Collingwood, Maurice 121, 124
Collingwood, R.G. 115
Collins, Daphne 113
Collins, Doreen 66
Collins, Jennifer 113
Collins, John 72, 84
Collins, Mrs Rose E. 84, 92, 94
Collins, Robin 123
Conrad, Joseph 124
Coombes, Mrs 75
Cooper, Jack 115, 121
Cork, Mr. 74, 75
Cork, Mr and Mrs 72, 77
Cork, Mrs 41, 51
Cork, Mrs Emily 31
Cork, Mrs Emily Victoria May (née Hillman) 26
Cork's, Mrs. 22, 60
Couchman, Mrs 118
Countess of Huntingdon 95, 100
Cox, Miss Sylvia 65, 68, 69, 75, 95, 117, 118
Craft, Rev E C 102
Craft, Phil 131
Cranford, Robin 123
Crockford 120

Croxton, Chas 100
Croxton, Molly 93, 118
Cruttenden, Charles 82
Cruttenden, Miss 72, 91, 92, 94, 95
Cullen, Mrs Vera 116
Cullen's 80
Curtis, Henry 11
Curtis, Major 55
Cyril 114

D

Daisy 4
Dale, Jennifer 93
Dale, Len 19
Dance, Mrs L 118
Daniels, Jim 100
Danton, Colin 124
David Greig's 36
Davies family 82
Davies, Keith 122
Davies, Roy 110, 111
Davison, Mrs Mary 92
Davison, Rowena 92
Davis, Rosie 56
Dawkins, James 11, 12
Dawkins, William 11
Dawson, Ada 33
Dawson, Charles 33
Dawson, Elaine, Graham and Rex 34
Denne, Mr G.H. 82
Denne's 16
Dickinson, Miss 66
Dinnage, Les 121
Divers, Daisy 4
Divers, Ellen Ivy 4
Divers, Jesse John 5
Divers, Matilda 4
Divers, Percy John Gore 4
Dobbin family 84
Dodge, George 100
Dodge, Peter 93
Dodson, Mrs Florrie Mona 78
Donohue, Miss J 118
Draper Hunt, Mr G.E. 66, 67, 68
Dreaver, Jean 91, 94, 95
Dungey, Clement 2
Dungey, David 2, 115
Dungey, Erica 119
Dunn, Ted 100
Dunn, Lovona 100
Dunn, Malcolm 100
Durkan, Barbara 122

E

Easterbrook, Mr. 58
East, Mr and Mrs 108, 109, 130
Edal, Conrad 105
Eddington Edmonds, Mrs B 118
Edgell, Miss 113
Edmonds, Margaret 26
Edmonds, R.Q. 32, 38, 60, 70, 73, 124
Edwards, Fred 81, 100
Edwards, Helen 93
Eley, Mr 89
Eliot, T.S. 1
Elks, Colin 105, 110
Elliot, Major E. 115
Elliott, Miss Bertha 90
Engleheart, Rev. G.H. 120
Epsom, Joseph 128
Evans 73

Evans, Dan 56
Evans, Dr [Catherine] 34
Evans, Miss 94
Evill, the Revd. William Ernest 4

F

Fabb, Betty 100
Fabb, Mrs Alice 116
Fagg, Pat and Richard 124
File, Emma 119
File, Paul 47
File, Shirley 130
Finns 47, 50
Fitzpatrick, Peter 123
Fitzpatrick, Shelby 132
Fleets 70
Fleming, Ian 123
Fletcher, Tim 13
Float, Denise 127
Foad, Elizabeth 119
Ford, Mrs A. 101
Fraser, Hugh 8
Freeman, Jane 96
French, George 71, 122
French, H.R. 122
French, Mabel 122
French, Mrs Clara 122
Fullager, Stan 100
Fuller, Sgt W.F. 67, 115

G

Gammon, Dot 61
Gammon, Ella 61
Gardener, Ray 76
Garwood, Douglas 129
Garwood & Nye 129
Gauden, Selwyn 76
Gaulle, De 29
Gausden, Revd. P.J. 37, 96
Gay, Ivor 115
Gay, Mrs Nancy 92
Gay, Peter 93, 98
Gee, William 82
George, Lloyd 23
Gerald Van Loo 124
Gibson, Guy 123
Gilbert, Anthony 79
Gilling, Sam 109, 114
Gill, Michael 73, 84
Gisby, Eric 93
Golder, Ben 123
Goodman, Roger 82
Grant, Captain 36
Grant, William 11, 12
Grayling, Mrs Margaret 118
Grayling, R.C. 115
Green, Basil 103, 106
Green, Dr. 75
Green, Madeleine 106
Green, Miss Flo 106
Greenwood, Tom 106
Griffiths, Joy 130
Grivas, Colonel 24
Gross, Charlie 108, 109
Gruska, Franciszek 83
Gurney 16

H

Hadlow, Albert 100
Hadlow, Mrs 97
Haggis, C. 115
Haimes, Thomas 88
Hall, Brian 110
Hall, Miss 93, 95
Hamilton, James 108, 109, 113, 114
Hammond, Bill 100
Hammond, Violet 66
Hampshire, Mr and Mrs 72
Hampton, Janie 81
Hardinge, George Edward Charles, 3rd
    Baron Hardinge of Penshurst 29
Hardinge, Lady 26
Harding, Miss Kathleen 106
Harris, Christine 92
Harris, Mrs M 118
Harris's 106
Harrisson, Margaret 127
Harrisson, Martin 122
Harrisson, Patrick 122
Harvey, Bill 100
Harvey, Dr M.S. 115
Harvey, George 102
Harvey, John 110
Hawkins, Mrs Dolly 114
Hawkins, Veronica 114
Haydon 51
Haydon, Fanny Margaretta 8
Haydon, Revd G.P. 8, 120
Headley, Monica 4, 11, 62, 88, 99, 118
Headley, Paul I'Anson 82
Healey, Denis 30
Hedger's 72
Henson, Basil 8
Hichens, Miss 91, 94, 95
Higham, Roger 124
Hill, Colonel Peter Edward, C.B., R.A. 6
Hill, Derek Ingram 124
Hilton, Mr 17
Hoare, Jack 50
Holdstock, John 62
Holdstock's 16
Holland, Dennis 93
Holloway, Anne 127
Holmes, Bill 46
Holmes, Frank 19
Holmes, Mrs Ivy (née Giles) 43, 44, 45
Holmes, Leslie 46
Mrs Nellie 73, 79
Holmes, Sgt E.E.C. 46
Holness, Michael 110, 111
Holness, Mrs Kathleen 92
Homersham 60, 110
Homersham, Arthur Douglas 13
Homersham, Arthur Henry 13
Homersham, C. 19, 52
Homersham, F. Stanley 13
Homersham, Mick 110, 111, 112
Homersham, Mrs Louisa 52
Homersham, Rose Matilda 15
Homersham, W.E. 19
Homersham, William E. 14, 19, 52
Hopkins, R. 19
Howells, Mrs 91
Hue-Williams, Anthony 104
Hughes, Tommy 55

I

Impett, Mr. Charles 47, 71
Ince, Dr A. Godfey 17, 52, 57, 71, 75, 78, 80

J

Jakeman, Patricia 93
Jameson, Mr Edward 12
James, William 4
Jannat, Maureen 127
Jarnell, Paul 93
Jarvis, Chris 110
Jenkins, Dave 121
Jenkins, Frank 115
Johncock, Audrey 72, 84
Johncock, Bob 71, 72
Johncock, Roy 72
Johnson, Brian 124
Johnson, Dr T.S. 12
Johnson, Frank 51
Johnstone, Lady Elizabeth 29
Johnston, Margaret 74
Joiner, William 63, 65, 115
Jones, Ernest 100
Jones, Marion 93
Jones, Trevor 115
Jordan, Bill 92

K

Keem, Gay 61
Keem, Gerald 92
Keem, Kay 61
Keem, Martin 129
Keem, Sharon 61
Keem, Terence 93
Kemp, Roy 92
Kennett, Mrs Irene 116
Kent, Michael 128
Kent, Sybil 127
Kenworthy, Major C.H.H. 53, 82
Kidner, R.W. 7
King George V1 21
Kington, Sally 113, 120
Kipling, Rudyard 29, 124
Kirkham, Alfred 78
Kirkham, Johnny 78
Kirk, Sharon 119
Knight, Mr Nelson 64

L

Ladley, John 110, 112
Lamb, Rose 93
Lambton, General 14
Lane, John 32
Lansdoff 107
Larkins, David 110, 111
Larkins, Jean 91, 118
Larkins, Ron 100
Lawrence, Bob 100
Leachman, Miss D.M. 121
Leeds, Edward 120
Lee, Rev R.W. 102
Lewis, Penny 88
Lindsell, Mrs G M 118
Line, Bill 110
Line, John 20, 35, 65, 76, 110, 111, 112, 121, 124
Line, John (Captain) 110
Line, Mr Dick 110

Line, Mrs Gertrude 62
Lipyeat, Jimmy 110
Litten, Veronica 99
Llewellyn, Ross 19, 22, 37, 55, 56
Lock, George 20
Lock, Joan 8
Lodge, Linda 60
Longley, David 105, 110, 111
Longley, Malcolm 121
Louch, Marion 119
Louise, Dorothy (nee Ladd) 62
Lovely, H. Clyde 115, 123
Lowther, Ivy (nee Dalton) 22
Lucas, Mrs Louisa 82
Luck, Bert 122
Lyons, Edward and Edith 40
Lyons, Vera 73

M

Mack, Cecelia 107
MacKenzie, June 81
Mack, Gertrude 107
Maile, Geoff 19
Maile, Reg 77
Makarios, Archbishop 24
Malory, Thomas 124
Mansfield, F.W. 61
Marley, Betty 127
Marriots 80
Marsh, Betty 74, 77, 127
Marsh, Betty (née Bull) 57
Marsh, John 88
Marsh, Mick 110
Marsh, Miss 4
Marsh, Peter 57
Martin, Dave 111
Martin, David 110
Mason, Miss 76, 91
Matthews, Alf 115
Maud Bouldin, Mrs Florence Emily (née Lyons) 40
Mavin, Mrs 89
Maxse, Miss Olive 26
Maxse, Mr. Leo 29
Maxted, Frederick 25
May, Arthur 82
Mayo, Doris 93, 100
Mayo, James 93, 100
Mayo, Joan 93
McCarthy, Revd Father Joseph B. 72, 115
McCormick, Mollie 52, 57
McGeorge, Miss 26
McIntosh, Dr R.A.C. 53, 95, 115, 121
McIntosh, K.H. 1, 3, 11, 12, 37, 60, 88, 90, 101, 115, 123
McIntosh, Kinn 33, 120, 121, 128, 131
McKenzie, Mary 122
McNeill, Ronald 28
McNulty, Larry 110
Mearns, Miss M 118
Mercer, Mr R.M. 12
Metherell, Ann 118
Metherell, Jill 118
Middleton, Miss 43
Milner, Lady 26, 29, 31, 32, 38, 39
Milner, Lord 27, 28, 30, 31, 32, 38, 39, 124
Misses Tates, The 106
Moat family, The 85
Moat, H. 87
Moat, Ian B. 75

Moat, John 85
Moat, Obadiah 23
Moloney, Dr 120
Montgomery, Frank 65
Moran, Sheila 61
Moran, Wendy, Brian, Liz, Michael 61
Morgan, Len 115
Morgan, Mr C. 89
Morley 27
Morris, Albert 64
Morris, Ethlebert 64
Morris, Miss Jane 62, 63
Morris, Mr. Jesse 37
Morris, Mrs 77
Morris, Mrs. 109
Morris, Mrs Nellie 109
Morris, Roy Thomas Edward 62
Morris, Thomas 62
Mrs. Ryan's 51
Munro's 107
Munton, Shirley 92, 118
Murray, Bob 110, 111
Murray, John 32
Murray, Mrs Kathleen 64
Murray, Pam 113
Murray, Ron 62, 91
Murrays 113

N

Neame, Edward 10
Neame, Mrs Margaret 10, 11
Neames 77
Neaves' 77
Neaves, Charlie 58
Neaves, Les 131
Neaves, Monty 77
Needham, Mrs Madge 127
Nethersole, Sir Michael Henry Braddon 24, 115
Newbury, Angela 119
Newing, Irene (née Dunn) 100
Newing, Mrs E 116
Newing, Roy 101
Newman, Miss Margaret 66, 67, 90, 118
Newman, Percy 100
Newson, Mr 130
Nice, Philippa (née Gross) 109
Noah 71
Nye, George Arthur 51, 52, 129, 130

O

Oaks, Mr. 52
Occleshaw, Michael 124
O'Flyn, Kate 119
Ogden, Bert 121
Ognall, Leopold Horace 123
Oldaker, Revd. W.H. 53
Olwen 114
Oppitz, Leslie 7
Osborne, Peter 123
Ovenden 105
Ovenden, Mrs Mary (nee Homersham) 64

P

Paget, Major 115
Paine, Nick 113, 114
Paine, Robert & Phyllis 113
Paine, Sally 108, 109, 113
Paine, Sandra, 114, 114
Palmer, William 93

Palmer, Willie 110, 111, 112
Parker, Mr 73, 77, 91, 109
Parker, Mrs. 109
Parker, Richard 123
Partington, Mrs Daphne 10
Patterson, Mr David 105
Paul, Janet 117
Pay, Mrs Vera 116
Payne, Nurse 52
Payne, Derek 121
Payne, Mr Royce 96
Pay, Roger 110, 111
Peakall, Brian 125
Peel, Alan 110
Peel, James 49
Peel, June 72, 84
Peel, Ken 93, 110, 111
Peel, Mr. 51, 59, 94
Peel, Mrs. 43
Peels 49
Petts, Mr. 107
Petts, Stella 92
Phillips, Percival James 58, 60
Philpott, Mr and Mrs 37
Pickford family 84
Pickfords 113
Pickford, Terry 62
Pidduck, Great Uncle William Gilbert 116
Piper, Sandy 23
Pitcher, H. 115
Pope, Ann 107
Popes 70
Pope, Thomas H. 3, 17, 36
Porter, Bernard 121
Portman, Eric 62
Post 51
Powell, Miss 102
Powell, Miss Jessie 94, 106
Powells, Misses 106
Prankerd Phelps, Thomas 124
Price, Albert 77
Price, Fred and Dorothy 33
Price, Peter 91, 92, 110, 111, 112, 121
Prior, Mr Albert 36, 71, 80
Prosser, Mr and Mrs W.E. 39, 43
Pugh, Elizabeth 38
Pugh, Sir Arthur 22, 38, 115
Purkiss, Mrs R.G. 118
Pye, Mr Bill 130
Pye's 130

Q

Quayle, Anthony 8

R

Rabbit, Lily 50
Race, Margaret 92, 118
Raffety, Mr.B.R. 53
Ralphs, Mrs. Jean 101
Ramsey, Mrs. 70
Ratcliff, Gillian 33
Ratledge, Ronald 68
Raven, Miss J E 75, 101, 117, 118
Ravine, Miss 43, 44, 76
Reed, Mrs 44
Reidinger, Hugo 88
Reid, Jimmy 15, 80
Reid, Mrs Mary 116
Reeves Revd C.V. 102
Rice, Sir William 116
Richardson, Ian 8

Richardson, Megan 76
Riley, Captain 85
Risdon-Brown, Monica 90
Risdon-Brown, Mrs Elizabeth 90
Risdon-Brown, Revd. Samuel 4, 72, 83, 91, 115
Roberts, Mr and Mrs Ellis 37
Robey, George 45, 110, 113
Robey, Janice 113
Robinson, Alf 59, 62
Robinson, Bilby 104, 105,107
Robinson, Freda 113
Robinson, John 115
Robinson, Mrs Dolly 64
Rogers, Harry 122
Rogers, Jean 93
Rogers, Ken 92, 110, 111, 112, 121
Rogers, Mrs 122
Rode, Bishop of Dover 54
Rose, Mrs. 54
Rose, Roy 19
Ross, Mr A.J. 117
Rowe 107
Rowland, Mrs Peggy 92
Roy, Agnes 92
Roy, Mrs Muriel 82
Ruck, Brenda 93

S

Saffrey, Jack 100
Sage, R.C. 115
Salmon, Doris 73
Saul, Gladys 52
Scott, Mr Robert 94
Seath, Bill 104
Seath, Mrs S. 84
Seaths 106
Seath, Sidney 104
Setterfield, Lilian Mabel 80
Setterfields 46
Sharratts, the 106
Shaw, John 55
Shephard, Ben 89
Shirref, Lizzie (née Gross) 108, 109
Simmonds, Mrs 89
Simpson, Jessie 90
Simpson, Miss Louise 90
Sim, Sheila 62
Skinner, Mr 11
Skinner, Mrs. 91
Skyrme, Joy 73
Slingsby 47
Smith, Brian 91, 92
Smith, Eileen 113, 114
Smith, F. 19
Smith, Ivy Ethel 60
Smith, Lenny 62
Smith, Miss G.H. 91, 93, 94
Smith, Molly 127
Smith, Norman 101
Sotheby 27
Southon 82
Southon, Mr 77
Spiller's, Dorothy 73
Spillett, Maurice 115
Spillett, Mrs Ida 116
Spindler, Mr 46
Spratt, Elsie and May 63
Stanbridge 51
Standing, Derek 122
Stanley 70, 71, 72

Stanley Bush, Mrs 84
Stanley, Dave 121
Stanwix, Mrs B L 118
Steele, Miss 26
Steinbeck, John 124
Steinhilper, Ulrich 123
Stennett, Heather 1, 3, 40, 43, 60, 74, 85, 101, 129
Stennett, Mrs Philip 44
Stephens, Mrs Olive 115
Stevens 105
Stewart, Joan 44
Stewart, Sid 44
Stilwell, Gill 124
Stilwell, Mike 124
Stockbridge, Alison 119
Sutherland-Leveson-Gower, Millicent 25
Sutton, Mary 127
Swain, Alan, Alec, Dollie, John, Hettie and Richard 63

T

Tamsitt brothers 62
Taplin, Mrs 100
Taylor, Joseph 102, 104, 105
Taylor, Kathleen 117
Terry, Richard 11
Tharps, Misses 51, 74, 77, 79
Thomas, George 37
Thomas, Muriel 22, 35, 37, 56
Thomas', The 20
Thompson, Bill 100
Thompson, Doris (née Mayo) 93
Thompson, Geoffrey 122
Thompson, Kath 60, 61
Thompson, Mrs Elizabeth 122
Thompson, Mr Wm 122
Thompson, Ned 80
Thompsons 77
Thompson, William 23
Todd, Betty Dorothy 62
Todd, David 62, 93
Todd, Elizabeth 119
Todds 113
Tompsett, Joanne and Jacki 119
Tomson and Wotton 16
Townsend, William 123
Toynbee, Arnold 124
Tritton, Paul 19, 64, 107
Truscott, Mary 118
Tuff, Percy 52, 77
Tugwell, George 100
Twyman, Michael 92
Twyman, Mrs 101
Tyler, Mr 52
Tywnne, John 123

U

"Uncle Mac" (Derek McCulloch) 90

V

Vidler, Mr David 64
Villiers-Stuart, Mr 113
Vinaver, Eugene 123, 124
Vye's 130

W

Waite, Herbie 55
Waite, Michael 105
Wallace, the Revd. George Lindsay, M.A.
     1900-1921 6
Walter, Stella 127
Wanstall, Ron 110
Wanstall, Ronald 93
Wanstall, Ronnie 111
Ward, Revd. J.Neville 123
Ward, Valerie 93
Warren, General Sir Charles 8
Warren, Sir Charles 9, 120
Weal, Dorothy 51, 127
Webb, Irene 57
Webb, Sarah 93
Webb, Vera 124
Weeks-Dungey 2
Weeks, William 2
Wells, Brian 110, 111
West, Lou 127

Westons 77
Westwood, Eric 82
Wheeler, Michael 93
White 51
White, Mr 77
Whittaker, Cyril 114
Whittaker, Ellen 75, 118
Whittaker, Elvina 114
Whittaker, Fred 50, 100
Whittaker, Janet 93
Whittaker, Mrs 114
Whittaker, Percy 64
Whittaker, Reggie 91, 92, 110, 111, 112
Whittaker, Sid 114
Whittaker, Tony 110, 111, 112
Wilde, Meredith and Oscar 26, 27
Wild, J.B. 61, 115
Williams, A. Susan 32
Williams, Father 113
Williams, G. 115
Williams, Len 131

Williams, Mrs Gymneth 116
Williams, Rev T.G. 67, 94
Williams, Watkin W. 8
Willson, Mrs Pamela (nee Butler) 89
Wilson, Guy 120
Wilson, Stanley 128
Wood 82
Wood, Mrs. 70
Wood, Mrs Jack 81
Wood, Owen 19
Wood, Thomas 82
Wooldridge, W. 19
Worrell, John 121
Wotton, Mr 5, 16, 106
Wright, Stan 110
Wyborn's 51

Y

Yeomans, Brian 92
Young, Harry 66, 82